Study Guide to Ac

SOCIOLOGY

Third Edition

David B. Brinkerhoff
Lynn K. White
University of Nebraska-Lincoln

Prepared by

Charles K. O'Connor
Bemidji State University

Charles L. Mulford
Iowa State University

WEST PUBLISHING COMPANY
St. Paul New York Los Angeles San Francisco

COPYRIGHT © 1991 by   WEST PUBLISHING CO.
.610 Opperman Drive
P.O. Box 64526
St. Paul, MN 55164–0526

98 97 96 95 94 93   8 7 6 5 4 3 2

ISBN 0–314–81740–9

CONTENTS

STUDY GUIDE PREFACE

Welcome to your study guide that accompanies SOCIOLOGY by Brinkerhoff and White. Brinkerhoff and White have written an outstanding text that is interesting, well organized, and very readable. This study guide has been carefully designed in consultation with them to help you in your efforts to successfully comprehend the course material. Each chapter is keyed directly to the corresponding chapter in the text, and contains a series of exercises that will allow you to actively participate in the learning process.

To achieve the greatest success in the course, we suggest you first carefully read the whole chapter paying very close attention to the key terms printed in boldface type. Your ability to master these concepts and to apply them to a variety of situations will be an important factor in doing well in the course. Also, don't forget to include in your studies the "Focus on" and "Issues" section of each chapter.

Once you are reasonably satisfied that you have a solid grasp of the chapter, turn to the study guide and carefully examine each of the learning objectives. The learning objectives are the key to success because they are the concepts that have been singled out as the most important in each chapter. Failure to master these most basic learning objectives will undoubtedly lead to poor performance on examinations. Keeping this in mind, thoroughly and completely answer each learning objective. If you have a difficult time understanding a particular objective, return to the text and review the appropriate portion of the chapter. If you still have difficulty understanding what is important in the text, you may wish to turn to the chapter outline in the study guide for a brief overview of the topic. If you have truly mastered the material in the chapter you should be able to successfully complete each objective.

Next, begin the process of self-testing. Start with the matching and fill-in-the-blank questions. Answer each and turn to the key at the back of the study guide to correct your answers. If any of the answers are wrong, review the applicable learning objective and turn to the page indicated and find the correct response in the text. Now try the multiple choice questions, again checking the key and looking up the correct answer in the text. Finally, you should try writing out detailed answers to the essay questions and comparing your answer to the test.

If you have diligently done all that has been suggested, then you should have mastered the chapter. You are ready to move on to the next chapter and, ultimately, the examination.

Good luck and best wishes,

Charles L. Mulford
Charles K. O'Connor

Chapter 1

The
Study
of
Society

LEARNING OBJECTIVES

1. Define sociology and discuss how it is distinct from other social sciences.

2. Discuss what is meant by the term "sociological imagination" and explain how social outcomes may be beyond the control of the individual.

3. Describe the impact of the industrial revolution on traditional values and beliefs.

4. Discuss how sociology uses the scientific method.

5. Identify the major contributions and key concepts associated with each of the following individuals: Compte, Marx, Durkheim and Weber.

6. Discuss how participation in society can be both confining and rewarding to the individual.

7. Recount the historical development of sociology in America focusing upon the role played by W.E.B. DuBois, Jane Adams and the University of Chicago.

CHAPTER 1

8.   List the assumptions underlying structural-functional theory and note the questions used to assess the consequences for the operation of social structures.

9.   Define the following: function, dysfunction, manifest function and latent function.

10.   Note the assumptions underlying conflict theory and identify the two major questions asked by conflict theorists.

11.   Describe the basic approach and guiding assumptions of symbolic interaction theory.

12.   Discuss the strengths and weaknesses of structural-functional, conflict and symbolic interaction theory.

13.   Analyze the practice of prostitution using any or all of the three major theory groups.

14.   Differentiate between macrosociology and microsociology.

15.   Contrast basic sociology and applied sociology and note the different contexts where each is practiced.

16.   Where are most sociologists employed and what are their chief activities?

17.   Note the employment opportunities that exist for sociologists outside of universities.

18.   How does sociology function to bring the concerns of the average citizen to the attention of policy makers?

CHAPTER OUTLINE

I.   What is Sociology?

      A.   Sociology is the systematic study of social structures and how they affect human behavior.

2

B.   Sociology is one of the social sciences, and as such, shares an emphasis on the <u>scientific method</u>, as the best approach to knowledge. This means relying upon critical and systematic examination of evidence by objective observers.

    1.   The subject of scientific sociological inquiry is <u>social structure</u>, or a relatively distinct set of social positions whose interactions are governed by shared norms.

        (a) All the social sciences are interested in somewhat differing patterned social regularities.

            (1)   Sociology focuses upon societal level causes while psychology focuses upon individual factors.

C   The <u>sociological imagination</u> is the ability to see personal experience within the context of social structure (<u>Mills</u>).

    1.   The sociological imagination allows us to see our personal troubles within a broader social and historical context.

        (a)   Problems of this nature are often beyond the control of individuals and may require changing the structure of society to affect a solution.

        (b)   This concern for solving social problems has been important to sociology since its founding over 100 years ago.

II.   The Emergence of Sociology

A.   The emergence of sociology coincided with the rise of the industrial revolution in western Europe during the 18th and 19th centuries.

    1.   The industrial revolution produced radical changes in the basic structures of society.

        (a) The newly discovered methods of science were now turned upon society in order to understand and possibly control the tumultuous changes that occurred.

B.   The founders of sociology were philosophers, economists and preachers and included Comte, Marx, Durkheim and Weber.

    1.   <u>August Comte</u> (1798-1857) was considered the founder of

sociology.   In fact, he even coined the term sociology.
(a) He urged the application of science to human
affairs and called the process <u>positivism</u>.
Scientists could thus learn the laws of social
behavior and eventually predict and control that
same behavior.
  (1)   Comte stressed that the study of sociology
  requires a concern for both the sources of order
  (<u>statics</u>) and continuity and the sources of change
  (<u>dynamics</u>).

2.   <u>Karl</u> <u>Marx</u> (1818-1883) was a philosopher, economist,
social activist and the highly influential originator of
contemporary conflict theory.
(a) Marx viewed poverty, inequality and alienation
as the products of capitalism and private
property.   Thus he sought to eliminate capitalism.
(b) Social institutions such as the family, law, etc. all
develop after and adapt to the economic
structure.   The idea is called <u>economic</u>
<u>determinism.</u>
(c) The <u>dialectic</u> (<u>Hegel</u>) is a three step process of
social change in which every idea fosters a
counter idea which conflicts with it.   Over time
they blend to produce a new idea.   The steps
are called the <u>thesis</u>, <u>antithesis</u> and <u>synthesis</u>.
(d) Applying the dialectic to capitalism shows the
ruling class (thesis) in conflict with the working
class (antithesis).   Marx predicted that
communism would emerge as the new economic
system (synthesis).
(e) Marx argued that the sociologist should be an
activist and help change society.

3.   <u>Emile</u> <u>Durkheim</u> (1858-1917) was a French scholar who
was devoted to understanding the stability of society and
the importance of social participation for individual
happiness.
(a) Durkheim studied the balance between regulation
and individual freedom in society.
(b) Positivism should be used to investigate social
facts.   This included an emphasis on clarifying

concepts, objectivity and discovering cause and effect relationships.

    (1)   The social integration arising out of community standards is constraining for the individual while at the same time providing a sense of satisfaction.

    (2)   Suicide may result when an individual is either too constrained (<u>fatalistic</u>) or too unrestrained (<u>anomic</u>) by society.

(c) Durkheim believed that sociologists should be objective observers only interested in facts. This view still dominates sociology today.

4.   <u>Max</u> <u>Weber</u> (1864-1920) was a German economist, historian and philosopher whose work provides the theoretical base for half a dozen areas of sociological inquiry.

(a) In order to understand the behavior of the individual it values were necessary for the rise of the economic system of capitalism.

(c) Sociology for Weber must be practiced so as to be <u>value</u> <u>free</u>.

C   Sociology in the United States shared the same intellectual roots as European sociology and featured a concern with social problems, a reforming rather than a radical approach and an emphasis on the scientific method.

1.   The pioneers included <u>W.E.B.</u> <u>DuBois</u> who studied ethnic inequality and racism and <u>Jane</u> <u>Adams</u> who was one of the first members of the <u>American Sociological Society</u>.

2.   Today America leads the world in the number of sociologists and nearly every college in the country features a program in sociology.

(a) American sociology is still oriented to both the practical and the theoretical.

III.   Current Perspectives in Sociology

A.   <u>Structural - functional</u> theory has its roots in natural sciences and in the analogy between society and an organism. This perspective directs attention to identifying the structures of society and how they function.

1. The assumptions of structural functionalism.
    (a) Stability - whether or not a structure or social pattern contributes to the maintenance of society.
    (b) Harmony - as the parts of an organism work together for the good of the whole, the parts of society are also characterized by harmony.
    (c) Evolution - social structures evolve and adapt to new needs and demands including the elimination of unnecessary structures.
        (1) It is also called <u>consensus theory</u>.
2. Structural-functional analysis involves two important steps.
    (a) The first step is to determine the nature of the social structure.
    (b) The second step is to assess the consequences for the operation of the social structure in terms of stability, harmony, etc. This includes looking for positive consequences called <u>functions</u> and for negative consequences called <u>dysfunctions</u>.
        (1) Further distinctions may be made between <u>manifest functions</u> and <u>latent functions</u>.
3. An evaluation of structural-functional theory shows that in practice a strong emphasis is placed upon judging structures primarily by the degree to which they contribute to the maintenance or status quo of society.
    (a) Structural-functional theory tends to produce a static and conservative analysis of social systems that appeals to those who wish to preserve society and not to those who seek to change it.

B. <u>Conflict theory</u>
    1. Conflict theory addresses the points of stress and conflict in society and the ways that they contribute to social change.
    2. The three primary assumptions of conflict theory are:
        (a) <u>Competition</u>. Competition over scarce resources is characteristic of all human relationships.
        (b) <u>Structured Inequality</u>. Inequality is built into social structure with those who benefit striving to maintain their advantage.

        (c) <u>Revolution</u>. Change occurs as a result of conflict between competing interests. It is often abrupt and revolutionary.

   3. Conflict analysis.

        (a) Conflict theorists ask two basic questions. They are:

           (1) Who benefits from structured inequality?

           (2) How do they maintain their advantage?

   4. Evaluating conflict theory shows that it produces a critical picture of society that focuses on conflict while ignoring stability in society.

        (a) A critical view of society runs counter to the value free approach of most sociologists.

C   <u>Symbolic interactionism</u> addresses the subjective meanings of human acts and the processes through which people come to develop and communicate shared meanings. Consequently, this perspective focuses on the everyday aspects of social life.

   1. Symbolic interactionists use three basic premises in the study of human behavior. They are:

        (a) The importance of symbolic meanings,

        (b) meanings grow out of relationships and

        (c) meanings are negotiated.

   2. Individuals both shape and are shaped by the relationships they experience.

   3. An evaluation of symbolic interaction theory shows that its focus is on small groups and daily face-to-face interaction. It explains how roles and social structure become an inseparable and natural part of human existence.

        (a) The major weakness stems from a lack of emphasis on large societal structures.

D.   Each theoretical perspective can be used as a photographer uses interchangeable lenses, i.e. to accentuate some aspect of the social scene.

   1. Conflict theory and functionalism are better suited for the study of larger social structures, or <u>macrosociology</u>, while symbolic interactionism is better suited to the study of interactions among individuals or <u>microsociology</u>.

CHAPTER 1

IV. Sociologists - What do they do?

    A.   The majority of sociologists are employed in college and university settings where they teach and do research.
1. Sociologists teach over two million students annually. The goals of teaching sociology are:
   (a) to provide a better understanding of society, and
   (b) to help students understand how social structure shapes individual experience.
2. Many professors as well as other sociologists employed in government, industry and nonprofit organizations engage in research.
   (a) <u>Basic</u> or <u>pure sociology</u> seeks to understand some aspect of human behavior.
   (b) <u>Applied</u> <u>sociology</u> seeks to provide immediate practical answers to problems.
3. Individual sociologists share many of the same concerns about social problems with the general public.
   (a) By combining these concerns with objective research findings, sociology has become a powerful tool for shaping government policy in the public interest.

MATCHING

A. Comte

B. W.E.B. DuBois

C. Marx

D. Durkheim

E. Weber

F. Manifest function

G. Anomic Suicide

H. Structural-Functional
    Theory

I. Conflict Theory

J. Symbolic Interactionism

K. Pure Sociology

L. Jane Adams

M. Microsociology

N. Applied Sociology

O. Fatalistic suicide

____ 1. Early studies to understand and combat racism.

____ 2. Provides immediate answers to practical problems.

____ 3. Inequalities in power and rewards are built into the social structure.

____ 4. Concerns about the balance between regulation and freedom.

____ 5. How individuals are shaped by relationships and social structure.

____ 6. Applied Hegel's dialectic to economic change.

____ 7. Positivism.

____ 8. Recipient of the 1931 Nobel Peace Prize.

____ 9. Value free sociology

____ 10. Consequences of too much societal regulation.

CHAPTER 1

FILL IN THE BLANK QUESTIONS

1. _____ is the philosophy arguing that the social world can be studied with the same scientific accuracy and assurance as the natural world.

2. The dialectic consists of three steps called _____ , _____ , and _____ .

3. _____ emphasized the necessity of studying the subjective meanings of human actions.

4. Providing a sexual outlet for the kinky is a _____ function of prostitution.

5. Urban life during the early years of industrialization was characterized by _____ , _____ and dynamic change.

6. Marx regarded private property and capitalism as the causes of _____ and _____ _____.

7. _____ rejected _____ idea that economic factors were the determinants of all other social relationships.

8. Three features have characterized U.S. sociology; they are, a concern with _____ _____, a _____ approach and an emphasis on the _____ _____.

9. Sociology in the United States has always been oriented towards the _____ as well as the _____.

10. _____ , _____ and evolution are the three assumptions behind structural-functionalism.

11. Positive consequences are called _____ and negative consequences are called _____.

12. Structural-functional and conflict theories emphasize the _____ sociological level of analysis while symbolic interactionism emphasizes the _____ sociological level of analysis.

13. A major weakness of ____ theory is that it ignores the larger social relationships that constitute society.

14. Making the connection between personal troubles and the larger context of social structure requires one to use the ____ ____.

15. Science requires the ____ and ____ examination of evidence before reaching any conclusion.

MULTIPLE CHOICE

1. The unique province of sociology:

   a. systematic study of social structure.
   b. use of scientific method.
   c. an interest in people.
   d. emphasis on individual factors such as motivation and intelligence.

2. Public issues are different from personal troubles in that:

   a. issues affect a few people and require personal adjustments.
   b. issues affect a few people and require structural adjustments.
   c. issues affect a large number of people and require structural adjustments.
   d. issues affect a large number of people and require personal adjustments.

3. He coined the term "sociology" and was the first major figure concerned with the science of society:

   a. C. Wright Mills.
   b. August Comte.
   c. Herbert Spencer.
   d. Emile Durkheim.

4.   Karl Marx saw all human relationships stemming ultimately from the:

     a.   family.
     b.   education.
     c.   religion.
     d.   economy.

5.   Durkheim's concept of "collective conscience" refers to:

     a.   instincts.
     b.   middle-class norms.
     c.   community standards of morality.
     d.   influence of national leaders.

6.   Founder of sociology who rejected Marx's ideas and emphasized the role of values in the foundation of economic systems:

     a.   Emile Durkheim.
     b.   Auguste Comte.
     c.   Max Weber.
     d.   C. Wright Mills.
     e.   Herbert Spencer.

7.   When members of an athletic team do what is expected of them during a contest, a sociologist would say that they are:

     a.   intelligent.
     b.   a social structure.
     c.   talented
     d.   motivated.

8.   An example of a public issue:

     a.   John can't find a part-time job to help pay his tuition.
     b.   John's girl friend is angry.
     c.   John received a grade of F.
     d.   many students find it difficult to pay for their tuition.

9. If parents wished to use Durkheim's perspective on regulation and freedom when bringing up these children, they would:

   a. balance regulation and freedom.
   b. provide maximum freedom.
   c. always be strict and when in doubt overregulate.
   d. be noncommittal with regard to expectations.

10. If one's purpose is not only to study society but to reform it, this would be most consistent with the ideas of:

   a. Weber.
   b. Marx.
   c. Durkheim.
   d. Comte.

11. Being able to see a life in the context of social structure illustrates:

   a. value freedom.
   b. sociological imagination.
   c. dialectic.
   d. biological evolution.

12. The belief that sociology should be value-free means that sociologists should be concerned with:

   a. what is rather than what ought to be.
   b. identifying the major values of a free society.
   c. analyzing how values affect individual behavior.
   d. making recommendations about how to make a better society.

13. A major concern of symbolic interaction:

   a. development and communication of shared meanings.
   b. competing interest groups.
   c. social order.
   d. integrated wholes.

14. The theory most likely used by a sociologist whose analysis of athletics is guided by the question, Who is receiving benefits; who is being hurt by athletics?

    a.   structural functionalism.
    b.   conflict.
    c.   symbolic interactionism.
    d.   macrosociology.

15. A guiding assumption of Marx's theory of social change:

    a.   the dialectic.
    b.   stability.
    c.   harmony.
    d.   evolution.

16. The theory that can be most directly linked to the ideas of Emile Durkheim:

    a.   conflict
    b.   symbolic interactionism.
    c.   structural functionalism.
    d.   dramaturgy.

17. This theory places less emphasis on the importance of value-free sociology:

    a.   structural-functionalism.
    b.   positivism.
    c.   symbolic interaction.
    d.   conflict.

18. This theory addresses the question of social organization and how it is maintained:

    a.   structural functionalism.
    b.   conflict.
    c.   symbolic interaction.
    d.   positivism.

19. Of particular importance for the emergence of sociology in western Europe:

    a.   industrial revolution.
    b.   wars.
    c.   decline or morality.
    d.   government scandal.

20. This school established the first course in sociology:

    a.   Harvard
    b.   Michigan.
    c.   Berkeley.
    d.   Yale.

21. Early sociology in this country was characterized by an interest in:

    a.   social problems.
    b.   theoretical issues.
    c.   revolution.
    d.   preserving rural society.

22. The majority of sociologists in the U.S. are employed in this sector:

    a.   government.
    b.   business.
    c.   higher education.
    d.   nonprofit organizations.

23. The founders of sociology all came from this part of the world:

    a.   South America.
    b.   Europe.
    c.   Africa.
    d.   Asia.

24. The most important contribution of sociologists to public policy debates:

   a. specify the values and preferences of elites.
   b. convert leaders to economic determinism.
   c. upgrade the values of leaders.
   d. be objective and represent interests of ordinary people.

25. Students who gain the ability to see even the intimate realities of their own lives in the context of social structure can be said to:

   a. have a sociological imagination.
   b. have verstehen.
   c. be experiencing anomie.
   d. be aware of latent functions.

26. If the trend continues for more and more sociologists to take jobs in business of in government, increasingly they will emphasize:

   a. pure research.
   b. a disregard for prediction and trend analysis.
   c. work that breaks with the traditions of American sociology.
   d. applied research.

27. Compared to other social sciences, the unique province (emphasis) of sociology is a concern for:

   a. scientific method.
   b. social structure.
   c. patterned social regularities.
   d. human behavior.

28. Generalizing from the factors that encouraged the development of sociology in the 19th century, which condition would lead to the further development of sociology?

   a. rapid social change.
   b. stability.
   c. disregard for social problems.
   d. disillusion with science.

29. The two founding fathers of sociology who played key roles in the debate over the primacy of economic forces versus social and religious values:

    a. Karl Marx and Max Weber.
    b. Karl Marx and Emile Durkheim.
    c. Max Weber and Herbert Spencer.
    d. August Comte and Herbert Spencer.

30. Based upon Durkheim's early research on suicide, one can expect that suicides may increase when society allows:

    a. too little or too much freedom.
    b. too little freedom.
    c. too much freedom.
    d. too much regulation.

ESSAY QUESTIONS

1. Discuss how the industrial revolution helped to break down traditional values, beliefs and behavior.

2. Discuss what is meant by the concept of the "Sociological Imagination."

3. Explain how conflict theory appeals to the "have-nots" in society and how structural-functional theory appeals to the "haves" in society.

4. Describe the process used by the structural-functionalist assessing the consequences for the operation of a given social structure.

5. Discuss how sociological research has become a powerful tool influencing public policy decisions.

Chapter 2
Doing
Sociology

LEARNING OBJECTIVES

1.   Define what is meant by the concept science and contrast it to common sense.

2.   Note the goals of scientific research and describe how the research process helps to achieve these goals.

3.   Outline the steps of the research process.

4.   Differentiate between the following concepts: variable, independent variable, dependent variable and control variable.

5.   Use the following terms to discuss the relationship between observation and theory: theory, hypotheses, correlation, induction and deduction.

6.   Explain the role played by operational definitions in the research process.

7.   Discuss what a sample is and note how one would go about selecting a sample.

8.   Outline the procedures, advantages and disadvantages of the controlled experiment, the sample survey and participant observation.

9. Compare and contrast the panel and cross sectional research designs.

10. Note some alternative research strategies to experiments, surveys and participant observation studies.

11. Outline the research methodology and results for each of the three studies noted as examples of sociological research.

12. Discuss the ethical issues associated with the experiment, the survey and participant observation research.

13. Define replication and note how it is used in the pursuit of scientific knowledge.

14. Describe the role played by professional journals in screening and distributing sociological research findings.

15. Discuss the relationship between marijuana smoking and school performance.

16. Note the kinds of harm that might befall human subjects in social research and outline the protections they enjoy as subjects.

17. Discuss the problems encountered by sociologists who are pressured to find solutions to pressing social problems.

CHAPTER OUTLINE

I. The Application of Science to Sociology

    A. Sociology is an academic discipline that uses the procedures of science to critically examine common sense explanations of human behavior. Science can thus be considered an extension of common sense.
        1. Science is a way of knowing that requires an objective and critical approach to empirical evidence.
            (a) An objective approach requires that evidence be evaluated in a fair manner without personal bias.
            (b) A critical approach means that all research results are

carefully examined to see if they meet strict technical standards.

    (1) Generally, results are only accepted after they have been <u>replicated</u>.

(c) <u>Empirical</u> refers to evidence that it is confirmed by human senses.

(d) While science cannot guarantee finding the truth, it is the best means we have for seeking and validating knowledge.

    (1) In sociology, science allows us to examine highly charged social issues and to produce answers that stand up to critical evaluation by objective observers.

II.   A Primer on Sociological Research

  A.   The research process has two goals: description and explanation. There are four steps to achieve these goals.

    1.   <u>Gathering data</u>.

    2.   <u>Finding patterns</u> may involve the discovery of <u>correlations</u> or an empirical relationship between two variables.

    3.   <u>Generating theories</u>.

       (a) A <u>theory</u> is an interrelated set of assumptions that explains observed patterns.

       (b) Theory always goes beyond known facts and includes untested assumptions that explain empirical evidence.

    4.   <u>Hypotheses</u> are statements about the empirical relationships we expect to observe if our theory is correct.

       (a) New data arising from hypotheses testing may be the basis for a revised theory.

       (b) This new theory will again be subject to empirical test and the research process begins anew.

    5.   The process of science can be viewed as a continuously turning wheel that moves from data to theory (<u>induction</u>) and from theory to data (<u>deduction</u>).

  B.   Sociological research involves several basic principles of research.

    1.   Sociological research focuses upon <u>variables</u> or the measured characteristics that vary from one individual or group to the next.

       (a) When we hypothesize a cause and effect relationship

between two variables, the cause is called the <u>independent variable</u> and the effect is called the <u>dependent variable</u>.

2. The research process requires exact specifications for the measurement of variables. These exact procedures are called <u>operational definitions</u>.

3. Sampling involves taking a systematic selection of representative causes from a larger population and involves two separate processes.
   (a) The first requires that one acquire a list of the population that you want to study.
   (b) The second requires that a representative sample be drawn from the list.
      (1) A random selection process generally assures an unbiased sample.

C   Evaluating sociological research.
   1. Professional researchers are obligated to share their research findings with their peers and to subject their work to objective and critical scrutiny. The primary mechanism for this is the professional journal.
      (a) When a research project is completed, the results are summarized along with a detailed description of the sample and the operational definitions and submitted to a professional journal for review.
         (1) Over 90% of these reports are rejected as not meeting the highest standards of the discipline.
      (b) Research reports making it into professional journals represent only the finest work done by scientists.
         (1) These reports are the basis for the research quoted in most sociology texts.

III. Three Strategies for Gathering Data

A.   An <u>experiment</u> is a method in which independent variables are manipulated in order to test theories of cause and effect.
   1. A controlled experiment requires that the researcher create two equivalent groups, impose the independent variable on one group (<u>the experimental group</u>) and not in the second group <u>the control group</u>). If the dependent variable appears only in the experimental group, a cause and effect relationship

can be assumed between the independent and dependent variable.

(a) Serious limitations arise with experiments.

    (1) First, experiments are often unethical because they expose subjects to harm.

    (2) Subjects often behave differently in experimental settings than they would in everyday life. This phenomena is called the guinea pig effect.

    (3) The artificiality of many laboratory settings reduces our confidence in generalizing the results of these experiments to the more complex setting of the real world.

(b) Because of these limitations relatively little sociological research utilizes the controlled experiment.

B.   Survey research involves asking a relatively large number of people the same set of standardized questions.

    1.   Because large samples are used, survey research is an ideal methodology for providing evidence on incidence, trends and differentials.

    2.   Most surveys use a cross-sectional design which takes a sample or cross-section of the population at one point in time.

        (a) Control variables can be utilized to eliminate background factors in order to better understand the relationship between the variables being studied.

    3.   Panel designs follow a sample over a period of time during which some portion of the sample experiences the independent variable.

        (a) Panel designs are expensive and time consuming.

    4.   Despite the use of control variables, panel designs and cross-sectional designs are less efficient than experiments in demonstrating causation.

        (a) Another problem of these survey designs is the misrepresentation of data known as the social desirability bias.

C   Participant observation is a method that seeks to examine the contexts of human interaction and their meanings for the individuals involved.

    1.   The major elements of this method are interviewing,

participating and observing.

    (a) The data produced is usually unrepresentative and unsystematic as a sample; conversely it is very rich data on the few individuals involved.

    (b) Examining real behavior, uncooperative populations and deviant behavior is best suited to participant observation technique.

    (c) In order to validate the findings of a study other scientists may engage in replication.

D.   Alternative strategies exist, many of which focus upon the analysis of social artifacts rather than people.

IV. Examples of Sociological Research

A.   Aneshensel, Fiedler and Becerra studied teenage sexual activity in Los Angeles County. They sought to describe the frequency, trends and differentials of sexual activity among Mexican American and Anglo women 13-19 years old. Their goal was to understand the relationship between sexual activity and teenage pregnancy.

    1. The sample consisted of over 1,000 young women selected through a detailed and exhaustive sample of households.

    2. The questionnaire itself was developed from 50 long informal interview sessions.

    3. The overall frequency of sexual intercourse was 50 percent.

    4. Ethnic differentials showed that Anglo women were more sexually active than Mexican American women.

        (a) Conversely, Mexican American women had significantly higher rates of pregnancy.

           (1) Women from broken homes had the highest probability of becoming pregnant due to their higher frequency of sexual activity and lower frequency of using contraception.

    5. Aneshensel, Fiedler and Becerra conclude that the prevention of pregnancy among the sexually active is a most pressing intervention priority.

B.   Elliot Liebow conducted a participant observation study of street

corner men in a slum in Washington, D.C.
1.   Liebow sought to uncover the relationship between the social structure of their community and what meanings the street corner men attached to their behavior.
    (a) A key relationship was to one's work which usually consisted of low-paying, unskilled dead-end jobs that robbed a man of his self-esteem and self-respect.
2.   The typical response was to reject work and hang out on the street corner where a set of shadow values permitted fictional accommodations that permitted them to be men again.
    (a) The shadow values included the theory of manly flaws that rationalized their behavior by saying that they were too manly to fill a man's role, hold a job, or submit to authority.
        (1) This explanation required neither social activism or self-hate.

C   Swartz and Gottlieb conducted an experiment on the by-stander effect where the research question centered upon the circumstances under which bystanders will intervene to help a stranger.
1.   A laboratory setting was chosen to carefully control the circumstances of the investigation and to avoid ethical problems.   Two experimental conditions were created.
    (a) Group one consisted of students who believed that they were the lone bystander and that the victim knew of their presence.
    (b) Group two consisted of students who believed that there were other bystanders in the area who could help and that the victim was unaware of their presence.
2.   In the experiment, the subjects (N=127) were randomly assigned to each treatment condition and each was shown a video scene where they believed a person in a nearby room had been a victim of an attack.
3.   While 89% of the subjects eventually made some attempt at help, the speed varied with the experimental treatment.
    (a) The maximum response occurred when the subject was the only bystander; however, when others were present, responsibility to help was not clearly defined and people were hesitant to help.

CHAPTER 2

V. The Ethics of Social Research

    A.   Most universities and professional associations have established strict codes of ethics and committees to oversee research with human subjects.
            1.   Subjects should not come to any physical, social or psychological harm due to their participation in research studies.

    B.   Sociological research raises few ethical issues and subjects are not likely to be harmed if ethical practices are followed.
            1.   A.S.A. code of ethics includes the following:
                (a) Subjects are entitled to the rights of biographical anonymity.
                (b) Sociologists must take the culturally appropriate steps to secure informed consent and to avoid the invasion of privacy.
                (c) Participation in research must not expose subjects to substantial risk of personal harm including embarrassment, mental trauma, physical harm, job loss or legal penalty.
            2.   The major ethical issue in sociological experiments focuses on the fact that deception is almost always involved which may be stressful and harmful to the research subjects.
            3.   Survey research raises few ethical issues due to the highly voluntary nature of participation in surveys.
            4.   Participant observation research raises the biggest ethical questions which center upon two issues.
                (a) An observer may not inform subjects they are being observed.
                (b) The observer must entitle the subjects to biographical anonymity and protect their identity.

VI. Sociology and Social Policy

    A.   Research on controversial social issues walks a tightrope between the demands for scientific standards and the social demands for immediate solutions.
            1.   Difficulties arise for the sociologist when problems arise too quickly for rigorous research designs or they may rise to the top of the political agenda before enough research has been

done.
(a) The sociologist is often caught between political reality and scientific standards.

MATCHING

A. Panel design

B. Experiment

C. Dependent variable

D. Induction

E. Replication

F. Deduction

G. Independent variable

H. Correlation

I. Social desirability bias

J. Operational definition

K. Participant observation

L. Hypotheses

M. Guinea-pig effect

N. Survey

O. Empirical

___ 1. An empirical relationship between two variables.

___ 2. The cause.

___ 3. Evidence confirmed by human senses.

___ 4. Expensive and time consuming.

___ 5. The ethical issue is the possibility of harm.

___ 6. Most common sociological research methodology.

___ 7. People behave differently under scientific observation.

___ 8. Ethics of biographical immunity.

___ 9. From theory to observation.

___ 10. Tendency to color the truth.

CHAPTER 2

FILL IN THE BLANK QUESTIONS

1. Science is not divorced from ____ ____ but is an extension of it.

2. Science requires an ____ and ____ approach to ____ evidence.

3. The research process has two goals: ____ and ____.

4. The four steps to the research process are gathering ____, finding ____, generating ____ and testing ____.

5. The American Sociological Association code of ethics guarantees subjects ____ ____, informed consent, privacy and protection from a substantial risk of ____ ____.

6. Survey research is the ideal methodology for providing evidence on the ____ , ____ and ____.

7. ____, ____ and ____ are the three major elements of participant observation research.

8. The strength of the ____ ____ method is the detail about the context of behavior it is able to gather.

9. Sampling requires that you first get a list of the population and that you get a ____ ____ from that list.

10. The assertion that a man is too much of a man to fulfill his expected role is explained by Liebow's theory of ____ ____.

11. Schwartz and Gottlieb found that the most favorable conditions under which a victim may receive help from a stranger is when one is a ____ and ____ bystander.

12. The ____ is a methodology that has the disadvantage of using unrepresentative samples in highly artificial situations.

13. The ____ ____ specifies how variables are to be measured.

14. Aneshensel, Fiedler and Becarra found that young women who did not live with their natural parents were ____ likely to be sexually active, ____ likely to use contraception and ____ likely to become pregnant.

15. Mexican American women had a ____ frequency of intercourse and a ____ frequency of pregnancy when compared to Anglo women.

MULTIPLE CHOICE

1. Science differs from other methods of acquiring knowledge in that science:

   a. required empirical evidence.
   b. is systematic.
   c. is divorced from common sense.
   d. is modern.

2. The first step in the research process begins with:

   a. gathering data.
   b. define the problem more specifically.
   c. choosing a research design.
   d. analyzing data.

3. The variable in a hypothesis that precedes or causes the other variable in the hypothesis:

   a. sample.
   b. dependent.
   c. independent.
   d. cause.

4. The exact procedures that we use to measure variables:

   a. sampling.
   b. operational definitions.
   c. observations.
   d. induction.

5. This strategy calls for a group of people to be surveyed at several points in time:

    a.   random sampling.
    b.   developing an operational definition.
    c.   random design.
    d.   panel design.

6. Used to look at two variables simultaneously:

    a.   independent variable.
    b.   cross-tabulation.
    c.   hypothesis.
    d.   operational definition.

7. Social scientists who use the general research process follow this sequence of steps:

    a.   data, finding patterns, theory.
    b.   theory, finding patterns, data.
    c.   data, theory, finding patterns.
    d.   finding patterns, data, theory.

8. Consider this hypothesis: students who use marijuana will have lower grades. What is the independent variable?

    a.   sex.
    b.   year in school.
    c.   marijuana use.
    d.   grades.

9. Let's suppose that you have been asked to help draw a sample of students with the object being to evaluate a newly proposed grading system. Which statement would you want to guide your sample selection?

    a. with a population of 25,000 students, a sample of 25 is okay.
    b. since seniors are more experienced, only include seniors in the sample.
    c. randomly select 500 students from all students registered for the sample.
    d. a random sample of 500 students from among those taking a course in Introductory Sociology will be used.

10. The experiment has been most useful in the:

    a. study of small group interaction.
    b. search for frequencies and trends.
    c. study of undesirable behavior.
    d. study of uncooperative persons.

11. In the hypothetical study of marijuana use and grades, neighborhood quality was what kind of variable?

    a. independent.
    b. dependent.
    c. control.
    d. social desirability.

12. To determine if both marijuana use and good grades are determined by social class one could:

    a. develop better samples.
    b. improve on operational definitions.
    c. introduce a control variable.
    d. focus upon whole individuals and not variables.

13. The most difficult task in sampling:

    a.   getting an accurate list.
    b.   introducing a control variable.
    c.   interpreting frequencies.
    d.   interviewing people.

14. This method of obtaining data has serious limitations because a researcher cannot expose subjects to an independent variable that might harm them:

    a.   survey.
    b.   questionnaire.
    c.   controlled experiment.
    d.   field studies.

15. In a study of marijuana use and grades, it was decided to categorize the students into subgroups such as sex, year in school, or major. This technique is called:

    a.   introducing a causal variable.
    b.   analyzing a frequency.
    c.   cross-tabulation.
    d.   developing a cross-sectional design.

16. Participant observation includes three elements. Which is not one of the elements?

    a.   interviewing.
    b.   participating.
    c.   observing.
    d.   large and representative samples.

17. Suppose that you have been asked to help conduct a study of students' interests and concerns. Data are to be obtained by analyzing the kinds of magazines that are found in the rooms of students. What kind of research strategy would this demonstrate?

    a.   controlled experiment.
    b.   survey.
    c.   participant observation.
    d.   artifact study.

18. If the objective is to document trends in adolescent sexual activity, one should turn to:

    a.   controlled experiments.
    b.   participant observation.
    c.   introspection.
    d.   survey research.

19. The major criticism of the research that looked at the possible side effects of birth control pills or the study of black men who had syphilis:

    a.   poor samples.
    b.   asking about unimportant issues.
    c.   studies were unethical and irresponsible.
    d.   studies should have been longitudinal.

20. Excellent device for demonstrating causal relationships:;

    a.   participant observation.
    b.   cross-sectional design.
    c.   panel design.
    d.   controlled experiment.

21. The major ethical issue that arises in experimental research:

    a.   putting ideas in peoples' heads.
    b.   not asking if people are willing to be studied.
    c.   deception about the research purpose.
    d.   high costs.

22.   In the study of adolescent sexual activity, researchers found that the best predictor of a person becoming pregnant was:

a.   age of person.
b.   social class of person.
c.   race of person.
d.   coming from a broken home.

23.   The research by Schwartz and Gottlied is one of the recent studies in the bystander tradition spawned by the Kitty Genovese incident.   Subjects in this condition were most likely to offer aid when:

a.   others are present, and others know that student is there.
b.   others are present, nobody knows that student is there.
c.   no others are present, others know that student is there.
d.   no others are present, nobody knows student is there

24.   Which is not included in the American Sociological Association's code of ethics?

a.   biographical anonymity for research subjects.
b.   experiments never to be used.
c.   protection of research subjects' privacy.
d.   no personal harm for research subjects.

25.   Science has been described as a continuously turning wheel.   Which is not true of this wheel?

a.   never-ending.
b.   no beginning point and no end.
c.   you must start with observation.
d.   investigator moves continuously between observations and theory.

26.   One clear advantage of participant observation is:

a.   can see behavior in context.
b.   excellent for analysis of cause-and-effect.
c.   limited to small, non-representative samples.
d.   can be done with large, random samples.

27. The best method for gathering data in a study of consumer preferences needed for a national advertising campaign:

    a.   participant observation.
    b.   controlled experiment.
    c.   survey.
    d.   social artifacts.

28. Participant observation is considered appropriate for all but one of the following:

    a.   studying undesirable behavior.
    b.   studying behavior rather than attitudes.
    c.   studying individuals without regard for social contexts.
    d.   studying uncooperative populations.

29. Various surveys have found that students who use marijuana get worse grades. The major weakness of this research that limits its usefulness for policy is:

    a.   cause not proven.
    b.   small samples.
    c.   poorly written survey questions.
    d.   research not timely.

30. If scientists practice this in their research, they will take a skeptical attitude toward new research findings:

    a.   be critical.
    b.   be objective.
    c.   be empirical.
    d.   discourage replicated studies.

ESSAY QUESTIONS

1. What is the advantage of using the scientific approach if it cannot guarantee finding the "truth"?

2. Explain the ethical issues that arise in social research using human subjects.

3. Compare and contrast the panel and cross sectional research designs and describe a study where each would be preferable.

4. Outline the advantages of sample survey research as compared to the controlled experiment and participant observation research.

5. How good is published sociological research?

Chapter 3
Culture

LEARNING OBJECTIVES

1.   Discuss the difference between society, culture, material culture and nonmaterial culture.

2.   Define and distinguish between the following terms: values, norms, folkways, mores, laws, sanctions, informal sanctions and formal sanctions.

3.   Define and discuss the difference between subculture, counterculture, elite culture and popular culture.

4.   List those values Americans say are important and note those values <u>sociologists</u> identify as being central and significant to the understanding of American culture.

5.   Identify and describe the major American values of the 1980's.

6.   Use the concept of sociobiology to discuss the existence of cultural universals.

7.   Discuss how culture is uniquely human.

8.   Discuss the role language plays in the development of human culture.

CHAPTER 3

9. Outline the linguistic relativity hypothesis.

10. Explain what is meant by cultural relativity and ethnocentrism.

11. Outline how the environment, technology, isolation and diffusion influence cultural variability and the rate of cultural change.

12. Note how the dominant cultural theme of Inis Beag can inhibit social change.

13. How do structural functionalism and conflict theory differ in their view of culture?

14. How is culture problem solving, relative and a social product?

15. Discuss why a knowledge of both biological and social factors are necessary in order to understand human behavior.

16. How is the south a uniquely regional subculture?

17. Discuss how culture is "produced" in America.

18. Discuss the pro's and con's of the ELA.

CHAPTER OUTLINE

I. Culture

    A. <u>Culture</u> is the total way of life shared by the members of a society.
        1. There are two categories of culture: <u>material culture</u> and <u>nonmaterial culture</u>.

    B. Within sociology there are two approaches to the study of culture.
        1. Structural functionalism treats culture as the underlying basis of interaction.
        2. Conflict theory focuses more upon culture as a social product and stress why particular aspects of culture develop.

II.   Culture and Biology

    A.   Biological factors help explain what is common to humankind across societies while culture explains why people and societies differ from each other.

        1.   Sociologists share the <u>cultural perspective</u>, they believe that culture is <u>problem solving</u>, <u>relative</u> and that it is a <u>social product</u>.

            (a) Cultural patterns have evolved to solve basic human problems.

                (1) Functionalists argue that these solutions have evolved over time by trial and error and that they endure because they work.

                (2) Conflict theorists note that these solutions work better for some people than for others and that elites have manipulated culture in order to maintain their advantages.

            (b) The solutions adopted by different cultures vary greatly. Therefore each cultural trait can only be evaluated using the idea of <u>cultural relativity</u>.

                (1) Failure to do so results in <u>ethnocentrism</u>, a natural but undesirable practice that can diminish other and different ways of thinking and feeling.

            (c) Some elements of culture are deliberately produced, thus making it a social product, not a biological product.

                (1) People learn culture and as they do, they modify and change it.

                (2) Culture depends upon a unique human attribute: language.

                (3) Language allows humans to change their culture at a very rapid rate thus freeing us from the slow process of genetic evolution.

        2.   The <u>biological perspective</u> of culture focuses upon <u>cultural universals</u> or the basic similarities shared by all cultures.

            (a) <u>Sociobiology</u> is the study of the biological basis of all forms of human behavior. It assumes that all life forms, including humans, have developed through evolution and natural selection.

(b) Most sociologists are more concerned with contemporary issues of understanding how biological and social factors work together to determine human behavior.
(1) Udry's research has explored the social and biological factors in puberty.

3. Both culture and biology must be considered in understanding the human condition.

III. The Carriers of Culture

A. Language is the ability to communicate in symbols.
1. Language is a carrier of culture; it embodies values and meanings.
(a) A loss of language may mean a loss of culture.
2. Language also shapes and confines our perceptions.
(a) The linguistic relativity hypothesis argues that grammar, structure and categories used in a language affect how one sees reality.
3. The use of a particular language can serve as a symbol in and of itself.
(a) Distinct languages can symbolize group or cultural differences.

B. Shared ideas about desirable goals are called values.
1. While many values may be universal, i.e., stability, security, strong family ties, etc. The guidelines for achieving them varies dramatically from culture to culture.

C. Cultural guidelines or shared rules of conduct are called norms.
1. Norms specify the means for achieving socially valued ends.
(a) Customary and habitual ways of doing things called folkways.
(b) Mores are norms that have strong feelings of right and wrong associated with them.
(c) Laws are norms that are officially enforced.

D. Social control refers to conforming to the norms of society.
1. Conformity is encouraged by sanctions -- rewards for conformity and punishments for deviance.

(a) Sanctions may be formal or informal.

(b) Normative behavior and actual behavior may differ.

E.   Variations in lifestyle are typical of modern societies.
1.   Groups sharing the overall culture but maintaining distinctive values, norms and life-styles are culled <u>subcultures</u>.
2.   Groups whose unique values, norms and lifestyles conflict with the dominant culture are called <u>countercultures</u>.

F.   <u>Societies</u> are groups of interacting individuals who share the same territory and are bound together by economic and political ties.

IV.   Cultural Variation and Change

A.   Cultural variation and change can in good part be explained by reference to such factors as the <u>environment</u>, <u>social isolation</u>, <u>technology</u> and <u>dominant cultural themes</u>.
1.   The physical and natural environment of an area sets the stage for the cultural adaptations of society.
(a) Environmental conditions can include climate, terrain and natural resources.
2.   Isolation or the absence of contact with other societies tends to perpetuate cultural patterns and slow the rate of change.
(a) Isolation may be geographical or social in nature.
(1) The unique culture of the island of Inis Beag arose and is maintained by physical and social isolation.
(b) Isolation tends to produce ethnocentrism.
3.   Technology, or the technological position of a society, can enhance the degree of cultural variation between societies. It can also have an impact on the rate of social change within a society.
4.   Social change can be accelerated by <u>diffusion</u>, the spread of cultural traits when one culture comes into contact with another.
(a) The industrial revolution and western practices of colonialism have produced rapid social change through diffusion.
(b) The technology of mass communications has greatly accelerated the process of international diffusion.

5. A dominant cultural theme gives a distinct character and direction to a culture, thus contributing to greater cultural variation.
    (a) A dominant cultural theme may also function like ethnocentrism to create barriers to interaction.

V. American Culture

A. American values are those things Americans feel are worth pursuing.
    1. Survey research asking Americans what they value the most, shows that a good family life, good self image, good health and a feeling of accomplishment are very important.
    2. Observation of American behavior shows three major categories of values significant to understanding our culture.
        (a) The importance of work.
        (b) The importance of achievement and success.
        (c) The importance of being moral.
    3. An important changing value that has taken on much prominence in the last decade is self-fulfillment.
        (a) This raises a question of the proper balance between commitment to others.
        (b) Other changing values include a reduced emphasis on work and a greater emphasis on consumerism.
        (c) While most American norms remain stable, there is a general acceptance of variation in the ways that people pursue major cultural values.
        (d) Despite these changes American values are quite stable.
    4. American society is characterized by great diversity and many subcultures. Highly visible subcultures center upon geographic or regional variations in lifestyles.
        (a) American countercultures include radical groups like white supremacists and punkers.
    5. Elite culture refers to art, opera, etc., while popular culture is what people like and what people do.
        (a) In the United States, the production of both popular and elite culture depends upon public support and financing.
            (1) Popular culture relies heavily upon market forces like commercial television programming.

(2) Elite culture often turns to private wealth or government support.

(3) The government may try to control the production of culture through legislation and regulation.

MATCHING

A. Values   ____ 1. The carrier of culture.

B. Subculture   ____ 2. Units of territorial organization.

C. Ethnocentricism   ____ 3. Shared rules of conduct.

D. Culture   ____ 4. A trait must be evaluated within the context of its own culture.

E. Isolation

     ____ 5. The spread of cultural traits.

F. Elite Culture

     ____ 6. Shared ideas of desirable goals.

G. Norms

     ____ 7. Punkers and white supremacists.

H. Counterculture

     ____ 8. Inis Beag

I. Evolution

     ____ 9. The customary, normal, habitual way a group does things.

J. Cultural Relativity

K. Language   ____ 10. Art, opera, symphony.

L. Folkways

M. Society

N. Diffusion

O. Mores

CHAPTER 3

FILL IN THE BLANK QUESTIONS

1. Culture is ___ ___, ___ and a ___ ___.

2. The ___ ___ ___ argues that grammar, structure, and categories used in language affect one's perception of reality.

3. The traditional form of Catholicism practiced in Ines Beag is best described as a ___ ___ ___.

4. Rewards for conformity and punishments for deviance are called ___.

5. The resistance to the E.L.A. reflects the notion that one's language can serve as a ___.

6. Norms associated with strong feelings of right and wrong are called ___.

7. Within the United States, a baseball bat would be classified as an item of ___ ___.

8. Culture depends upon a unique human attribute: ___.

9. ___ theorists are more interested in the determinants of culture.

10. ___ focuses upon the biological and evolutionary bases of social behavior.

11. An American reacting negatively to the unique culture of Inis Beag could be guilty of being ___.

12. Recent research indicates that ___ is the major American value of the 1980's.

13. The major changes in American values are a growing emphasis on ___, a reduced emphasis on ___ and a greater emphasis on ___.

14. Many of the things that were clearly wrong a generation ago are increasingly being ___ by the American public.

15. Subcultures generally share the dominant values but differ in their ____ and ____.

MULTIPLE CHOICE

1. Included as an element of material culture:

   a. tools.
   b. beliefs.
   c. values.
   d. norms.

2. An informal norm that specifies customary habitual ways of behaving:

   a. more.
   b. law.
   c. folkway.
   d. value.

3. A group of people who share the dominant culture of society but who also maintain a distinct set of values, norms, and lifestyles:

   a. counterculture.
   b. subculture.
   c. society.
   d. nationality.

4. A capacity or gift not shared by man with other animals:

   a. distinguish and sign gestures.
   b. combine gestures into rudimentary sentences.
   c. speak true language.
   d. potential for abstract reasoning.

5. Not a contributor to cultural variability and change:

    a. technology.
    b. isolation.
    c. environment.
    d. biological inheritance.

6. Refers to the total way of life shared by members of society:

    a. norm.
    b. value.
    c. subculture.
    d. culture.

7. Professor Brown wore blue jeans to a faculty reception. Several friends kidded Brown about his dress. Brown had violated a:

    a. more.
    b. law.
    c. folkway.
    d. value.

8. John has noticed that his boss smiles and is pleased when John gets to work at the office a bit early, or stays a bit late. John is being influenced by:

    a. values.
    b. informal sanctions.
    c. formal sanctions.
    d. mores.

9. An example of a counterculture:

    a. religious group.
    b. occupational group.
    c. ethnic group.
    d. punkers, or delinquent gangs.

10. When American abroad say that "they really find these people strange" they are:

    a.   being ethnocentric.
    b.   expressing cultural relativism.
    c.   identifying with a counterculture.
    d.   expressing a wish for more cultural variability.

11. Betty has just taken a position with a different corporation. She is quite frustrated because the office machines are different, the business forms are unfamiliar and her co-workers use many terms that she hasn't heard before. She is reacting to:

    a.   a subculture.
    b.   diffusion.
    c.   a counterculture.
    d.   mores.

12. The "Goddess of Liberty" constructed by Chinese students illustrates:

    a.   ethnocentricism.
    b.   cultural diffusion.
    c.   invention.
    d.   traditional Chinese isolationism.

13. Values and norms can be evaluated in terms of their generality and immediacy. Which is true:

    a.   norms have more immediate but less general influence on behavior.
    b.   norms have less immediate and less general influence on behavior.
    c.   values have more immediate and more general influence on behavior.
    d.   values have less general and less immediate influence.

14. Marxists pay particular attention to this factor when they attempt to explain cultural change and variability:

   a.   technology.
   b.   environment.
   c.   values and norms.
   d.   biological factors.

15. The cultural equivalent of geographic isolation:

   a.   ethnocentrism.
   b.   cultural relativity.
   c.   cultural universal.
   d.   diffusion.

16. Sociobiology is emerging as an important theoretical perspective in the U.S.   At this time most social scientists:

   a.   openly identify with this theory.
   b.   think that both social and biological factors play a role.
   c.   have adopted this theory but still reject evolution as an important process.
   d.   are rejecting culture as a source of variation in human behavior.

17. Ethnocentrism means using norms and values of our own culture as standards to judge the practice of others.   Which is true about ethnocentrism:

   a.   it is always bad.
   b.   seldom acts as a barrier to understanding.
   c.   it is not altogether bad.
   d.   it is instinctual.

18. Which is not the most common orientation toward culture shared by sociologists?

   a.   it is based upon biological inheritance.
   b.   it is problem solving.
   c.   it is relative.
   d.   it is a social product.

19. Not identified as a central value of Americans:

    a.   loyalty to the group at all costs.
    b.   good health.
    c.   freedom of choice.
    d.   living up to one's potential.

20. The punk counterculture is particularly attractive to:

    a.   middle-class youth.
    b.   young women.
    c.   young men.
    d.   youth outside the mainstream.

21. Not a major factor in the development of sexual repression on Inis Beag:

    a.   cultural diffusion.
    b.   harsh environment.
    c.   limited land supply.
    d.   religion that stresses fear of damnation.

22. The value with the most support of Americans:

    a.   work for a better America.
    b.   a good family life.
    c.   strict moral code.
    d.   having an exciting life.

23. With regard to elite culture, most Americans think that government should:

    a.   provide more funding.
    b.   set standards for good art.
    c.   provide less funding, but set standards for good art.
    d.   not provide funding and not set standards for good art.

24. If a person wants to really understand the culture of a different society, it is necessary to first:

    a. do away with all ethnocentrism.
    b. learn the language.
    c. become familiar with societal values.
    d. visit the country.

25. If trends in American culture continue, we can expect to see:

    a. massive changes in values and norms.
    b. wider variations in the means used to achieve values.
    c. a rejection of popular culture.
    d. a decline in the importance of a good family life.

26. If social change continues at a rapid rate, with inequalities increasing in our society, we can expect to have:

    a. fewer subcultures.
    b. more subcultures.
    c. more subcultures and countercultures.
    d. more countercultures.

27. While many Americans continue to be influenced by traditional values, research has provided evidence of a new value that is prominent now. It is the value that stresses:

    a. hard work and activity.
    b. self-fulfillment.
    c. practicality and efficiency.
    d. achievement and success.

28. Which is not a basis for the most prominent subcultures in the U.S.?

    a. intelligence.
    b. region.
    c. ethnicity or race.
    d. class.

29. This factor operates to perpetuate differences in societies:

    a. diffusion.
    b. geographical isolation.
    c. adoption of technology.
    d. rejection of cultural themes for cultural universals.

30. Which is not true about laws and norms?

    a. mores and norms with strong feelings of right and wrong.
    b. not all violations of mores result in legal punishment.
    c. laws can not be used to create norms.
    d. laws not enforced can become dead-letter laws.

ESSAY QUESTIONS

1. Identify those values that are central and significant to the understanding of American culture and then discuss the impact of the rapid social change of the last decade upon these values.

2. Discuss how structural functional and conflict theory approach the understanding of American culture.

3. What is ethnocentrism, how does it arise and how might it be seen as both helpful and harmful to a given society?

4. Discuss the role played by the environment, isolation and technology in producing cultural variation.

5. Differentiate between culture, material culture and non-material culture. Select an item of material culture and note how it is both a result of culture and an influence upon culture.

Photo Essay:

Environmental Damage: A Cultural Product

1. The average American generates ____ pounds of garbage per week.

2. Environmental damage is a product or our ____ and ____ ____.

3. Very high levels of ____ and ____ are part of the American way of life.

4. The ____ ethic is the basis for much of our current environmental policy.

5. The utility ethic tolerates environmental damage in exchange for ____ and ____.

6. The ____ ethic stands in opposition to the utility ethic.

7. The value changes created by changes in the physical and social environment may be hurried by changing the ____ and ____ environments in which people make decisions.

8. Who owns the water and the air and the whooping crane? The answer is ____.

9. Because resources are owned in common, no one person has a ____ ____ in taking care of them.

10. In contemporary nations...the ____ is the guardian of the environment.

1. Which is NOT an environmental problem?

   a. health hazards.
   b. lack of knowledge.
   c. toxic waste.
   d. overuse of nonrenewable resources.

2. The largest truth is that many of our environmental problems are caused by:

   a. farm practices.
   b. uncaring manufacturers.
   c. those who illegally dump wastes.
   d. values and cultural practices.

3. Which is NOT an element of American life-style that contributes to environmental damage?

   a. expensive lawns.
   b. carpooling.
   c. use of polystyrene.
   d. disposable diapers.

4. Where in the industrialized world is acid rain destroying forests?

   a. the U.S.
   b. Canada.
   c. Japan.
   d. entire world.

5. The sociological imagination suggests that to save the Spotted Owl and other species we will have to:

   a. stop all cutting forests.
   b. import more owls.
   c. change values.
   d. make individuals more responsible.

6.   ____ are the most common set of environmentally relevant values.

   a.   bioethics.
   b.   utility ethics.
   c.   animal rights.
   d.   economic determinism.

7.   Which is NOT consistent with utility ethics?

   a.   if animals get in the way, we are free to exterminate them.
   b.   really no need to be concerned about toxic waste.
   c.   acid rain may be affecting our health.
   d.   above all else, jobs and prosperity come first.

8.   Which is NOT consistent with the biocentric ethic?

   a.   humankind is different and separate from nature.
   b.   the earth is more than just a resource.
   c.   it is our duty to preserve nature.
   d.   people can't put their rights above those of other species.

9.   Generally, the utility ethic emphasizes:

   a.   preservation over development.
   b.   guaranteeing the future over securing the present.
   c.   protecting humankind over nature.
   d.   disregard for development.

10.   The "tragedy of the commons" principle suggests that:

   a.   common people can't understand environmental issues.
   b.   resources held in common may be abused.
   c.   common sense is all that is required to understand environmental issues.
   d.   individuals are too quick to take action against polluters.

Chapter 4
Social Structure

LEARNING OBJECTIVES

1. Define each of the following terms and describe the relationship between them: social structure, status, role, social network and institution.

2. Differentiate between achieved statuses and ascribed statuses using examples for each.

3. Use the example of race to demonstrate how our lives are patterned by status membership.

4. Discuss the difference between role strain and role conflict.

5. Discuss four different factors influencing role performance.

6. Explain why social roles must be negotiated.

7. Explain what is meant by the concept of a social institution and describe the five basic institutions.

8. Outline the emergence of separate institutions and discuss the extent to which institutions are independent or interdependent.

CHAPTER 4

9. Compare and contrast the conflict and functional views of the role of social institutions.

10. Explain the differences between the four types of societies.

11. Discuss the impact of forced relocation and the subsequent changes on the social institutions of the Ojibwa of Grassy Narrows.

12. Discuss how both alcoholism and its cure can be tied to social structure.

CHAPTER OUTLINE

I. Social Structure

    A. Social structures are recurrent patterns of relationships. These relationships can be both enabling and constraining.
        1. A social network is an individual's total set of relationships.

    B. A status is a specialized position within a group.
        1. Statuses are either ascribed or achieved.
        2. Sociologists wish to identify the available range of statuses, determine their distribution, assess the consequences and ascertain how these statuses may be combined.
            (a) Analysis using these four dimensions reveal how our lives are patterned by status membership. Race is a prime example.

    C Roles are sets of norms that specify the rights and obligations of each status and define how the occupants of a status ought to act and feel.
        1. While statuses are fixed, role behavior varies considerably.
        2. Role performance can be influenced when incompatible demands are present.
            (a) Role strain occurs when incompatible demands are built into a single status.
            (b) Role conflict occurs when incompatible demands exist between multiple statuses.
            (c) Adequate role definition, appropriate sanctions and the availability of basic resources also influence role

performance.

3.   The <u>negotiated order</u> refers to the fact that the norms of any social structure are never complete and thus require some improvisation or negotiation.

II.   Institutions

    A.   <u>Institutions</u> are enduring complex social structures that provide ready-made answers to basic human needs. Institutions thus provide for stability and provide an important regulating vitality.

       1.   The basic institutions are the family, economy, government, education and religion.

           (a) Historically all institutions were subsumed within the family institution.

               (1) Increasing complexity in society led to the development of more specialized institutions.

               (2) Institutions are dynamic and are characterized by change.

               (3) The Mormon Church had to alter many of its practices in order to be integrated into the dominant institutions of American society.

       2.   Institutions can lose their regulating vitality when rapid social change occurs.

           (a) The Ojibwa of Grassy Narrows had their institutions destroyed by policies enacted by the Canadian government.

               (1) The result was massive social disorganization applied to everyday living.

           (b) In many cases the social trauma experienced by individuals can only be cured by altering the institutions of society.

       3.   Institutions are interdependent; the elements of each affects the others and is affected by them.

    B.   The role played by institutions is interpreted differently by structural-functional and conflict theorists.

       1.   Structural-functional theory argues that institutions regulate human behavior and provide the basis for social order through encouraging conformity, stability and predictability in social interaction.

2.   Conflict theory acknowledges the regulatory role played by institutions but interpret this as reducing innovation and freedom while favoring one group over another.
   (a) Institutions are thus oppressive and function as mechanisms for disguising inequality.

III. Types of Societies

A.   Society is the population that shares the same territory and is bound together by political and economic ties.
   1.   Historically many types of societies have developed with major changes within the economic institution.

B.   Hunting, fishing and gathering societies are characterized by subsistence economies where there is no surplus, technology is limited and small bonds are organized by kinship ties.

C   Horticultural societies occurred with the first breakthrough from subsistence economies with the development of agriculture.
   1.   Technology is limited but effective in producing a surplus which allows for the formation of a class hierarchy and the emergence of institutions outside of the family.

D.   Agricultural societies emerged as greater surpluses were produced by expanded technology.
   1.   Many people were freed from direct agricultural production producing a greater degree of inequality, a complex class system, permanent urban settlements and the further differentiation of institutions from the family.

E.   Industrial societies occurred when surpluses were greatly increased by mechanical, electrical and petroleum energy sources.
   1.   Increasing numbers of people have now been freed from direct industrial production and the social institutions, knowledge and technology have all been radically altered.

MATCHING

A. Role

B. Industrial societies

C. Social structures

D. Role conflict

E. Horticultural societies

F. Structural-functional theory

G. Status

H. Agricultural societies

I. Ascribed status

J. Conflict theory

L. Role strain

K. Institutions

M. Achieved status

N. Social network

O. Hunting, fishing and gathering societies

____ 1. Institutions provide the basis for social order.

____ 2. Contradictory expectation in two or more statuses.

____ 3. Specialized position within a group.

____ 4. Enduring structures meeting basic human needs.

____ 5. Sets of norms specifying rights and obligations for a status.

____ 6. Incompatible roles within a single status.

____ 7. Institutionalized patterns help maintain inequality.

____ 8. Permanent settlements.

____ 9. An individual's total set of relationships.

____ 10. Bare subsistence, no surplus.

FILL IN THE BLANK QUESTIONS

1. The adult women of Grassy Narrows were forced to become ____ of goods, rather than ____.

2. There is a significant disadvantage to holding the status of ____ in American society.

3. The the first breakthrough from subsistence economy to economic surplus was the development of ____.

4. The basic building block of society is the ____.

5. ____ ____ are recurrent patterns of relationships.

6. The patterns of social structure in our lives are both ____ and ____.

7. When contradictory expectations are built into the same status ____ ____ can occur.

8. Institutions are enduring social structures that meet ____ ____ ____.

9. The analysis of social structure revolves around three concepts: ____, ____ and ____.

10. The Mormon Church in Utah is an example of ____ ____ of institutional ____.

11. Often the individual is not the cause of a social problem, instead the cause lies within the ____ ____.

12. An important determinant of institutional development is society's ability to produce an economic ____.

13. People must be motivated to meet their role expectations by a system of ____.

14. Adequate role performance requires both basic ____ and ____.

15. According to the notion of the ____ ____, the norms of any social structure are never complete.

MULTIPLE CHOICE

1. A recurrent pattern of relationships is referred to as a:

    a. social structure.
    b. role.
    c. sanction.
    d. value.

2. A set of norms specifying the rights and obligations associated with a specific status:

    a. norms.
    b. value.
    c. role.
    d. social structure.

3. A specialized position within the social structure is called a:

    a. network.
    b. social structure.
    c. status.
    d. group.

4. An enduring social structure that provides ready-made answers to basic human problems?

    a. role.
    b. value.
    c. institution.
    d. group.

5. The kind of society with the most marked degree of homogeneity:

    a. horticultural.
    b. hunting, fishing and gathering.
    c. agriculture.
    d. industrial.

6. This is optional, meaning that it can be earned in a lifetime:

    a.   achieved status.
    b.   social institution.
    c.   ascribed status.
    d.   role.

7. Not a characteristic of institutions:

    a.   endures for generations.
    b.   complex set of roles and statuses.
    c.   relatively easy to change.
    d.   addresses human needs.

8. Pete is unhappy at work. His supervisor is inconsistent and keeps giving Pete different jobs to do and expects Pete to get them all done. Pete is suffering from:

    a.   role strain.
    b.   value conflict.
    c.   role conflict.
    d.   role segmentation.

9. Relatively few people can expect to find good jobs in agriculture today. This illustrates which sociological status concern?

    a.   identification.
    b.   distribution.
    c.   consequences.
    d.   combinations.

10. Which is NOT true about institutional interdependence?

    a.   none stand alone.
    b.   norms and roles in different institutions are usually compatible.
    c.   never an important mechanism for change.
    d.   interdependence reinforces social stability.

11. In a positive form these reinforce conforming role behavior. In a negative form they discourage non-conformity. They are:

    a.   roles.
    b.   values.
    c.   sanctions.
    d.   norms.

12. Which is most likely to be the correct order in the development of institutions in a society?

    a.   economy first, then family.
    b.   religion, then family.
    c.   family first, then economy.
    d.   leisure first, then education.

13. As hunting and gathering gives way to agriculture, one can expect:

    a.   a decrease in population size.
    b.   a decrease in division of labor.
    c.   an increase in inequality.
    d.   a drastic reduction in the peasant population.

14. Conflict theorists emphasize that institutions have this negative affect:

    a.   reduce innovation.
    b.   help to pattern conduct.
    c.   help people learn what is approved.
    d.   produce conformity and stability.

15. It is thought that this institution leads the way in triggering institutional change and complexity:

    a.   family.
    b.   economy.
    c.   religion.
    d.   government.

16. The Ojibwa became a broken society because of:

    a. low motivation.
    b. too few resources.
    c. role conflict.
    d. interference by the Canadian government.

17. Both conflict and functionalist sociologists have attempted to explain how and why institutions change. What is the contribution of these theories?

    a. conflict theory is most useful.
    b. functionalist theory is most useful.
    c. the two theories address different questions and each is useful.
    d. neither has proven to be very useful.

18. According to theory, a complex set of interdependent institutions first develops in a (an) ____ society.

    a. horticultural.
    b. industrial.
    c. hunting and gathering.
    d. agricultural.

19. The leading cause of deaths in the community of Grassy Narrows:

    a. alcohol or drug-induced violence.
    b. pneumonia.
    c. industrial accidents.
    d. famine.

20. Not included as a basic institution:

    a. family.
    b. economy.
    c. government.
    d. leisure.

21. The Mormons who migrated to Utah challenged traditional institutions. This economic organization challenged the economic institution:

    a. polygamy.
    b. People's Party.
    c. United Order.
    d. Edmunds Act.

22. The agricultural revolution that led to the development of agricultural societies occurred about:

    a. 500 years ago.
    b. 5,000 years ago.
    c. 50,000 years ago.
    d. 100,000 years ago.

23. Which has NOT been a result of the industrial revolution?

    a. increasing the number of people engaged in food production.
    b. increased urbanism.
    c. increase in institutional complexity.
    d. substitution of mechanical for animal energy.

24. Compared the the national average, which is true about Native Americans and alcoholism?

    a. overall level of alcohol abuse is low.
    b. less likely to die in motor vehicle accidents.
    c. less likely to die from alcoholism.
    d. lack of good jobs increases the likelihood of alcoholism.

25. Some are born poor but work hard and become very successful business managers. This is illustrative of:

    a. ascribed status.
    b. achieved status.
    c. role strain.
    d. institutional interdependence.

26. As societies develop and become more complex their institutional structure changes, too. Which is likely to develop as a new institution in these circumstances?

    a.   family.
    b.   economy.
    c.   religion.
    d.   medicine.

27. Generally, which is true about variability found in American society?

    a.   almost complete variability in roles and statuses.
    b.   usually little opportunity to "negotiate order."
    c.   more in roles than in statuses.
    d.   more in statuses than roles.

28. Which trend is more likely to be true for the Mormon church in the U.S.?

    a.   decline in political influence in Utah.
    b.   decreased economic power.
    c.   successful in challenging conventional institutions.
    d.   will remain a central institution in Utah.

29. Each institution can be seen providing a solution to a universal problem. This institution provides for community coordination and defense:

    a.   family.
    b.   government.
    c.   religion.
    d.   education.

30. Based upon what has been learned about factors affecting role performance, bosses should:

    a.   help to reduce role strain.
    b.   pay all workers the same.
    c.   leave roles a bit vague.
    d.   encourage workers to obtain their own resources.

ESSAY QUESTIONS

1.   Discuss the historical role played by economic surplus in the change from hunting, fishing and gathering societies to industrial societies.

2.   Discuss how the values of freedom and equality embodied in the early American political institution have come to permeate the other institutions of our society.

3.   Define role strain and role conflict and discuss three methods of resolving the difficulties arising from participation in multiple roles.

4.   Using structural-functional and conflict theory, describe the extent to which social institutions both enable and constrain.

5.   Review the problems at Grassy Narrows and discuss how the situation that resulted could not be blamed upon the individuals involved, and how the solution to the problems rests in the social structure.

Chapter 5
Groups, Networks, and Organizations

LEARNING OBJECTIVES

1. Explain what is meant by the terms social structure and social process and then differentiate between exchange, cooperation, competition and conflict.

2. Differentiate between group, aggregate and category.

3. Explain how size and proximity influence group interaction.

4. Note the characteristics of the following communication patterns: all channel network, circle pattern, chain pattern and wheel pattern.

5. Discuss how social cohesion and social control function in small groups.

6. Explain what choice shifts are and note the difference between a tame shift, risky shift and group think.

7. List the characteristics of primary and secondary groups.

8. Differentiate between the following: expressive activities, instrumental activities, social networks, strong ties, and weak ties.

9. Explain what a voluntary association is, list the correlates of participation and note what advantages accrue to the members.

10. Discuss how gift giving enhances social ties.

CHAPTER 5

11. Differentiate between complex organizations and bureaucracy.

12. Contrast the classic model of organizations with the notion of an organizational culture.

13. Briefly describe each of the drawbacks attributed to bureaucracy: ritualism, alienation and structural inequality.

14. Discuss how complex/bureaucratic organizations differ from the "alternative forms" of organizations.

15. Explain how the Japanese model of organizations combines elements of traditional western bureaucracies and elements stressed by Japanese culture.

16. How can we use our knowledge of group process and structure to foster cohesion in American communities.

CHAPTER OUTLINE

I. Group Processes

A. Social structure implies something that is rigid and unyielding, yet it has an important dynamic element to it. It is process as well as framework.

B. All interaction can be included in the concept of social processes: the forms of interaction through which people relate to one another. Social processes are concerned with the dynamic aspect of society. Four such processes regularly occur.
1. Exchange occurs when people voluntarily undertake interaction in the expectation of receiving some reward.
(a) Exchange is one of the most basic processes of social interaction.
(b) Exchange relationships are governed by the norm of reciprocity.
(1) Unequal benefits may result from exchange.
2. Cooperation occurs when both parties work together for something that none could reach individually.

(a) unequal benefits may also result from cooperation.

3. <u>Competition</u> is a form of interaction that involves a struggle over scarce resources. The struggle is governed by norms and values.

    (a) When norms are violated competition may erupt into conflict.

        (1) Competition often results in change.

4. When individuals or groups in competition attempt to neutralize, injure or eliminate their rivals, <u>conflict</u> occurs.

    (a) A certain amount of conflict is always present in society.

        (1) Positive and negative consequences may follow.

        (2) Conflict between groups may raise solidarity within the respective groups.

        (3) Conflict within a group is seldom positive.

II. Groups

A. When two or more persons interact together within a shared social structure and recognize mutual dependency it is called a <u>group</u>.

    1. Members share a social structure specifying statuses, roles and norms as well as a feeling of mutual dependency.

    (a) This differentiates groups from <u>categories</u> and <u>aggregates</u>.

B. Group influence is vital in determining behavior, perception and values.

    1. This may happen consciously (<u>Asch</u>) or unconsciously.

C. Interaction in groups is influenced by a host of factors.

    1. As the size of the group increases, the time available for individual participation decreases and the distribution of skills to solve problems increase. Interaction becomes more impersonal, more structured and less personally satisfying and democracy replaces consensus seeking.

    2. Interaction is more likely to occur between group members who are in proximity or physically close to one another. This has been demonstrated by observing housing patterns, small groups and committees.

    3. Interaction of group members can be either facilitated or retarded by patterns of communication. Four basic patterns are: the <u>all channel network</u>, <u>circle pattern</u>, <u>chain pattern</u> and <u>wheel pattern</u>.

> (a) Physical location and seating patterns influence communication patterns in groups.
>
> 4. Social cohesion is defined as the degree of attraction members feel towards a group.
>   (a) A cohesive group has strong feelings of attachment and dependency.
>   (b) Factors leading to cohesiveness in groups are small size, similarity, frequent interaction, long duration and a clear line between insiders and outsiders.
> 5. Social control exercised by groups is usually informal and includes sanctions with the threat of exclusion being the most effective.
> 6. An outgrowth of group processes is decision making.
>   (a) Groups make decisions by achieving consensus. The convergence to consensus is called choice shift and it may take several forms.
>   (1) The risky shift is convergence upon an adventurous decision while the tame shift is convergence upon a conservative decision.
>   (2) Groupthink is an apparent convergence that occurs when members suppress critical thought. Real opinions are hidden in order to be supportive in the decision making process.

D. One can belong to a variety of types and groups.
   1. Primary groups (Cooley) are characterized by intimate, face-to-face association and cooperation.
       (a) The major function of primary groups is providing social integration and emotional support for individuals. This form of behavior is called expressive activity.
           (1) Primary groups tend to be intimate, face-to-face, permanent, small in size, informal and are characterized by loyalty and nontraditional decision making.
   2. Secondary groups are formal, large, impersonal and are formed to accomplish some specific task, i.e., instrumental activity.
       (a) Secondary groups engage in temporary, formal and anonymous interaction.
   3. Preindustrial society featured primary groups that served both expressive and instrumental needs.

      (a) Modern society has shifted a great deal of interaction to secondary groups even to the extent of using some secondary groups to meet expressive needs.

      (1) Some see this as weakening social control in society.

III. Social Networks

A.   A <u>social</u> <u>network</u> is an individual's total set of relationships with others.

    1.   Social networks consist of either <u>strong ties</u> or <u>weak ties</u>.

      (a) Strong ties are characterized by intense, intimate sharing and weak ties have little intensity or intimacy.

      (1) Gift giving can reinforce social ties.

      (2) Weak ties consist of many small gifts, not large ones.

B.   <u>Voluntary associations</u> are nonprofit organizations designed to allow individuals to pursue their shared interests collectively.

    1.   Participation in voluntary associations is related to personal satisfaction, self-esteem, political effectiveness and a sense of community.

    2.   Voluntary associations can mediate between primary and secondary groups. Participation meets intimacy needs while providing a greater sense of control over our immediate environment, it is called the <u>meditation hypothesis</u>.

    3.   Voluntary association participation can be predicted by urban residence, social class, age, gender and religion.

C.   Social ties also occur within communities where close physical proximity encourages social interaction.

    1.   Strong communities are characterized by dense, cross-cutting social networks.

    2.   Weak ties with neighbors increases social control and cohesion while decreasing deviance and fear of crime.

    3.   Some advocate <u>network intervention</u> to create social ties in communities.

IV. Complex Organizations

A.   <u>Complex organizations</u> are large formal organizations with complex status networks.

1. Complex organizations have made massive improvements in the standard of living while contributing to a more impersonal social environment.
2. <u>Bureaucracy</u> is a special type of complex organization. It is characterized by explicit rules and a hierarchical authority structure, designed to maximize efficiency.
    (a) <u>Weber</u> developed a framework to analyze bureaucratic structures. It consists of the following characteristics: division of labor and specialization, hierarchy of authority, system of rules and regulations, impersonality, efficiency and employment through technical qualifications.
    (b) Formal rules alone cannot be used to determine day-to-day behavior in bureaucracies.
        (1) <u>Organizational culture</u> refers to the pattern of norms and values that affect how work is actually carried out in an organization.
        (2) Successful organizational cultures occur when employee interaction creates cohesion.
        (3) Often people evolve their own way of doing work and ignore the formal rules.
3. The degree of bureaucratization is related to how predictable or unpredictable organizational activities are.
4. Organizations may be criticized because they stifle initiative (ritualism), reduce worker satisfaction (alienation) or create structured inequality.

B. Many alternative organizations have arisen in recent years in an effort to counter the hierarchical authority relations typical of bureaucratic organizations.
    1. <u>Collectives</u> emphasize democracy and consensus, minimize rules, shun authority, rely on personal and moral appeals, eliminate advancement and status distinctions, use nonmaterial rewards and deemphasize specialization and technical expertise.
        (a) The demand for consensus and democracy means some sacrifice in efficiency.
        (b) The tendency for an elite to dominate such organizations is called the <u>iron law of oligarchy</u>.

C. A more bureaucratic alternative is the Japanese model that draws upon western efficiency and Japanese traditions. This model has four principle components.

1. Permanent employment means a commitment to employ the worker for life.

2. Internal labor markets mean that higher level positions are filled from below and within the organization.

3. There is a relative absence of blue collar or white collar status distinctions.

4. Participatory decision making involves all levels in decision making, not just management.

MATCHING   I

A.	Voluntary association	___ 1. Fostering communication with one's neighbors.
B.	Secondary group	___ 2. Consensus centers upon a more adventurous plan.
C.	Groupthink	___ 3. All parties expect rewards.
D.	Expressive	___ 4. Major sources of intimacy.
E.	Network intervention	___ 5. How business is actually carried out in organizations.
F.	Group	___ 6. Activities providing integration and emotional support.
G.	Exchange	
H.	Primary group	___ 7. People temporarily clustered together.
I.	Organizational culture	___ 8. Convergence occurs when true feelings are not shared.
J.	Weak ties	___ 9. Formal, large and impersonal
K.	Risky shift	___10. Activities that are task oriented.
L.	Bureaucracy	
M.	Instrumental	
N.	Aggregate	
O.	Complex organizations	

MATCHING   II

A.   Elite domination

B.   Employ specialists

C.   Control and supervision

D.   Collectives

E.   Collectivist organizations

F.   Voluntary associations

G.   Conflict

H.   Ritualism

I.   Standardize activities

J.   Weber

K.   Strong ties

L.   Groupthink

M.   Japan

N.   Make bureaucracy more efficient

O.   Weak ties

____ 1.   Meeting socioeconomic needs without bureaucratic regulation.

____ 2.   Original model of bureaucracy.

____ 3.   Division of labor.

____ 4.   Permanent employment.

____ 5.   Low intensity and intimacy.

____ 6.   Unregulated struggle over scarce resources.

____ 7.   Hierarchy of authority.

____ 8.   Iron Law of Oligarchy

____ 9.   Intense, intimate, emotional

____ 10.   Rigid adherence to rules.

FILL IN THE BLANK QUESTIONS

1. When the norms governing interaction are violated ____ may turn into ____.

2. Community cohesion is fostered by many of the same factors that create cohesion in ____ ____.

3. If you do something for somebody, they are then obligated to return the favor. This is called the ____ ____ ____.

4. ____ is when people work together to achieve shared goals.

5. The breakdown of traditional primary groups has forced us to rely upon ____ ____ even for expressive needs.

6. As the ____ of a group increases, practical utility may be gained at the expense of individual satisfaction.

7. Within collectives the demand for consensus and full participation means some   sacrifice of ____.

8. Through participation in ____ we meet some of our needs for association and intimacy while achieving greater control over our immediate environment.

9. Voluntary associations that cut across class and racial lines create links in the community that foster ____ and ____.

10. Two distinct features of groups are shared ____ ____ and mutual ____.

11. The most effective group control technique is ____.

12. Group memberships are vital in determining our ____, ____ and ____.

13. The major purpose of primary groups is ____ ____.

14. The degree of attraction members feel towards a group is called ____ ____.

15. The most efficient communication pattern is the ____ ____ ____ which allows for maximum participation.

MULTIPLE CHOICE

1. The ABC Agency is trying to attract customers away from the XYZ Agency. Which process is at work?

    a. conflict.
    b. exchange.
    c. competition.
    d. cooperation.

2. Groups that are characterized by impersonality and rationality:

    a. secondary group.
    b. primary group.
    c. aggregate.
    d. association.

3. Not a characteristic of secondary groups by design:

    a. inefficiency.
    b. numerous divisions.
    c. many roles.
    d. ties of authority and subordination.

4. This consists of all people to whom we are linked by ties of affection, association or business:

    a. primary group.
    b. social network.
    c. association.
    d. business.

5. Not included as a characteristic of the Japanese model of organizations:

    a. permanent employment.
    b. bottom-up management.
    c. centralized decision making.
    d. emphasis on small-group responsibility.

6. Which is NOT necessarily a characteristic of groups?

    a. small.
    b. informal or formal.
    c. mutual dependency.
    d. interaction.

7. Hispanics, welders, and students are examples of:

    a. groups.
    b. categories.
    c. aggregates.
    d. associations.

8. When pressures to agree are strong, people hide their real opinions. This is known as:

    a. risky shift.
    b. group think.
    c. tame shift.
    d. a bureaucratic decision.

9. The closest approximation to an ideal primary group:

    a. work group.
    b. family.
    c. peer group.
    d. adult friendships.

10. If social workers wanted to seek out people having the fewest voluntary organizational memberships, they should most likely concentrate on people who:

    a. are from lower classes.
    b. are urban.
    c. are relatively young.
    d. are male.

11. John is going to open a new business. He wants to organize the work so that each person has specific responsibilities and can become an expert in that work. Which characteristics of bureaucracies should be emphasized?

    a. division of labor and specialization.
    b. hierarchy.
    c. system of rules.
    d. impersonality.

12. ___ are nonprofit organizations designed to allow individuals an opportunity to pursue interests collectively.

    a. small groups.
    b. voluntary associations.
    c. bureaucracies.
    d. aggregates.

13. It is thought that voluntary associations mediate (provide a bridge) between primary and secondary groups. This is called the:

    a. primary group hypothesis.
    b. secondary group hypothesis.
    c. mediation hypothesis.
    d. integration hypothesis.

14. This person is given credit for developing the framework for understanding bureaucracies:

    a. August Comte.
    b. Karl Marx.
    c. Max Weber.
    d. George Mead.

15. Theory would tell us that collectivist organizations will be LEAST effective if this factor is present:

    a. high personal involvement.
    b. consensus.
    c. emphasis on rules.
    d. democracy.

16. Theorists have proposed that there may be a shift taking place from a reliance on primary groups to a reliance on secondary groups. From society's point of view, what is the most likely result of this shift?

    a. social control will most likely increase.
    b. some persons may crave more emotional support than they will receive.
    c. people will become less reliant upon secondary groups, too.
    d. people may turn to secondary groups for both instrumental and expressive needs.

17. Which factor would most likely reduce the cohesion of a group?

    a. major increase in size.
    b. increased similarity among members.
    c. increased interaction.
    d. increased distinction between insiders and outsiders.

18. Network theory suggests that we should expect to find that:

    a. weak ties do not exist in primary groups.
    b. strong ties do not exist in secondary groups.
    c. weak and strong ties exist in primary and secondary groups.
    d. only strong ties exist in primary groups.

19. The communication pattern with the greatest equality of participation:

    a. circle.
    b. chain.
    c. wheel.
    d. all-channel.

20. These are most likely to be characterized by intimate and face-to-face interaction:

    a. secondary groups.
    b. voluntary organizations.
    c. primary groups.
    d. aggregates.

21. The most important factor affecting a person's number of strong ties is:

    a. sex, with males having more ties.
    b. educational level.
    c. residence.
    d. age.

22. This factor is NOT associated with membership in voluntary association membership or participation:

    a. region.
    b. social class.
    c. age.
    d. gender.

23. Most persons in the U.S. are employed by:

    a. government.
    b. large complex organizations.
    c. farmers.
    d. small businesses.

24. This kind of work organization is designed to avoid too much hierarchy and regulation:

    a. collectivitst.
    b. bureaucracy.
    c. Japanese model.
    d. voluntary.

25. These are a major source of solidarity and cohesion, reinforcing our interaction in society:

    a. aggregates.
    b. groups.
    c. categories.
    d. bureaucracies.

26. Persons are most likely to participate in deviant acts when:

    a.   primary groups encourage deviance.
    b.   primary groups discourage deviance.
    c.   secondary groups encourage deviance.
    d.   secondary groups discourage deviance.

27. Efforts to strengthen communities should be most successful in communities that are characterized by:

    a.   high levels of interaction.
    b.   high growth.
    c.   heterogeneity.
    d.   large size.

28. In general, it can be concluded that people with multiple and meaningful ties to groups and organizations are:

    a.   less able to cope.
    b.   healthier.
    c.   subject to less stress.
    d.   more likely to be deviant.

29. The primary factor affecting the degree of bureaucratization found in an organization:

    a.   size.
    b.   age.
    c.   complexity.
    d.   degree of uncertainty.

30. Gifts have important consequences for networks.   Gift giving:

    a.   demands direct and immediate reciprocity.
    b.   marked by many small gifts builds strong ties.
    c.   is more popular among males.
    d.   is most often used to "buy" friends.

ESSAY QUESTIONS

1. Discuss how gift giving can maintain and enhance social ties.

2. Explain how the mediation hypothesis works.

3. How do complex organizations or bureaucracies differ from the so called collectives?

4. Discuss how social cohesion and social control function in small groups.

5. Compare and contrast primary groups and secondary groups.

6. Critique complex organizations.

Chapter 6
The Individual and Society

LEARNING OBJECTIVES

1. Define socialization.

2. Know the difference between nature and nurture.

3. Describe the effects of childhood neglect and deprivation.

4. Differentiate between the self and a self concept and identify the parts of the self and then describe the operation of the looking glass self.

5. Discuss the relationship between role taking, role playing, significant other and generalized other.

6. Describe how we develop role identities, a situated identify and an identity salience hierarchy.

7. In what ways do the interactionists and structuralists attempt to explain the relationship between self concept and social roles.

8. Describe how individuals actively negotiate and create their own identities.

9. Describe how people occupying the same status tend to develop similar personalities and self concepts.

CHAPTER 6

10.   What is primary socialization and why is it so critical?

11.   Note the impact of day care on children.

12.   Discuss the impact of family instability on children.

13.   Why is adolescence seen as a difficult period and what impact do peers, family and schools have upon adolescents?

14.   Describe the relationship between self esteem and success among adolescents.

15.   What is the relationship between work roles and self concept for adults?

16.   Describe what is meant by the concept of resocialization and note the role of total institutions in the process.

17.   What is the impact of the mass media upon children?

CHAPTER OUTLINE

  I.   The Self and Self Concept

       A.   Each individual <u>self</u> is a combination of unique attributes and normative responses.
            1.   These two parts of the self are called the <u>I</u> and <u>me</u> by <u>G. H. Mead</u>.
                 (a) The I is the spontaneous part of the self and the me is the self as a social object.
                 (b) The I and the me interact to create daily behavior.
            2.   The <u>self concept</u> is the part of the self that we are aware of.
                 (a) The self and the self concept are social products developed through social relationships.
                     (1) It includes all of the images one has of themselves in which they interact.

  II. Learning to be human: The beginning steps

       A.   The necessity of nurture

1. We have a biological endowment referred to as <u>nature</u>.
2. Love, attention and interaction or <u>nurture</u> are required for us to survive and to achieve our inherited potential.
3. Without nurture physical, mental and social maturation suffer. Key studies by <u>Spitz</u> and <u>Harlow</u> demonstrate these effects.

III. <u>Symbolic interactionism</u> is a theoretical framework that emphasizes the subjective meanings of human acts and the processes through which we develop and communicate shared meanings.

    A. The <u>Interaction School</u> holds that people are actively involved in creating and negotiating their own roles and self concepts.

        1. The <u>looking glass self</u> is <u>Cooley's</u> term for a self concept that is based upon how we think we appear to others.

          (a) We actively define our self concept through interpretations of our perceptions of others and by selecting from among a range of looking glasses.

            (1) These interpretations are real in their consequences. (<u>W. I. Thomas</u>).

        2. Mead argued that we learn norms and acquire our self concept through <u>role taking</u>. This involves imagining ourselves in the role of the other in order to figure out what criteria others will use to judge our behavior.

          (a) This is a lifelong process with role playing and role taking being influenced first by the <u>significant other</u> and later by the <u>generalized other</u>.

          (b) The individual is an active agent in the construction of his or her own self concept. The self is <u>negotiated</u> through the selective use of looking glasses and significant others.

            (1) <u>Self-esteem</u> is the evaluative component of the self concept; it is our judgment about our relative self worth compared to others.

    B. The <u>Structural School</u> focuses upon the self as a product of social roles in which one is constrained and shaped in important ways by society.

        1. A <u>role identity</u> is the concept we have of ourself in a specific role. A self concept is the composite of one's role identities.

          (a) The concept of <u>situated identity</u> implies that we have no unified identity, but instead we have multiple role identities

that are used in specific situations.
    (b) We rank role identities in an <u>identity salience hierarchy</u> thus allowing us to choose the most preferable role in a given situation.
2.   The structural school also studies the processes through which people who share a social status tend to develop into similar sorts of people.
    (a) People sharing the same status experience the same kinds of constraints and demands and will tend to develop similar personalities and self concepts.
    (1) Social class is perhaps the most important of these structured statuses.

V.   Role Identity and Self Concept Over the Life Course

A.   One's self concept and initial roles are learned in childhood and learning continues throughout the life course.
1.   Sociologists are interested in two aspects of this process.
    (a) The first is an interest in the process of learning new roles necessary for participation in social institutions. This is called <u>socialization</u>.
    (b) Another interest centers upon how changing roles affects one's self concept and identity.

B.   Early childhood socialization is called <u>primary socialization</u> because it occurs first and is critical to later development.
1.   Personality and self concept are first formed here.

C   The most important agent of socialization is the family, which provides the basic nurturance required for normal human development.
1.   Early learning in the family setting includes the mastery of language, the acquisition of basic skills and preparation for experiences outside the family.
2.   Personality and self-concept are strongly influenced by childhood experience including the family's race, social class and religion.
3.   Unstable family backgrounds contribute to problems for children when they reach adolescence and adulthood.

D. Preschool and day care are experiencing increasing numbers of children as their mothers enter the work force.
   1. To date research shows no ill effects of "quality" day care on children.
      (a) Few American day care centers qualify as "quality" centers with trained, stable staff in appropriate numbers for the number of children served.
      (b) Children in "low" quality centers are more likely to experience inadequate socialization.

E. Among children ages 6 to 18, the school and the peer group are particularly important.
   1. In each case <u>anticipatory socialization</u> occurs that prepares them for adult life.
      (a) Schools function to impart specific skills, necessary abilities and society's central cultural values.
      (b) The school also teaches impersonal rules, regulations and authority patterns necessary for careers.
   2. Extended levels of education coupled with working parents creates a social vacuum which may be filled with peer inter-action in which learning takes place.
      (a) While peers exert some influence on each other, parents' values are still important.
      (b) Peer interaction facilitates the development and validation of the self-concept while providing an arena for practicing role taking and learning roles that adults don't teach.
   3. Adolescence is a difficult time in which the self concept must adjust quickly to many rapid changes.
      (a) Self-esteem may be difficult to sustain during these changes.
         (1) Low self-esteem may spiral into poor decisions which further lower self-esteem or high self-esteem may lead to good performance and to even higher self-esteem.

F. Adult role identities and socialization can extend 60 years or more in which many changes occur which can have a powerful effect upon one's self concept and personality.
   1. A significant part of our lives is spent at work.
   2. <u>Kohn</u> contends that work influences our self concept and behavior.
      (a) Traits developed on the job are also valued in the home.

3. Occupation is the dominant status in most people's lives and as such influences their self concept and non-work roles.
    (a) Loss of a job may be a major blow to one's self concept which can increase anxiety, depression and physical illness.

G. Adulthood can be seen as a gradual process of role accumulation.
    1. Role accumulation is positive because multiple roles anchor us in confirming social relationships. We know who we are.

H. Socialization is a lifelong process that begins in childhood and continues as we learn new roles and renegotiate our self concept throughout our lives.
    1. Resocialization occurs when we abandon our self-concept and way of life for one that is radically different.
    2. Resocialization requires isolation from one's past environment.
        (a) Total institutions (Goffman) are facilities in which all aspects of life are strictly controlled for the purposes of radical re-socialization; they include prisons, mental hospitals and the military.
    3. Resocialization may not always require the use of total institutions.
    4. Changing the self concept usually requires a change in activities and relationships.

I. Throughout life the mass media bombards us with messages.
    1. Media information is an important means of supporting and validating what we already know.
    2. Adults actively filter media content through the mechanism of selection perception.
    3. Children spend a great deal of time watching television while still in their formative years.
        (a) The actual effects of television on children are quite controversial and highly debated.
        (b) Much of the debate centers upon the impact of television violence on children.
            (1) Eron found a strong correlation between viewing and violence in young men who preferred to watch violent programs as children.

(2) Television violence appears to desensitize the viewer, put violence in a positive light and present violent role models.

MATCHING   I

A. Liebow   ____ 1. Total institutions

B. Mead   ____ 2. Media violence and children

C. Goffman   ____ 3. Looking glass self

D. Eron   ____ 4. Each generation faces the same social structure with the same results.

E. Harlow and Harlow
                    ____ 5. Deprivation in children.

F. Dornbush
                    ____ 6. Situations defined as real are real in their consequences.
G. Cooley

H. Kohn   ____ 7. Deprivation in monkeys.

I. W.I. Thomas   ____ 8. Adolescent peers.

J. Spitz   ____ 9. Role playing and games

                    ____ 10. Work and Self Concept

CHAPTER 6

MATCHING   II

A.   Role accumulation

B.   Negotiated identity

C.   Resocialization

D.   Total institutions

E.   Role taking

F.   Socialization

G.   The I

H.   Looking glass self

I.   Self concept

J.   Me

K.   Primary socialization

L.   Generalized other

M.   Self esteem

N.   Situated identity

O.   Identity salience hierarchy

____ 1.   When we abandon our self concept and way of life for something radically different

____ 2.   Putting ourselves in the role of another.

____ 3.   Our awareness of social norms.

____ 4.   Stability provided to adults occupying multiple roles.

____ 5.   The evaluative part of the self concept.

____ 6.   Early childhood learning.

____ 7.   The role identity in a specific situation.

____ 8.   Spontaneous and creative part of the self.

____ 9.   A self concept that is based on how we think we appear to others.

____ 10.   Facilities in which all aspects of life are strictly controlled for the purposes of radical resocialization.

FILL IN THE BLANK QUESTIONS

1. ____ ____ ____ is the ranking of an individual's various role identities in order of their importance.

2. The ____ school focuses upon the self as a product of institutionalized social roles.

3. People occupying different structural positions tend to have different ____ and different ____.

4. The child that experiences family instability is more likely to experience personal and social problems in ____ and ____.

5. Low quality day care centers are characterized by ____ and ____ staff and high ____ ratios.

6. Primary socialization refers to ____ development and ____ learning which occur in early childhood.

7. The ____ ____ is the composite of expectations of all the other role players with whom we interact.

8. The ____ school focuses upon the active role of the individual in creating the self concept.

9. Because each of us has multiple statuses and roles, we have multiple ____ ____.

10. ____ ____ is the role learning that prepares us for roles that we are likely to assume in the future.

11. The self is a complex blending of unique ____ and ____ responses.

12. ____ is the process of learning roles, statuses, and values necessary for participation in social institutions.

13. Research shows that most adolescents are more concerned about their ____ opinion than about their ____ opinion.

14. Adolescence is a difficult period because of the rapid adjustments required by the ___ ___.

15. For adolescents there is a spiraling relationship between ___ ___ role performance and ___.

MULTIPLE CHOICE

1. The orphans studied by Rene Spitz were more likely to die because of:

    a. too little individual attention.
    b. infectious disease.
    c. physical abuse.
    d. birth defects.

2. The emphasis in socialization is on:

    a. development of personality.
    b. participation in informal group activities.
    c. learning roles, norms, and values.
    d. nurturant activities.

3. The theoretical framework that emphasizes interaction, negotiation and role taking:

    a. moral development.
    b. developmental theory.
    c. behaviorism.
    d. symbolic interaction.

4. During this socialization, a child develops personality and self-concept, acquires language and becomes aware of significant others:

    a. primary socialization.
    b. resocialization.
    c. anticipatory socialization.
    d. continuing socialization.

5. The most important socialization agent:

    a. the family.
    b. peers.
    c. schools.
    d. mass media.

6. This prepares people for the roles that they will likely assume in the future:

    a. primary socialization.
    b. anticipatory socialization.
    c. resocialization.
    d. interaction school.

7. John had planned his schedule so that Sunday evening would be free for studying, but he decided to go to a movie with several friends when they stopped by and asked that he come with them. John was following his:

    a. me.
    b. looking glass self.
    c. significant other.
    d. negotiated self.

8. Jill is attending her first school dance. She doesn't know the new steps, imagines that her date is disappointed in her and knows that she is a complete disaster. This is an example of:

    a. the looking glass self.
    b. peer pressure.
    c. impression management.
    d. positive reinforcement.

9. John thinks of himself as a professor at work but a husband and father at home. This concept refers to the role identity used in a particular situation:

    a. situated identity.
    b. self esteem.
    c. I.
    d. role taking.

10. Prisons and drug treatment centers make deliberate efforts to force people to change their established self-concepts and ways of behaving. This process is referred to as:

    a. socialization.
    b. primary socialization.
    c. behaviorism.
    d. resocialization.

11. Self-esteem is our own judgment of our worth. Which is true about self esteem?

    a. we think better of ourselves than others do.
    b. very changeable from situation to situation.
    c. we typically downgrade ourselves.
    d. people with high self-esteem are conservative and resist new ideas.

12. To best understand the process of anticipatory socialization, one should concentrate on:

    a. socialization in work groups.
    b. role accumulation in adulthood.
    c. socialization in school and peer groups.
    d. socialization in total institutions.

13. In the case studies of socially isolated children, the main independent (causal) variable was:

    a. social deprivation
    b. uncaring parents.
    c. inadequate self-concept.
    d. poor nutrition.

14. Which is NOT a premise of the structural school of symbolic interaction?

    a. roles are allocated.
    b. self-concept is determined by roles.
    c. individual is less active in creating a self concept.
    d. roles are negotiated.

15. Research and theory suggest that children who are placed early in quality daycare centers are more likely to:

    a. become alienated from parents.
    b. become dependent.
    c. become high achievers.
    d. suffer high anxiety.

16. Which is least likely to result to adolescents because of peer socialization?

    a. more concern for peers' opinions than for parents' opinions.
    b. provision of a looking glass self unclouded by love or duty.
    c. provision of an arena for practicing role taking.
    d. provision of a mechanism for learning social roles that adults don't want to teach.

17. Research by Kohn suggests that people who have boring and highly routine jobs are more likely to:

    a. suffer depression and physical illness.
    b. value order and discipline at home.
    c. oppose subordination and routine in non-work settings.
    d. become democratic spouses and parents.

18. Theory and research suggest that role accumulation in adulthood:

    a. usually leads to role strain and conflict.
    b. is usually a good thing.
    c. is good for males but not for females.
    d. usually leads to ambiguities about one's identity.

19. According to Provence and Lipton who compared physically healthy, institutionalized infants with infants raised at home, the institutionalized infants showed definite signs of mental retardation:

    a. during the first few weeks of life.
    b. by three months of age.
    c. by twelve months of age.
    d. by 24 months of age.

20. Which is NOT a step in the development of a looking-glass self?

    a. others provide us with verbal evaluations of our behavior.
    b. we imagine how we appear to others.
    c. we imagine how others judge us.
    d. we develop feelings about the judgments that we imagine are made about us.

21. Which is NOT a total institution?

    a. monastery
    b. factory.
    c. prison.
    d. mental hospital.

22. Important sociologist who described the "I" and "me" aspects of self:

    a. Jean Piaget.
    b. B.F. Skinner.
    c. W.I. Thomas.
    d. George Mead.

23.   In studies of aggression among persons in the U.S., this factor has been identified as the best predictor of how aggressive a male would be by 19 years of age:

   a.   violent television programs be preferred when 8 years of age.
   b.   number of siblings.
   c.   social class.
   d.   race.

24.   It is estimated that children see as many as ___ murders on television by the time that they are age 16.

   a.   100,000.
   b.   100
   c.   20,000.
   d.   1,000.

25.   Generalizing from what has been learned about neglected children, the effects of neglect:

   a.   have been overestimated.
   b.   are severe and never reversible.
   c.   are severe but in some cases reversible.
   d.   always end in premature death.

26.   As children grow older, we can expect them to:

   a.   continue to respond to the expectations of significant others.
   b.   shift entirely from the expectations of significant others to the generalized other.
   c.   respond to the expectations of both significant others and the generalized other.
   d.   become autonomous and respond neither to significant others nor to the generalized other.

27. Children of divorce are less likely to:

    a.   achieve high education.
    b.   marry early.
    c.   have children while unmarried.
    d.   have their marriages break.

28. When individuals are described as active in "negotiating" their own identity, this means that:

    a.   complete freedom of choice exists in accepting or rejecting judgments of others.
    b.   dominant roles become less important.
    c.   the influence of parents ceases to exist.
    d.   people select dominant roles in which they are likely to succeed and selectively perceive judgments of others.

29. Which kind of socialization is most likely to prepare people for responsibilities they will face as parents, spouses and workers?

    a.   primary socialization.
    b.   anticipatory socialization.
    c.   resocialization.
    d.   socialization in total institutions.

30. Researchers have concluded that television appears to encourage violence through certain mechanisms. Which is NOT one of these?

    a.   symbolic interaction.
    b.   desensitization.
    c.   role modeling.
    d.   apparent approval.

ESSAY QUESTIONS

1.   How influential is the mass media?

2.   Discuss the relationship between nature and nurture.

3. Discuss how the self and the self concept are social products that develop through relationships.

4. Compare and contrast the interactionist and structuralist schools.

5. Discuss how role identity and self concept change throughout the life course.

Chapter 7
The Sociology
of
Everyday Life

LEARNING OBJECTIVES

1. Define what is meant by the phrase "the sociology of everyday life" and discuss the basic premise of this approach.

2. Discuss the different directions that the EDL approach takes to everyday interaction.

3. Outline the basic assumptions of EDL including the concepts of the dialectic, biography, thick description and thin description.

4. How are encounters problematic and what issues must be resolved to manage the encounter?

5. Describe what is meant by "framing" and identity negotiation.

6. Discuss how the theater is an analogy to everyday life and note how non-verbal cues can support a role performance.

7. What is ethnomethodology? What is its central concern and what hypothesis and techniques are utilized?

8. What is identity work and what strategies does it entail?

9.   What is a spoiled identity and what strategies can be employed in an attempt to protect one's self-esteem?

10. Discuss the reasons for homelessness in recent years.

11. Define the following terms and describe how the homeless use each to maintain their self-esteem and develop positive identities: role distancing, role embracement and story telling.

CHAPTER OUTLINE

I.   The <u>sociology</u> of <u>everyday</u> <u>life</u>, or the EDL perspective, focuses on the social processes that structure our experience in ordinary face-to-face situations.

     A.   Concern for everyday life focuses on two different dimensions. One is the patterned regularities that govern everyday life and the other is the management of the ambiguous or problematic situations.

     B.   The routine nature of daily life is often taken for granted, yet distinct patterns exist for such phenomena as riding an elevator or simply managing the personal space around us.
          1.   <u>Civil</u> <u>inattention</u> can be used in public places to discourage intimacy.

     C.   Social life depends upon routine and predictable patterns of behavior (Goffman).
          1.   These help us organize and interpret our daily lives.
          2.   The most important routines are carried out through talk.

II. The EDL perspective utilizes four assumptions.

     A.   Culture is problematic in that many situations are unclear as to which rules apply and when.
          1.   This requires a constant stream of choices.

     B.   Choices may be seen as dialectic where a conflict exists between individual freedom and social constraint.
          1.   The outcome of these conflicting choices is never certain.

C. Each individual possesses a unique biography based upon his or her own personal history.
    1. No two persons are entirely identical.

D. Thick Description is the attempt to understand the subjective social worlds of individual actors in specific situations.
    1. Thick description is used in preference to thin description.

III. The management of everyday life requires the individual to utilize a series of strategies and techniques.

  A. Each encounter requires two basic steps.
    1. Determining what is going on.
      (a) A frame is roughly identical to a definition of the situation.
        (1) It is a set of explanations about the nature of the interaction taking place.
        (2) The frame is open to negotiation between actors.
    2. The second step is to determine what identities will be granted.
      (a) The identities are tied to the specific situation.
      (b) This is called identity negotiation or the process of trying to manipulate others into taking on certain identities. This is a verbal process.

  B. Dramaturgy (Goffman) views social situations as scenes manipulated by the actors in order to convey the desired impression to the audience.
    1. Interaction is seen through the analogy of the theater with its stage, sets, props, actors, audience, front region and back region.
    2. In real life one's mode of dress, body language, and nonverbal cues are all utilized to manipulate the definition of the situation.

IV. Ethnomethodology (Garfinkel) consists of the everyday strategies, folk methods and procedures that individuals use to study and organize their world.

  A. Interaction begins with a working hypothesis about what is going on. We then watch others' reactions.
    1. A central focus of this approach is to discover the common understandings individuals use in making sense of their world.

109

    (a) One such major hypothesis is that people are who they appear to be.

    (b) Another hypothesis is that others share our symbolic worlds.
        (1) This is a crucial assumption of all interaction.

    (c) Bringing common understandings into the open may be done by the use of <u>break experiments</u>.
        (1) Interaction is broken down when one deliberately fails to share symbolic worlds.

V.   <u>Identity work</u> consists of managing identities to sustain our self-esteem.

  A.   We manage our identities to maximize social approval.

  B.   Two techniques of identity work are avoiding blame and gaining credit.
    1.   Violating norms may require that we protect our self-esteem to avoid blame.
      (a) Most of the repair work involves verbal devices (accounts) in which we may try to successfully explain away our error and to restore a good image of ourselves.
    2.   Claiming credit is difficult to do without actually having to ask for praise.

  C.   <u>Spoiled identities</u> are those identities that are actively rejected by society.
    1.   One can manage these identities by two techniques, physically withdrawing from interaction or trying to pass.
    2.   Snow and Anderson found that the homeless used three basic strategies to manage a positive self concept.
      (a) <u>Role distancing</u> involves rejecting a role identity.
      (b) <u>Role Embracement</u> is being comfortable in a role identity and accepting it as salient and permanent.
      (c) <u>Story telling</u> is a form of identity talk in which one attempts to establish a positive non-street identity.
    3.   Two explanations for increased homelessness exist.
      (a) The first argues that deinstitutionalization of the mentally ill onto the streets is the root of the problem while the second points to increases in low paying jobs and a decrease in low income housing as causes for homelessness.

(b) Despite most of the homeless being able to maintain favorable self images, their health and living conditions are very poor. More low income housing is needed to meet their needs.

VI. Sociological Trends.

A. In the 1950s a deterministic view of society dominated.

1. In the last decade sociologists increasingly view social behavior as more negotiable and less rule bound.
    (a) The E.D.L. view reflects this change.
2. The view of life as problematic and negotiable counterbalances the more deterministic view of traditional sociology.

CHAPTER 7

MATCHING

A. Spoiled Identity

B. Frame

C. Ethnomethodology

D. Identity Work

E. Civil Inattention

F. Biography

G. Thin Description

H. Break Experiments

I. Reframing

J. Role Distancing

K. Dramaturgy

L. Thick Description

____ 1. Everyday strategies that individuals use to study and organize their world.

____ 2. Understanding the actors conceptual world.

____ 3. Interaction seen through the analogy of the stage.

____ 4. Identity rejected by society.

____ 5. When an individual rejects a role identity.

____ 6. Polite acknowledgement and then withdrawal.

____ 7. An answer to the question - what is going on here?

____ 8. Disrupting routines to cause trouble.

____ 9. Explains why each encounter is just a bit different from the rest.

____ 10. Managing identities to support and sustain our self-esteem.

FILL IN THE BLANK QUESTIONS

1. Norms about personal space are closely related to ___ ___.

2. Viewing interaction episodes as a ___ leads to the proposition that interaction is never completely programmed.

3. ___ ___ tells us why the actors did what they did and what it meant.

4. E.D.L. is closely identified with the ___ school of symbolic interactionism.

5. When our initial definition of the situation leads to greater perplexity, we may be forced to revise the ___.

6. Dress and body language are all examples of ___ ___.

7. ___ ___ determines the identity an actor will use in a specific situation.

8. ___ ___ consists of two general strategies, avoiding blame and gaining credit.

9. ___ has the purpose of establishing a positive non-street identity among the homeless.

10. One handles a spoiled identity by physically ___ and trying to ___.

MULTIPLE CHOICE

1. Which is likely to violate civil inattention in a public place?

   a. an averted gaze.
   b. silence.
   c. social withdrawal.
   d. striking up a conversation.

CHAPTER 7

2.   Methodological technique preferred by those engaged in the sociology of everyday life:

a.   surveys.
b.   thin description.
c.   thick description.
d.   experiment.

3.   Roughly identical to a definition of the situation:

a.   a frame.
b.   biography.
c.   keying.
d.   altercasting.

4.   A deliberate attempt to challenge common sense expectations that underlie social interaction:

a.   break experiment.
b.   cueing.
c.   framing.
d.   identity negotiation.

5.   Managing identities to support and sustain our self-esteem is called:

a.   ethnomethodology.
b.   framing.
c.   naturalistic inquiry.
d.   identity work.

6.   These are low in status and actively rejected by society:

a.   self concepts.
b.   spoiled identities.
c.   efforts to maintain personal space.
d.   the I and the me.

7. John stops briefly to say hello to a worker whom he supervises and is surprised to find the worker wants to tell him about a personal problem. John excuses himself as quickly as possible. Which principle is illustrated by John's behavior?

    a. the dialectic.
    b. total institution.
    c. biography.
    d. personal space.

8. Professionals such as medical doctors and lawyers make it a point to have their offices appear neat and well organized. They are showing a concern for their:

    a. front region.
    b. dialectic.
    c. back region.
    d. biography.

9. A chairperson of one sociology department always got to meetings early so that he could claim the chair at the end of the table. He was concerned about:

    a. body language.
    b. cueing status.
    c. dress.
    d. personal space.

10. An experienced office worker tells a new employee: "Above all avoid blame when things go wrong, and always take credit for work that goes right." This cynic has described:

    a. identity work.
    b. ethnomethodology.
    c. identity negotiation.
    d. dramaturgy.

11. When we fail miserably we may then have spoiled identities. One strategy is to explain that this is just a temporary situation and not a reflection of who we really are. This process is called:

    a. role enhancement.
    b. storytelling.
    c. role taking.
    d. role distancing.

12. Snow and Anderson used this research strategy as they passed as fellow homeless:

    a. experiment.
    b. survey.
    c. artifact.
    d. participant observation.

13. The sociology of everyday life is closely identified with this theory:

    a. conflict.
    b. symbolic interaction.
    c. functionalism.
    d. behaviorism.

14. Which is not an assumption of the everyday life prospective?

    a. the dialectic.
    b. biography.
    c. cultural universals.
    d. naturalistic inquiry.

15. Regarded as the "chief architect" of dramaturgical theory:

    a. George Mead.
    b. Erving Goffman.
    c. Max Weber.
    d. Karl Marx.

16. Ethnomethodology is closely linked to the work of:

    a. Herbert Spencer.
    b. Erving Goffman.
    c. Harold Garfinkel.
    d. Auguste Comte.

17. Not an assumption or a corollary of ethnomethodology:

    a. people are who they appear to be.
    b. others will trust our appearances.
    c. others share our symbolic worlds.
    d. belief that appearances can be deceiving.

18. Theory suggests that to gain credit it is best NOT to:

    a. brag.
    b. link yourself to high status people.
    c. be tactful.
    d. subtly remind others of your qualities.

19. Observation suggests that distances of up to ____ are reserved for intimates in this country.

    a. 3 feet.
    b. 6 inches.
    c. 4 feet.
    d. 18 inches.

20. The ultimate back region for most people:

    a. work.
    b. school.
    c. church.
    d. home.

21. Managing identities to sustain our self-esteem includes two strategies: avoiding blame and ___.

a. reframing.
b. nonverbal cueing.
c. gaining credit.
d. breaking.

22. Not included among those with spoiled identities:

a. mother on welfare.
b. traitor.
c. person with AIDS.
d. severely handicapped person.

23. This sociology theory dominated in the 1950s but came under serious question in the 1960s:

a. ethnomethodology.
b. dramaturgy.
c. sociology of everyday life.
d. structural functionalism.

24. A favorite theorist of structural-functionalists in the 1950s when they emphasized the power of institutionalized norms:

a. Max Weber.
b. George Mead.
c. Emile Durkheim.
d. Erving Goffman.

25. Based upon what sociologists have learned about personal space, professionals would probably interpret the need to share offices as:

a. punishing.
b. rewarding.
c. inefficient.
d. very practical.

26. Our self-esteem may suffer when we break norms or fail to live up to expectations. Most of the "repair work" is done by ____:

    a. withdrawing from the situation.
    b. attacking other people.
    c. offering excuses or justifications.
    d. pretending that nothing happened.

27. Generalizing from what has been learned about spoiled identities, a person arrested for a sex crime is most likely to:

    a. confess quickly.
    b. deny that he/she has anything in common with sex offenders.
    c. refuse to be interrogated.
    d. offer a disclaimer.

28. Generalizing from what was learned about children living in cities in the 1900s which is not likely to be an effective motivator of children:

    a. a variety of jobs.
    b. exciting places to spend money.
    c. personal profit from work.
    d. chance to work with parents.

29. Analysis of the causes and consequences of homelessness suggests that an obvious first step should be to ____.

    a. increase deinstitutionalization.
    b. provide more low-income housing.
    c. create more drug education programs.
    d. cut back on welfare programs.

CHAPTER 7

30. Dennis Wrong introduced the "oversocialized view of man" in the early
     1960s. This view called for sociologists to:

     a.   pay greater attention to the power of institutionalized norms.
     b.   view social behavior as more negotiable.
     c.   pay greater attention to the power of institutionalized roles.
     d.   reject the concept of socialization.

ESSAY QUESTIONS

1. Explain how dramaturgy, ethnomethodology and identity work all fit into
    the EDL perspective.

2. Discuss the four basic assumptions of the EDL perspective.

3. Explain how dramaturgy works in everyday life.

4. Discuss the causes of homelessness and how individuals so entrapped can
    manage positive self-esteem.

5. What is the relationship between identity work and self esteem?

Chapter 8
Deviance, Crime and Social Control

LEARNING OBJECTIVES

1. Explain what is meant by social control using the concepts of internalization, informal control and formal control.

2. Differentiate between nonconformity and deviance and discuss how deviance is relative.

3. Contrast the structural-functional, symbolic interactionist and conflict approaches to the study of deviance.

4. Specify how Merton uses the concepts of anomie and social structure to explain deviance. Note two shortcomings of this approach.

5. Describe Merton's four modes of adaption to anomie.

6. Identify the key elements of differential association and deterrence theories.

7. Define each of the following and note the role it plays in labeling theory: primary deviance, secondary deviance and the power to label.

8. Critique labeling theory.

CHAPTER 8

9. Identify each of the following: crime, deviance, victimless crime and street level justice.

10. Discuss how conflict theory explains deviance.

11. Summarize the key points for each of the following: murder, rape, robbery, assault, property crimes and white collar crime.

12. Explain the role played by age, gender, race and class in the commission of crimes.

13. Describe the function of each level of the criminal justice system.

14. Differentiate between retribution, reformation, specific deterrence, general deterrence and prevention.

15. Fully describe each of the different forms of community based corrections.

16. Discuss the problems of "getting tough on crime."

17. Who are the nation's prisoners and why?

18. Discuss how functional and conflict theorists view the role of the law in society.

19. How is the quality and quantity of the law related to the level of inequality in society.

20. Differentiate between rational law and substantive law.

CHAPTER OUTLINE

I. Conformity, Nonconformity and Deviance

    A. Social control consists of the forces and processes that encourage conformity. Three factors combine to create social control.
       1. Internalization is the process of building conformity to norms and values from our groups into our self concept.

2. Informal social control is self-restraint exercised because of a fear of what others may think.
3. Formal social controls are administrative sanctions such as fines and imprisonment.

B. Deviance refers to norm violations that exceed the tolerance level of the community and result in negative sanctions.
    1. Few acts are intrinsically deviant and most deviance depends upon the definition of the situation. The definition of what is deviant is relative.

C. The structural-functional theory sees deviance arising from a lack of integration in the structure of society.
    1. Merton drew upon Durkheim's concept of anomie, where the norms of society are no longer clear or applicable, to develop the strain theory of deviance.
        (a) There is a dislocation between the strongly held social goal of economic success and the means for achieving success that creates a condition of anomie that encourages individuals to commit deviant acts.
        (b) Adaptation to anomie may take the form of conformity or it may take the deviant forms of innovation, ritualism, retreatism, or rebellion.
        (c) Deviance is thus seen as arising from the social structure and not from individuals.
        (d) Critics argue that Merton sees deviance as an unnatural state arising from extraordinary circumstances when in fact deviance is a natural state of human affairs.
            (1) Conflict theorists argue that deviance comes only from competition over scarce resources.
            (2) Others see Merton's use of social class as an explanation for some deviance as inaccurate.

D. Symbolic interactionism sees deviance as being learned through interaction and involving the development of a deviant self concept.
    1. Differential association theory assumes that deviance is learned through the same mechanisms as conformity, i.e., through interaction with intimates (Sutherland).
        (a) Deviance is thus learned in one's neighborhood, on the job

or among friends and will occur when individuals find that they are rewarded more for criminality than for conformity.

2. Deterrence theory argues that deviance arises when sanctions provide insufficient rewards for conformity.

    (a) The primary blame falls on inadequate sanctioning systems but the individual still actively chooses to deviate or conform through a calculation of the costs and benefits.

    (b) When positive sanctions are systematically denied to some segments of society, these individuals have less to lose by choosing deviance.

    (c) Instrumental rewards, family ties and self-esteem are especially important deterrents to deviance.

3. Labeling theory is concerned with the processes by which the label deviant is attached to specific behaviors of individuals.

    (a) Becker contends that deviant behavior is behavior that people so label. Thus the label that people attach to an act is more important than the act itself.

        (1) The labels are attached by control agents.

    (b) Primary deviance is an individual's first impulse act of non-conformity, when a person accepts a deviant self concept and elects to play that role, secondary deviance occurs.

    (c) Individuals labeled as sick and not as bad, are entitled to treatment rather than punishment.

    (d) Three major criticisms are commonly mentioned regarding labeling theory.

        (1) The realitivistic approach to deviance limits its use to minor or victimless crimes.

        (2) Labeling also overlooks the causes of primary deviance.

        (3) It cannot explain repeated deviance by the yet unlabeled.

5. Conflict theory argues that economic pressures lead to crime and that class interests determine who is labeled as criminal.

    (a) The law rationalizes and supports the status quo by failing to punish any but the poor law breaker.

        (1) Lower class crime is thus a response to deprivation and exploitation.

II. Crime as Deviance

    A. Crimes are deviant acts that are subject to criminal or civil penalties.

In violating criminal or civil codes crimes can be classified as violating significant norms and thus constitute deviant behavior.

B.   The <u>Uniform Crime Report</u> summarizes crimes known to the police in several major categories called index crimes.

C.   Crimes involving the use of force or threat of force are called crimes of violence.
1.   Murder is the most violent and rarest of major violent crime.
(a) In 1988, 48% of all murder victims were black and 75% were male.
2.   Forcible rape accounts for only 7% of violent crime.
3.   Robbery involves personal confrontation and the threat or use of force.
4.   Assault or an attack for the purposes of inflicting severe bodily injury constitute nearly half of all violent crime.
(a) Violent assault is the most rapidly increasing index crime.
5.   Property crimes, which are not considered violent crimes, are by far the most frequently reported crimes.

D.   Crime rates are higher this decade than in the last decade.

E.   <u>Victimless crimes</u> are illegal acts of exchange for which there is no complainant.   Crimes typically included here are prostitution, gambling, homosexuality, etc.
1.   Efforts against victimless crimes are costly and time consuming activities that direct resources away from violent crime.
(a) Enforcement efforts are irregular and inconsistent.

F.   <u>White collar crime</u> is crime committed by people of respectability and high social status in the course of their profession.
1.   White collar crime is far more costly than common crime.
2.   White collar crime is obviously class related and for the most part these crimes go undetected and unreported.

G.   There are four major correlates of crime: age, sex, race and class.
1.   The highest crime rates are for the population 15 to 24 years of age with black males between the ages of 18 to 20 being the most likely to commit crimes.
(a) Younger people may experience lower self-esteem, a greater

gap between aspirations and opportunity and lack effective ties to conventional society.

(b) The young have less to lose by deviance and their delinquency is mostly a leisure time activity.

2. Males, consistent with their sex roles, are greatly overrepresented in crime, especially violent crime.

(a) Women typically are involved in minor crime and their rates have increased faster than the overall crime rates for males. Still, women are not typically involved in violent crimes.

3. Social class as such is not seen as a direct cause of crime itself. It appears that class is directly related to the type of crime committed.

(a) Lower class crime is typically of a direct and interpersonal nature while middle or upper class crime centers upon the misuse of power.

(1) Enforcement and incarceration are typically reserved for the lower class criminal.

4. Blacks and Hispanics are greatly overrepresented in crime statistics

(a) Most of the explanations for minority crime lie in the living conditions of disorganized neighborhoods and deprivation experienced by minority group members.

(1) Minority unemployment leads to unstable families and neighborhoods.

(2) Minorities appear to be more likely to commit some crimes and are far more likely to be singled out for attention by the criminal justice system.

III. The Sociology of the Law

A. Theories of the law.
1. The law serves three functions.
(a) It provides formal sanctions to encourage conformity and discourage deviance.
(b) It helps to settle disputes.
(c) It may be an instrument for social change.
2. Functionalists and conflict theorists disagree over the nature of the law.
(a) The law is indeed functional by maintaining order in society.

(b) The law may be used to dominate and to control others while maintaining a system of inequality.

3. Black argues that the "quality" and the "quantity" of the law depend upon the level of inequality in society.

(a) The greater the inequality in society, the more law there will be.

(b) The law works differently when the victim and the offender are status unequals than when they are status equals.

(1) The law mediates between status equals.

(2) The law is more punitive when statuses are unequal.

4. Weber distinguishes between rational law and substantive law.

(a) Rational legal procedures require the strict application of the law.

(b) Substantive legal procedures take into account the unique circumstances of the individual case.

(1) Sentencing outcomes show the law to be more substantive than rational where the nature of the decisions depends more upon the characteristics of the judge than upon the case.

IV. Formal Social Controls

A. The role of the police is to investigate and arrest persons suspected of committing crimes.

1. The police are in a unique and powerful position due to their ability to make arrests under conditions of low visibility and great discretion.

(a) The discretionary powers are best reflected in street-level justice or the decisions made by police in the initial stages of an investigation.

(1) This form of justice is relatively invisible and hard to evaluate.

B. The court system involves the prosecution of people who have been arrested as suspects in the commission of a crime.

1. Decision stages in the court system are critical in that negotiation and plea bargaining account for 90 percent of all convictions. They occur before a trial can be held.

2. Negotiation and plea bargaining are often involved in setting

the sentence for the guilty.
3. Sentencing varies greatly from jurisdiction to jurisdiction with prejudice and class bias playing a strong role.

C. The prison system is assigned the task of administering punishment to those convicted of crimes. Five rationalizations for punishment are <u>retribution, reformation, deterrence, general deterrence</u> and <u>prevention.</u>
1. Today prison populations are exploding. Increasingly the inmates are uneducated, unskilled, poor and black.
   (a) A crisis exists in our prisons due to overcrowding.
2. The utility of massive imprisonment is being questioned by new evidence showing that getting caught is more of a deterrent than the length of the sentence.
   (a) This leads some to argue for greater funding for the police.
3. Only one quarter of convicted offenders go to prison. The others are put into a <u>community-based</u> <u>corrections</u>.
   (a) Programs include probation, parole and the newer programs of intensive supervision probation or I.S.P.
4. Alternatives to the conservative approaches include attacking the root causes of crime - society itself. This includes:
   (a) reducing social impoverishment and inequality,
   (b) replacing unstable low-wage, dead end jobs with decent jobs,
   (c) enacting a supportive national family policy and
   (d) increasing the economic stability of communities.

D. The sociological perspective suggests that crime can be addressed more effectively by considering social institutions rather than individual criminals.
1. Symptomatic of this misplaced emphasis is the current war on drugs.
   (a) Attacking the suppliers will not diminish the social conditions that encourage drug use.

MATCHING I

A. Police   ____ 1.   More common than crimes of violence.

B. Murder   ____ 2.   Prostitution, gambling, pornography.

C. Women   ____ 3.   A very rare form of crime.

D. Deterrence   ____ 4.   Pent up aggression, diffuse hostility and violence.

E. Rational law

                        ____ 5.   Cost benefit decision to deviate.

F. Assault

                        ____ 6.   Commit more interpersonal crime.

G. Property crimes

                        ____ 7.   Reported rates have doubled in the past two decades.

H. Lower class

I. Mafia   ____ 8.   No increase in their participation in violent crime.

J. Middle class

                        ____ 9.   The root cause of minority crime.

K. Lower-class minorities   ____ 10.   Commit crimes involving power.

L. Victimless crimes

M. White collar crime

N. Street-level justice

O. Low quality employment

CHAPTER 8

MATCHING II

A. Courts

B. Social control theory

C Specific deterrence

D. Primary deviance

E. Rational law

F. Police

G. Retribution

H. U.C.R.

I. Substantive law

J. General deterrence

K. Blacks and Hispanics

L. Victimless crime

M. Prevention

N. White collar crime

O. Reformation

____ 1. Society punishes to revenge the victim.

____ 2. Low risk, high yield crime.

____ 3. Negotiated plea bargaining.

____ 4. Summary of crimes known to the police.

____ 5. Designed by society to scare us.

____ 6. Street-level justice.

____ 7. Incapacitating offenders.

____ 8. Police must find both the crime and the criminal.

____ 9. Following the letter of the law.

____ 10. Designed to scare the offender.

FILL IN THE BLANK QUESTIONS

1. Being expelled from class for cheating exemplifies ____ social control while fearing humiliation in front of your classmates demonstrates ____ social control.

2. Self-control occurs because individuals ____ the norms and values of their groups.

3. Minor rule violation constitutes ____ and significant norm violation is called ____.

4. In Merton's scheme, slavishly going through the motions prescribed by society is called ____.

5. Sutherland's theory of ____ ____ assumes that ____ is learned when one's associates favor ____ more than they do ____.

6. According to Black, both the quality and the quantity of the law are related to the level of ____ in society.

7. Becker contends that deviant behavior is any behavior people ____ ____.

8. The first impulsive act of deviance is called ____ ____.

9. Deterrence theory suggests that some deviate when it will enhance their ____ ____.

10. People who are arrested for criminal acts are overwhelmingly and disproportionately ____, ____ and ____ ____ ____.

11. ____-class individuals predominately commit interpersonal crimes while ____-class individuals commit crimes using power.

12. The structural-functional approach to deviance sees deviance as being ____.

13. America's emphasis on achievement and success leads to ____ according to Merton.

CHAPTER 8

14. According to Weber, ____ law takes into account the unique circumstances of the individual case.

15. According to conflict theory, crime is actually ____ prevalent among the poor.

MULTIPLE CHOICE

1. Social control, the forces that bring about conformity, rests largely on:

   a. self control and informal social controls.
   b. self control and formal social controls.
   c. formal social controls.
   d. self control.

2. Social scientists speak of deviance when:

   a. any norm is violated.
   b. when one feels guilty about a norm violation.
   c. when people violate society's significant norms.
   d. when persons in a group violate norms together.

3. Which is NOT true about behavior that is defined as deviance?

   a. many acts are intrinsically seen as deviant in all cultures.
   b. often depends on the circumstances .
   c. often depends on the individual's characteristics.
   d. often depends on the group whose norms and values are chosen as standards.

4. Continued and deliberate deviance that results from labeling:

   a. primary deviance.
   b. innovation.
   c. secondary deviance.
   d. white collar crime.

5. Which is NOT true about white collar crime?

    a. not listed on the UCR.
    b. easily detected.
    c. includes crimes by employees against companies.
    d. includes crimes by companies against the public.

6. Following guidelines from Max Weber, rational justice refers to:

    a. lenient enforcement of laws
    b. strict application of the law, regardless of fairness.
    c. enforcement of informal community norms but not laws.
    d. emphasis on unique circumstances of the individual.

7. Some parents may work very hard at getting their children to internalize the norms and values of their group. This means that they want their children to conform because of:

    a. informal social controls.
    b. self control.
    c. formal social controls.
    d. fear of the authorities.

8. Citizens sometimes complain that employees in government agencies are more concerned about following the rules, even when this doesn't make sense, than they are about helping citizens. Robert Merton would refer to these employees as:

    a. ritualists.
    b. conformists.
    c. innovators.
    d. retreatists.

9. Most citizens, and probably most sociologists, take this approach to law:

    a. conflict.
    b. structural-functional.
    c. symbolic interaction.
    d. labeling.

10. Data for the Uniform Crime Reports are obtained from:

    a. crimes known to police.
    b. random sample of householders who report any crimes that they have experienced.
    c. confidential reports by police informants.
    d. self report techniques.

11. An example of white collar crime:

    a. prostitution.
    b. homosexuality.
    c. false advertising.
    d. murder.

12. Studies of sentencing outcomes suggest that:

    a. law tends to be more rational than substantive.
    b. law tends to be more substantive than rational.
    c. sentences are highly correlated with the nature of crime.
    d. sentences vary by race and class of offenders and victims.

13. This theory of deviance was initially formulated by Durkheim:

    a. anomie.
    b. cultural transmission theory.
    c. social control theory.
    d. sociobiology.

14. According to Robert Merton's strain theory, innovation as deviance occurs when:

    a. persons accept both society's goals and means.
    b. persons accept society's goals but not the means.
    c. persons reject both society's goals and means.
    d. persons accept society's means but not the goals.

15. These theorists see deviance as an inevitable product of competition in society:

    a. anomie.
    b. conflict.
    c. cultural transmission.
    d. labeling.

16. This theory assumes that deviance is learned:

    a. anomie.
    b. differential association.
    c. labeling.
    d. social conflict.

17. According to Black's theory of law, both the quantity and the quality of law depends most upon:

    a. levels of inequality in society.
    b. gross national product.
    c. certainty of punishment.
    d. national character.

18. Theories of punishment suggest that if the goal of society is to revenge victims and society as a whole it will emphasize:

    a. general deterrence.
    b. prevention.
    c. retribution.
    d. reformation.

19. Which is true about the murder rate in the U.S.?

    a. a relatively rare form of crime.
    b. rate has changed dramatically in recent years.
    c. chance of being a victim greatest for white males.
    d. most victims are middle class.

20. The fastest-growing category of crime in the UCR:

    a.   murder.
    b.   rape.
    c.   robbery.
    d.   aggravated assault.

21. About what percent of the effort in the drug war in this country is going into law enforcement and not education?

    a.   70%.
    b.   10%
    c.   30%.
    d.   50%.

22. About what percent of criminal convictions are actually processed through public trials?

    a.   10 percent.
    b.   30 percent.
    c.   50 percent.
    d.   75 percent.

23. Which of the following BEST reflects the current "crisis of penalty" in this country?

    a.   rapidly increasing prison populations.
    b.   overcrowding.
    c.   inmate violence.
    d.   soaring costs.

24. About what portion of convicted offenders actually go to jail?

    a.   24 percent.
    b.   50 percent.
    c.   100 percent.
    d.   75 percent.

25. Researchers have found that this theory helps to explain why some youth
     become increasingly delinquent after contacts with powerful others
     whereas others eventually accept conformity and conventionality:

     a.   labeling.
     b.   anomie.
     c.   differential association.
     d.   control theory.

26. Only about 3% of the population reports being a crime victim each year, but
     if one is a victim he/she is most likely to be a victim of a:

     a.   robbery.
     b.   rape.
     c.   aggravated assault.
     d.   property crime.

27. If this theory is correct, we would expect crime among the lower class to
     rise during economic recessions when it becomes difficult to meet basic
     needs:

     a.   anomie.
     b.   differential association.
     c.   self-esteem.
     d.   conflict.

28. Murder is among the most violent of criminal acts. Victims are most likely
     to be:

     a.   unknown to their attackers.
     b.   rural residents.
     c.   black.
     d.   female.

29. Some persons are much more likely to be arrested for criminal acts. A characteristic of persons most likely to be arrested is:

    a.   old.
    b.   male.
    c.   female.
    d.   white.

30. If current trends continue, which factor is most likely to increase the number of convicted persons sent to community-based corrections?

    a.   more liberal view of paroles.
    b.   increased cost of imprisoning people.
    c.   more liberal view of probation.
    d.   decline in rate of imprisonment in recent years.

ESSAY QUESTIONS

1. Discuss how deviance is relative.

2. How does a sociological approach to crime suggest certain problems and solutions?

3. How effective have we been by "getting tough on crime?"

4. Use three examples to explain how Merton uses the concepts of anomie and social structure to account for deviance.

5. Why are most prisoners poor, uneducated and minorities and what can be done about it?

Chapter 9
Stratification

LEARNING OBJECTIVES

1. Explain the relationship between inequality and stratification.

2. Define what is meant by ascribed status and achieved status, and discuss the role played by each in caste and class systems.

3. Identify each of the following terms and note how it is used by Marx in his explanation of social classes: bourgeois, proletariat, class consciousness and false consciousness.

4. Explain what Weber means by reference to the concepts of class, status and power.

5. Outline the structural-functional theory of social stratification and the Marxian or conflict view of stratification. Don't forget to note the major shortcomings of each approach.

6. Note three assumptions of Beegley's synthesis and point out how this approach draws upon both structural-functional and conflict theory.

7. Define SES and explain how sociologists use occupation and self-identification to measure social class.

8. Point out inequities in the distribution of wealth and income in the U.S. and describe how social class makes a difference in our daily lives.

9. Differentiate between the following terms: social mobility, intergenerational mobility and intragenerational mobility.

10. Outline how the indirect inheritance model functions noting the factors that influence mobility.

11. Specify both the macro and micro factors in social mobility.

12. How do intelligence and achievement motivation operate to overcome the barriers to social mobility?

13. Outline the dominant characteristics of the upper class, the working class and the poor.

14. Explain the following terms: absolute poverty, relative poverty, culture of poverty and underclass.

15. Discuss the role played by ideology in justifying inequality in the U.S.

CHAPTER OUTLINE

I. Structures of Inequality

    A. Sociologists study that form of inequality called <u>stratification</u> in which social statuses within society are ranked on the basis of their access to scarce resources. Inequality becomes stratification under the following conditions.
        1. The inequality is institutionalized.
        2. The inequality is based upon membership in a status rather than on personal attributes.

    B. Two basic forms of stratification structures are caste and class systems.
        1. <u>Caste</u> structures exist where scarce resources are distributed on the basis of <u>ascribed</u> <u>statuses</u>.
        2. In a <u>class</u> <u>system</u>, scarce resources are distributed primarily on the basis of <u>achieved</u> <u>statuses</u>.

(a) Class systems permit <u>social</u> <u>mobility</u> which may be either upward or downward and may be measured <u>intragenerationally</u> or <u>intergenerationally</u>.

(b) Ascribed statuses like race or gender may also operate in a class system.

3. A class system is an ordered set of statuses, the actual number of which depends upon one's theoretical approach.

(a) <u>Marx</u> identified only two main classes. They are the <u>bourgeoisie</u>, or those who own the means of production and the proletariat who own nothing and must compete among themselves to sell their labor to the bourgeoisie.

(1) <u>Class</u> is thus determined by one's relationship to the means of production.

(2) Marx believed that a revolutionary movement to eliminate class differences would be likely to occur when <u>false</u> <u>consciousness</u> was replaced by <u>class</u> <u>consciousness</u>.

(b) <u>Weber</u> proposed three independent dimensions upon which to rank individuals. Like Marx, he chose class but he added status and party as two additional dimensions.

(1) <u>Status</u> is social honor expressed in one's lifestyle which is not to be confused with an economic ability to purchase goods and services.

(2) People from the same <u>class</u> are united in a unique lifestyle.

(3) <u>Power</u> is the ability to get others to act against their own wishes.

(4) Modern sociologists draw heavily upon Weber in constructing a composite measure of <u>social</u> <u>class</u> where a category of people share roughly the same class, status and power.

(5) Social class thus includes an emphasis on class, status, power and an element of self-awareness.

II. Inequality in the United States

A. The picture of inequality obtained depends upon how inequality is measured.

1. Self-identification simply asks people to identify what class they belong to.

(a) Answers vary considerably based upon the form of the question used.

2. Occupational prestige scales yield reliable and consistent results that order occupations in a prestige ranking.
   (a) Socioeconomic Status (SES) ranks individuals on combinations of variables, chief among which is occupation.

B. Economic inequality is present at high levels in all contemporary societies.
   1. Inequality in household income has changed little in the last 35 years.
   2. Wealth is highly concentrated and has been in America since at least the beginning of the 19th century.
      (a) The top 2% in income owned 26% of all assets in 1984.
      (b) The top 20% of households held 75% of all wealth in 1984.

C The consequences of social class are quite apparent in that class influences almost every behavior and attitude one has.
   1. While wealth and income inequality patterns are quite stable, some patterns have changed.
      (a) Middletown studies show that class differences are declining.
      (b) Two factors are noted: an increase in real income and a greater increase in public services.

III. Explanations of Inequality

A. Structural-functional theory was applied to social stratification by Davis and Moore who conclude that stratification is necessary and justifiable because it contributes to the maintenance of society.
   1. Society has important roles to fill and inequality functions to fill these roles, thus contributing to the maintenance of society.
      (a) Society must encourage those with talent to undergo extensive training to fill these roles.
      (b) Inequality in the form of significant financial rewards serves to motivate the talented to undergo training and to fill key roles.
      (c) Rewards are influenced by the unpleasantness and importance of the task as well as the talent required.
   2. Criticisms against functional interpretations of stratification systems focuses upon three major points.
      (a) High demand jobs can be artificially created by limiting access to them.

(b) Social class, etc. is probably a stronger predictor of high rewards than is talent or ability.

(c) Many highly paid positions do not really reflect their functional importance.

B. Marxian <u>conflict</u> <u>theory</u> explains inequality in terms of exploitation.
1. The bourgeois seeks to maximize profit by minimizing the amount of wages paid to the proletariat.
   (a) Inequality is thus a product of the division of labor and the ownership and control of private property.
      (1) Individuals who control the work of others also have power to pursue their self-interest.
2. Modern conflict theory emphasizes ownership less and sees those managers who actually control the organizations as the oppressors.
   (a) Manipulation and exploitation of the less powerful is still the focus of modern conflict theory.
3. Criticisms against Marxist theory centers upon the fact that people are unequal to begin with and that inequality is a major motivation for human labor.
   (a) Also, coordination and authority are functional.

C Beegley draws upon both functional and conflict theory in proposing a synthesis. There are three major postulates.
1. Power is the major determinant of scarce resources.
   (a) The powerful will use their power to benefit themselves.
2. The distribution of power is socially structured.
   (a) Advantages and disadvantages are maintained through private and public policy.
3. Individuals can make a difference.
   (a) Individual characteristics are not wholly determined by social structure, i.e., talent and ambition do play a role.

IV. Sorting People into Structures

A. <u>Micro</u> <u>level</u> factors or the characteristics of individuals affect the allocation of statuses.
1. The <u>indirect</u> <u>inheritance</u> <u>model</u> focuses upon the role of the family.
   (a) Education is a key to status attainment and one's social class

standing.

(1) The best predictor of education is one's parents' education.

(b) Parental education and social class directly influence the educational aspirations of a child.

(1) Aspirations are bolstered by home attitudes, help and family resources.

(c) Two factors not directly influenced by the family that influence status attainment are <u>achievement</u> <u>motivation</u> and <u>intelligence</u>.

B.   <u>Macro-level</u> factors or the character of the labor market also influences status attainment and individual achievement.

1.   Major changes in the structure of occupations during the past century have dramatically increased social mobility.

2.   The U.S. has a dual labor market consisting of one level (primary) containing good jobs and another level (secondary) for bad jobs.

(a) Women and minorities typically fall into the secondary labor market.

C.   The stratification system depends upon both macro and micro-level forces with some factors are best explained by macro forces while others are better explained by micro forces.

D.   An <u>ideology</u> is a set of norms and values that rationalize the existing social structure. Ideologies are built into the dominant culture of society.

1.   The major ideology justifying inequality in this country is the <u>American</u> <u>Dream</u> which states that success comes entirely from one's own efforts and that failure can only be blamed upon the individual.

V.   The Rich, the Working Class and the Poor

A.   The upper class is best characterized by inherited wealth.

1.   The wealth is cumulative and is managed to produce even more wealth.

2.   Most people in the upper class were born into considerable privilege before actually becoming members of the upper class.

3.   They share the fundamental values of private enterprise, limited government and due process.

B. The working class falls below the middle class and above the lower class.
   1. <u>Halle</u> summarizes the working class lifestyle as follows.
      (a) The majority are high school graduates who did not do well in school and failed to absorb middle class values.
      (b) Jobs can pay well but are not enjoyable.
         (1) Incomes may peak by age 25 and there may be no chance for promotion.
         (2) Economic insecurity, layoffs and plant closings are typical.
         (3) Most own their own home.
      (c) Work and leisure are clearly separated and sex segregated.
      (d) Sharp gender differences occur and are reinforced by class values.
         (1) Marriages are often unhappy.
   2. The future of this class seems bleak.

C. The poor or those living in poverty lack the amount of money or resources to meet the minimum requirements of a decent standard of living.
   1. In 1988 the figure for poverty stood at 31.9 million people.
   2. Poverty cuts across many dimensions of age, sex and race.
      (a) In 1988 46 percent of the poor were elderly and children.
         (1) The persistently poor are typically those living in a household headed by a black woman or the elderly.
   3. Poverty can be seen as either <u>absolute poverty</u> or <u>relative poverty</u>.
      (a) Few people in America are absolutely poor with most of the poor experiencing relative poverty.
      (b) Absolute poverty characterizes the homeless and the <u>underclass.</u>
         (1) The underclass are those who are unemployed and unemployable and constitute a miserable and useless substratum. They are on the bottom and they will stay there.
   4. The affluent, citing the American Dream blame the poor for their own condition. They are seen as lazy, inept, immoral or disabled.
      (a) White poor often accept this ideology while black poor are more likely to see structural factors lying at the root of poverty.
      (b) <u>Lewis</u> uses the concepts of a <u>culture of poverty</u> to explain the

persistence of the poor.

    (1) The poor develop values that are functional to their current living conditions because middle class values do not work for most of the poor.

    (2) These alternative values do not lead to mobility thus allowing the poor to survive but never improve their lot in life.

5.   Most sociologists conclude that structural problems in the American economy create a mismatch between opportunities and the people available to fill them.

  (a) Policies directed toward the problem of inequality follow three routes: taxing inheritances, outlawing discrimination and creating special education programs.

  (b) The working class is experiencing strong pressures for downward mobility due to the permanent loss of manufacturing jobs.

    (1) These good paying jobs are being replaced by poor paying jobs in the service sector.

  (c) The declining opportunities are enhancing the formation of an urban underclass.

MATCHING

A.	Class structure	____ 1. Status is fixed at birth.
B.	Status	____ 2. A society based upon achieved status.
C	Conflict theory	____ 3. Those who own tools and materials.
D.	Ideology	____ 4. Social honor.
E.	Relative poverty	____ 5. A composite measure of income, education, and occupation.
F.	Bourgeois	
G	Absolute poverty	____ 6. Davis and Moore.
H.	Caste structure	____ 7. American Dream
I.	Culture of poverty	____ 8. American norms and values.
J.	Structural-functional theory	____ 9. Inability to provide the requirements for life.
K.	Estate taxes	____ 10. Those who sell their labor.
L.	Proletariat	____ 11. Living for the moment.
M.	Middle class	____ 12. Origins of inequality in the division of labor.
N.	Ascribed status	
O.	SES	
P.	Modern conflict theory	

FILL IN THE BLANK QUESTIONS

1. The two basic forms of stratification structures are ____ and ____.

2. According to Beegley, ____ can make a difference.

3. ___ ___ is a lack of awareness of one's real position in the class structure and ___ ___ is an awareness of one's true class identity.

4. The three dimensions upon which to rank people, proposed by Weber, are ___, ___ and___.

5. The structural-functional theory argues that ___/ ___ are the means used by society to ensure people fill essential roles.

6. ___ ___ is a change in social class from one generation to the next.

7. ___ theory explains inequality as the result of class conflict.

8. Conflict theory overlooks the fact that ___ and ___ are functional.

9. Modern conflict theory sees the ___ as the oppressors.

10. Social class differences are less than 50 years ago because of an increase in ___ ___ and the extension of ___ ___.

11. A macro approach to social mobility would focus the characteristics of the ___ ___ while a micro approach would focus upon the characteristics of ___.

12. The role played by the family in influencing mobility is stressed in the ___ ___ ___.

13. Two factors influencing mobility that are not directly related to one's social class background are ___ ___ and ___.

14. An ___ is a set of values and norms that rationalize the existing social structure.

15. Economic insecurity, unenjoyable jobs and sharp gender differences characterize the ___ class.

MULTIPLE CHOICE

1. Which of the following is NOT an example of stratification?

   a. being born into a wealthy family.
   b. having an above average I.Q.
   c. being born an African American male.
   d. being a millionare who pays no income taxes.

2. This term means that a person may have a higher or lower occupation or social class than the parents did:

   a. career mobility.
   b. intergenerational mobility.
   c. intragenerational mobility.
   d. social mobility.

3. This indicator is based upon income, education, and occupation:

   a. class.
   b. status.
   c. power.
   d. socioeconomic status.

4. Family status and income provide children with surroundings and goals that ensure that they end up at the same place as the parents. This is referred to as:

   a. caste system effects.
   b. achievement motivation effects.
   c. intergenerational mobility.
   d. indirect inheritance model.

5. Oscar Lewis coined the term "culture of poverty" to explain why some people stay poor. Which value is emphasized in the culture of poverty:

    a. live for the moment.
    b. thrift.
    c. investment in the future.
    d. hard work.

6. This concept alerts us to macro economic processes that affect the poor:

    a. "culture of poverty."
    b. structure of opportunity.
    c. values such as hard work and thrift.
    d. ideology of the American dream.

7. Which is NOT true about occupational prestige as measured by the Occupational Prestige Scale?

    a. results are based on survey research.
    b. repeated tests yield consistent results over time.
    c. women rank occupations different than men.
    d. same ordering of occupations occurs in other Westernized societies.

8. Which is NOT a consequence of social class in the U.S.:

    a. people who have high levels of achievement motivation.
    b. babies born in poor neighborhoods are more likely to die before their first birthday.
    c. people who fail to graduate from high school are more likely to get a divorce.
    d. people with low incomes are more likely to be crime victims.

9. The major ideology that justifies inequality in the U.S.:

    a. liberalism.
    b. the American dream.
    c. conservatism.
    d. imperialism.

10. Each year, the U.S. government fixes a poverty level and determines who lives below that level. The category of persons most likely to be poor is:

    a.   female-headed households.
    b.   rural residents.
    c.   central city residents.
    d.   those over age 65.

11. Why are some people poor? Is it their own fault? A majority of Americans believe that being poor is caused by:

    a.   sickness.
    b.   values.
    c.   bad luck.
    d.   structural factors.

12. ____ is designed to reduce the direct inheritance of social position and create greater equality.

    a.   laws against discrimination.
    b.   laws outlawing social classes.
    c.   estate taxes.
    d.   special education programs.

13. In Marx's framework those who own the tools and materials necessary for their work are the:

    a.   bourgeois.
    b.   middle class.
    c.   proletariat.
    d.   government leaders.

14. Not an assumption of the Davis and Moore functionalist theory of stratification:

    a.   some roles in society are more important.
    b.   inequality in rewards is the means society uses to ensure that people play important roles.
    c.   inequality is seen as exploitation.
    d.   sees inequality as a rational response to a social problem.

15. A major criticism of the conflict perspective on stratification:

    a. an ideology that justifies inequality.
    b. the assumption that unequal financial rewards are needed to motivate people.
    c. ignores the fact that people are unequal.
    d. too much emphasis on the importance of inequality as a major motivator of human labor.

16. According to Beegley, who has tried to provide a general theory of contemporary stratification, which factor is the major determinant of the distribution of scarce resources?

    a. power.
    b. individual differences.
    c. luck.
    d. type of political system.

17. Alternative theories exist to explain why we have inequality and poverty. Governments, sometimes guided by social science theory and research, have developed policies with regard to the elimination of inequality. Which has NOT been a direct approach of social policy in the U.s.:

    a. taxing inheritance.
    b. outlawing discrimination.
    c. seeing the family as the root of both advantage and disadvantage.
    d. education opportunities.

18. Theorists who compare inequality and stratification note that:

    a. with stratification, inequality is institutionalized.
    b. inequality exists only in capitalistic societies.
    c. inequality is rare in today's societies.
    d. access to resources has little to do with either.

19. Occupation with the highest prestige in the U.S.:

    a. physician.
    b. college professor.
    c. accountant.
    d. police officer.

20. When Americans were asked whether they belong to the upper, middle, lower or working class, nearly half say middle class and nearly half say: ____.

    a. upper class.
    b. middle class.
    c. lower class.
    d. working class.

21. Which is true about inequality in the distribution of household income in the U.S.?

    a. it has declined dramatically in recent years.
    b. it has increased dramatically in recent years.
    c. it has changed little in recent years.
    d. it is present now but not present in the early years of our history.

22. In 1972 a team of investigators did a restudy of Middletown (Muncie, Indiana) and reported a marked convergence on all measures except one -- namely:

    a. percent unemployed.
    b. infant mortality.
    c. mental health.
    d. obesity.

23. Most millionaires in the U.S. pursued careers in:

    a. sports.
    b. business.
    c. professions.
    d. education.

24. About how many millionaires are there in the U.S.?

    a.   10,000,000.
    b.   5,000.
    c.   500,000.
    d.   100.

25. The single best predictor of eventual class in the U.S.:

    a.   race.
    b.   parents' education.
    c.   education.
    d.   intelligence.

26. Marx and Weber each included this dimension in their categories:

    a.   class.
    b.   status.
    c.   party.
    d.   family.

27. The best single predictor of eventual social class is education and best single predictor one's education is:

    a.   parents' education.
    b.   parents' occupation.
    c.   ambition.
    d.   intelligence.

28. The wealth of those with smaller estates is <u>more</u> likely to be invested in:

    a.   stocks and bonds.
    b.   their homes.
    c.   businesses.
    d.   other investments.

29. Which is NOT a characteristic of working-class families?

    a. strong normative gender differences.
    b. being unemployed and unemployable.
    c. owning their own homes.
    d. having little or no chance for promotion.

30. If current trends continue, most millionaires in the U.S. will be:

    a. under age 45.
    b. white and male.
    c. graduates of state public universities.
    d. self-made persons.

ESSAY QUESTIONS

1. Compare and contrast those who are wealthy to the working class and note how social class advantages and disadvantages seem to be transmitted from one generation to another.

2. Define SES and explain how sociologists use occupations and self-identification to measure social class.

3. Discuss how social class differences measured by sociologists actually reflect real differences in life style.

4. Explain how poverty can persist in American society.

5. Discuss the role played by ideology in justifying inequality.

Chapter 10
Racial and Ethnic Inequalities

LEARNING OBJECTIVES

1. Compare and contrast the concepts of race and ethnicity.

2. Define racism and note how race relations in America constitute a semi-caste system.

3. Define the following: majority group, minority group, conflict, accommodation, acculturation and assimilation.

4. Discuss how prejudice is facilitated by personal and institutional factors.

5. Describe how the self-fulfilling prophecy works.

6. Define discrimination, note its different forms and outline the relationship between prejudice and discrimination.

7. Fully identify each of the following: social distance, segregation and extraordinary solutions.

8. Outline the historical development of the melting pot and Anglo conformity in America.

9.   Note the distinctive historical, social and economic characteristics of black Americans.

10. Discuss the political, educational and economic changes experienced by African Americans in the last two generations.

11. Highlight the distinctive historical, social and economic characteristics of Hispanics, Native Americans, Jews, Japanese and other Asians.

12. Briefly outline the use of extraordinary solutions to the problems of American racial and ethnic minorities.

13. Discuss the relationship between prejudice, residential segregation, intermarriage and the prospects for minority assimilation.

14. Describe how the black underclass has been formed and why it is seen as a major social problem.

CHAPTER OUTLINE

I.   Race, Ethnicity and Inequality

    A.   Race and ethnicity constitute two major dimensions of inequality.
        1.   Race refers to a category of people whom we treat as distinct on account of physical characteristics to which we have assigned social importance.
        2.   An ethnic group is a category of people whose members are thought to share a common origin and important elements of a common culture.
        3.   Individual self-identity and institutional forces both work to create and maintain racial and ethnic statuses.
            (a) These statuses are not fixed and they change over time.
            (b) Subcultural differences exist for many of these statuses.
            (c) The key point to understand is that these are disadvantaged subcultures.

    B.   Caste, class and racism are special cases of stratification.

1. Conflict theory argues that groups gaining power create institutions that rationalize and perpetuate the status quo.
   (a) Racial advantages are maintained through racism or a belief that inherited physical characteristics provide the legitimate basis for unequal treatment.
   (b) The stratification characteristics of a semi-caste system apply to minority group, majority group relationships where the majority group maintains a strong advantage in the distribution of scarce resources.
      (1) Both race and class are critical factors in the maintenance of the semi-caste system.
   (c) Within minority groups the patterns of stratification are apparent in that income and wealth are unequally distributed.

II. Separate and Unequal: The Maintenance of Inequality

A. The maintenance of inequality is enhanced by establishing majority and minority groups.
   1. A majority group is culturally, economically and politically dominant and a minority group is culturally, economically and politically subordinate.
   2. Relations between minority and majority groups may follow several patterns including conflict, accommodation, acculturation or assimilation.

B. Interaction with minority group members can be controlled with regard to the intimacy and proximity involved.
   1. Social distance is the degree of intimacy and equality in relationships between two groups.
   2. Several processes encourage social distance.
      (a) Prejudice is irrationally based negative attitudes towards categories of people.
         (1) Prejudice is learned along with other norms, values and beliefs.
         (2) Prejudice can become institutionalized into the structure of society where the attitudes permeate the major institutions and social class structure.
         (3) Personal factors accounting for why some individuals

are prejudiced are <u>authoritarianism</u> and <u>scapegoating</u>.

    (4) Prejudice relies heavily upon stereotypes and operates through the mechanism of the <u>self-fulfilling prophecy</u>. If we stereotype a category of people, treat them according to the stereotype, then they will probably become much like the stereotype.

C. Prejudice is an attitude and <u>discrimination</u> is behavior in which individuals are treated unequally on the basis of their membership in categories.

    1. Public policy undercuts racism by outlawing discrimination.

    2. Prejudice and discrimination combine to form several patterns of behavior that include <u>bigots, friends, timid bigots</u> and <u>fair weather friends</u>.

D. Group differences are easier to maintain if social distance is enhanced by <u>segregation</u> or the practice of physically separating minority and majority group members.

E. The persistence of racial disadvantage through apparently neutral social processes is called <u>institutionalized racism</u>.

    1. Institutionalized racism operates through the <u>indirect inheritance model</u> and <u>majority rule</u>.

        (a) Majority rules is a more subtle form of racism that is now typical of the U.S.

F. Additional solutions exist in the form of rigid segregation, concentration campus, expulsion or extermination. These are referred to as <u>extraordinary</u> solutions.

III. Racial and Ethnic Groups in the United States

A. White immigration began in the 16th century with the English emerging as the majority group, a position not relinquished to this day.

    1. Those arriving after English domination were required to undergo acculturation and assimilation. Despite this fact, a myth arose in which it was believed that a physical and cultural blending of groups called a <u>melting pot</u> would occur.

2. The process of acculturation which actually occurred is called Anglo-conformity. The new immigrant groups came to adopt English language and customs.
 (a) Today, fewer Americans identify with an ethnic group.

B. African Americans constitute 12% of the population and are the largest racial minority.
 1. Their migration was involuntary and they are among the earliest of American immigrants.
  (a) Migration to northern industrial centers began in World War One and accelerated greatly after World War Two.
   (1) The last forty years have seen major gains for the black minority with outlawed segregation in the armed forces, desegregation of schools, passage of the Civil Rights Act and the passage of affirmative action legislation.
 2. Political gains commenced with the end of the civil war but they only became reality with the massive civil rights movements occurring in the 1960's and 1970's.
  (a) Black voter registration skyrocketed and black mayors have been elected in a number of major cities.
 3. Educational gains have centered upon the near equal high school graduation rates between whites and blacks. Major differences still exist throughout undergraduate and graduate level degree programs.
 4. Economic gains for blacks remain a major problem with black income continuing to lag behind white income.
  (a) Half of this is explained by the large number of female-headed black families created by high male unemployment and low male income.
   (1) Female headship is a rational response to low earnings.
  (b) Black unemployment rates are quite high and even when employed, their earnings are less than whites.
  (c) Black workers have less education and they also face discrimination which further widens the income gap.
 5. The major gains made by blacks in previous decades have stopped with several indicators showing worsening conditions for the last decade.
  (a) Improvement among working and middle-class blacks has

been more than offset by the problems of lower-class blacks.

(b) Familial structure, illegitimacy and lack of opportunity create a vicious circle entrapping a significant segment of the black population in permanent poverty.

C   Hispanics include Cubans, Puerto Ricans and Mexican Americans.

1.   Cubans first arrived in large numbers in 1960 with the displacement of the Cuban middle class by the Cuban revolution. Subsequent immigration has been from among the more disadvantaged.

2.   Puerto Ricans have a high incidence of female-headed households and have one of the lowest family incomes of any racial or ethnic group.

3.   Most Mexican Americans were not immigrants and half of them are third generation Americans who became citizens with the annexation of the southwestern states.

(a) Subsequent waves of immigration are mostly illegal and are spurred on by salary differentials between Mexico and the United States.

4.   Major problems confronting Hispanics center upon their very low levels of education and high rates of poverty. This is mostly attributed to recent immigration and problems with the English language.

(a) Hispanics are the fastest growing minority group. This raises several concerns:

(1) The S.E.S. of Hispanics is falling,

(2) Anglos and blacks fear them as economic competition and

(3) they are increasingly becoming segregated.

(b) Many suffer the triple problems of being poor, Hispanic and black.

D.   Jews have experienced thousands of years of prejudice and discrimination, thus helping to maintain a highly segregated and distinct culture.

1.   Jews through work and education enjoy mobility rates twice that of any other minority.

2.   Discrimination and prejudice against Jews and separatism by Jews are all declining, thus leading some to suggest that Jews may no longer be considered as minorities.

E. Asian Americans constitute 1.5% of our population and have surpassed the educational achievements of white Americans.
  1. Despite being a model minority, Asians still encounter discrimination in the form of restricted access to education, managerial positions and they are frequently the victims of violence.

F. Native Americans still remain predominately unacculturated and unassimilated.
  1. Prejudice and discrimination against Native Americans took the exclusive form of extraordinary solutions.
  2. This treatment, combined with the reservation system, has created a shattered culture with individuals who cannot find a home in modern society or in their past culture.

IV. Equality: Prospects and challenges.

  A. Progress towards assimilation reflects considerable inequality with regard to residential segregation.
    1. Restricting access to housing also restricts access to jobs and school.
    2. Residential segregation is greatest for blacks followed by Hispanics and Asians.
       (a) Suburbanization reduces but does not eliminate racial segregation.
    3. Income and education tend to separate Hispanics and Asians; race on the other hand, is a significantly greater barrier to blacks.

  B. The ultimate measure of assimilation is intermarriage.
    1. Marriage within ethnic groups remains substantial while racial intermarriage is so low that we are truly a separatist nation.

  C. African Americans are uniquely disadvantaged.
    1. Racism is the root cause of the problems faced by black Americans.
       (a) To break the cycle, prejudice and discrimination must be eliminated and affirmative action programs must be advanced.
       (b) Institutionalized racism must be attacked by better head

start programs, education and job training.

(c) Conflict theorists argue that capitalism itself must be dismantled to offset the entrenched power of Anglos over other minorities.

D. The black underclass poses special problems.

1. It arose with the decline in good paying urban manufacturing jobs and the disintegration of the black community.

2. Wilson contends that a national job policy, higher wages, universal health care, training, relocation and child care are needed for all Americans.

3. Conservatives believe that there are more than enough jobs available but that racism has intervened and established a culture of poverty.

4. Currently there is no public agenda aimed at the underclass.

MATCHING I

A.	Discrimination	____ 1. Extraordinary solutions.
B.	Scapegoat	____ 2. Inherited physical characteristics.
C.	Segregation	____ 3. Coexist as separate cultures in the same society.
D.	Amalgamation	
E.	Racism	____ 4. Blocked goal attainment.
		____ 5. End of identity as a distinct group.
F.	Race	
G.	Pluralism	____ 6. Share a common culture.
		____ 7. Physical and cultural blending.
H.	Prejudice	____ 8. Permit intimate social interaction.
I.	Accommodation	
		____ 9. Negative and irrational.
J.	Melting Pot	____ 10. Behavior, not an attitude.
K.	Ethnicity	
L.	Assimilation	
M.	Expulsion or extermination	
N.	Segregation	
O.	Social distance	

CHAPTER 10

MATCHING II

A. Cubans

B. Asian Americans

C. Mulattos

D. Native Americans

E. Mexican Americans

F. White ethics

G. Anglo conformity

H. Hispanics

I. Defensive pluralism

J. Vietnamese

K. African Americans

L. Haitians

M. Japanese

N. Canadians

O. Jews

_____ 1. Declining ethnic identity.

_____ 2. A specific form of U.S. acculturation.

_____ 3. Most are not immigrants, many are 3rd generation residents.

_____ 4. American concentration camps.

_____ 5. Largest racial minority.

_____ 6. Most unassimilated minority.

_____ 7. Highest average education of any major minority group.

_____ 8. First wave came in 1960.

_____ 9. Rate of upward mobility twice that of other immigrants.

_____ 10. Diverse cultural backgrounds, same ethnic group.

FILL IN THE BLANK QUESTIONS

1. Although there are physical differences between the races, the differences that count are those with ____ importance.

2. A ____ group is culturally, economically and politically dominant while a ____ group is culturally, economically and politically subordinate.

3. The process of ____ includes learning the language, history and manners of the dominant group.

4. Even when physical distance is absent, ____ ____ can be maintained by prejudice and discrimination.

5. ____ refers to attitude, ____ refers to behavior.

6. Both ____ and ____ are personal factors contributing to prejudice.

7. The striking economic disadvantage of African Americans can be attributed to two factors: ____ ____ ____ and ____ ____.

8. Two key characteristics of black Americans are that their immigration was ____ and blacks are among the ____ of all immigrants.

9. ____ ____ experience less racial segregation than do other nonwhite groups.

10. Decreased discrimination and high rates of intermarriage suggests that ____ may no longer be considered a minority.

11. The <u>most</u> important indicator of assimilation is ____ ____ and the <u>ultimate</u> indicator of assimilation is ____.

12. Data shows that ____ are the most highly segregated minority group living in urban centers.

13. Institutionalized racism works through the ____ ____ ____ and ____ ____.

14. The ____ are model minorities.

15. In fact, being ____ is a better indicator of poverty and unemployment than it was 25 years ago.

MULTIPLE CHOICE

1. A category of people who are socially defined as distinct because of inherited physical characteristics:

    a. ethnic group.
    b. race.
    c. majority.
    d. minority.

2. The degree of intimacy in the relationship between two groups is called:

    a. social distance.
    b. prejudice.
    c. discrimination.
    d. racism.

3. With this form of intergroup relations the minority group adopts elements of the culture of the majority group:

    a. conflict.
    b. accommodation.
    c. assimilation.
    d. acculturation.

4. A situation in which, by acting on the belief that something exists, it becomes real:

    a. institutionalized racism.
    b. self-fulfilling prophecy.
    c. discrimination.
    d. scapegoating.

5.   An extraordinary solution:

   a.   prejudice.
   b.   discrimination.
   c.   segregation.
   d.   rigid segregation.

6.   This concept called for interaction and assimilation among ethnic groups to the point that a new race would emerge in North America:

   a.   white ethnicity.
   b.   Anglo conformity.
   c.   majority rule.
   d.   melting pot.

7.   Which is NOT true about prejudice?

   a.   always negative.
   b.   irrational.
   c.   a barrier to interaction.
   d.   easily gives way to facts.

8.   More than any other minority, these people have remained both unacculturated and unassimilated.

   a.   blacks.
   b.   Native Americans.
   c.   Asians.
   d.   Jews.

9.   Which would NOT be considered a minority group:

   a.   whites in South Africa.
   b.   women in the U.S.
   c.   students.
   d.   blacks in the U.S.

10. The kind of intergroup relations practiced in Canada with its parallel cultures, each with its own institutions:

    a.   conflict.
    b.   acculturation
    c.   accommodation.
    d.   assimilation.

11. Setting unjustifiable prerequisites that exclude a disproportionate number of minority group members and unnecessary educational requirements for jobs are examples of:

    a.   prejudice.
    b.   institutionalized racism.
    c.   social distance.
    d.   prejudice.

12. To a significant extent, ethnicity has ceased to be a basis for stratification for these people:

    a.   African Americans.
    b.   white and Gentile Americans.
    c.   Hispanic Americans.
    d.   Native Americans.

13. Which is NOT true of prejudice:

    a.   its foundation is stereotyping.
    b.   it may be positive or negative.
    c.   it exists in spite of the facts.
    d.   personal and institutional factors cause prejudice.

14. It has been proposed that personal factors can cause prejudice. One personal factor discussed in the text is:

    a.   age.
    b.   sex.
    c.   authoritarianism.
    d.   political preference.

15. Social distance refers to:

    a. the degree of intimacy.
    b. residential segregation.
    c. social class differences.
    d. knowledge of other groups.

16. Prejudice is thought to ensure that when people from different groups interact with each other, they see not each other but only their conception of what the other is like. If this is true, by 1700 unless you were a member of this group you were a minority in the American colonies:

    a. French.
    b. English.
    c. Spanish.
    d. Dutch.

17. Not a factor that causes prejudice:

    a. cultural norms.
    b. biological differences.
    c. institutional patterns.
    d. personal factors.

18. ____ will result if relations between different groups leads to a struggle over scarce resources.

    a. conflict.
    b. accommodation.
    c. assimilation.
    d. acculturation.

19. This represented a startling example of prejudice by Americans during World War II:

    a. internment of West Coast Japanese Americans.
    b. refusal to allow blacks in the military.
    c. denial of voting rights for Americans with German ancestry.
    d. refusal of Japanese Americans to serve in the military.

171

20. Four combinations of prejudice and discrimination are possible. "Timid bigots" are:

    a. prejudiced and discriminate.
    b. prejudiced but do not discriminate.
    c. not prejudiced but do discriminate.
    d. not prejudiced and do not discriminate.

21. Public policy in the U.S. directed at racism is aimed almost entirely at reducing:

    a. prejudice.
    b. discrimination.
    c. social distance.
    d. stereotyping.

22. The largest racial minority in the U.S.:

    a. Hispanics.
    b. Japanese.
    c. blacks.
    d. native Americans.

23. The most highly segregated group in U.S. cities:

    a. Asians.
    b. Hispanics.
    c. Jews.
    d. blacks.

24. _____ are the most disadvantaged of all Hispanic Americans.

    a. Cubans.
    b. Puerto Ricans.
    c. Mexican Americans.
    d. Central Americans.

25. Scholars of race relations and stratification in the U.S. use this term to describe the system in operation today:

    a.   classes.
    b.   castes.
    c.   institutionalized racism.
    d.   semicaste.

26. Instead of a blending of all cultures in the U.S. what has happened is a special form of acculturation called:

    a.   the melting pot.
    b.   Anglo-conformity.
    c.   the American dream.
    d.   a "peculiar institution."

27. Although the 40 years following World War II have seen rapid social change, this goal has NOT been accomplished by black Americans:

    a.   economic parity with whites.
    b.   segregation banned in the military.
    c.   school segregation outlawed.
    d.   affirmative-action laws passed.

28. The largest group of Hispanics in the U.S. are:

    a.   Cubans.
    b.   Puerto Ricans.
    c.   Mexican Americans.
    d.   persons from Central America.

29. Between 1880-1920, Jewish immigrants to the U.S. came mainly from:

    a.   Germany.
    b.   Eastern Europe.
    c.   Near East.
    d.   Far East.

30. Which of the following accurately depicts the rank ordering of high school graduation rates?

    a.   whites, Hispanics, blacks.
    b.   blacks, whites, Hispanics.
    c.   Hispanics, blacks, whites.
    d.   Hispanics, whites, blacks.

ESSAY QUESTIONS

1.   Compare and contrast the concepts of race and ethnicity. In what ways may they be different and in what ways may they overlap?

2.   If racism is the root cause of the underclass, how can we combat it?

3.   Explain the relationship between prejudice, social distance and residential segregation.

4.   Discuss the relationship between Anglo conformity and rising ethnic awareness.

5.   Explain how race relations in America constitute a semi-caste system.

Chapter 11

Sex
and
Gender

LEARNING OBJECTIVES

1. Differentiate between sex and gender.

2. What are gender roles and what are the determinants of a woman's status.

3. Describe how early socialization and the looking glass self operate to produce gendered identities, attitudes and personalities.

4. Discuss how gender identities and gender norms influence achievement, family roles, education and labor force participation for both men and women.

5. Describe how society is structured to disadvantage some in education, on the job, in politics, religion and even in daily interaction.

6. Outline the disadvantages for males in a male-dominated society.

7. Describe how the division of labor concept in structural-functional theory can be functional and discriminatory at the same time.

8. Explain how conflict theory uses the concept of a split labor market in accounting for the subordination and exploitation of women.

9.   Carefully outline how gender inequities are maintained by the social-
      ization process, learned expectations, sexism and sexual harassment.

10.   Note the key differences between liberal, socialist and radical feminist
      thought.

11.   What is the relationship between viewing violent pornographic materials
      and men's attitude toward women?

12.   Note the particular problems faced by women of color as they confront
      both sexism and racism.

CHAPTER OUTLINE

I.   Sexual Differentiation

      A.   In all societies sex, or one's biologically differentiated category, is
            the basis for differentiation.
            1.   Gender refers to the expected dispositions and behaviors that
                  cultures assign to each sex.
            2.   While the biological sexes are only two, the rights, duties and
                  obligations assigned to men and women, or gender roles, differ
                  greatly from culture to culture.
                  (a) Within a given culture, gender roles vary by race, class
                      and subculture.

      B.   There are two important cultural universals. In all cultures child
            care is a female responsibility and women have less power than do
            men.
            1.   Three factors determine the status of women, they are:
                  (a) the degree to which bearing, nursing and rearing children
                      ties her to the house,
                  (b) the degree to which economic and child rearing duties
                      overlap in or near the home,
                  (c) and the degree of physical strength necessary for sub-
                      sistence activities.

II. Gender Roles Over the Life Course.

A. Many characteristics are <u>gendered</u> or considered more appropriate for one sex than another.
   1. We think that women and men ought to act in specific, different ways. This is reflected in <u>gender norms</u>.

B. Developing a gendered identity requires that we see ourselves through the eyes of others. As they treat us in sex typed ways, we develop a <u>gender identity</u>.
   1. Early childhood socialization develops highly rigid stereotypes about gender in young children.
      (a) Boys are punished more often for cross sex behavior than girls.
   2. Actual differences in the aptitudes and personalities of girls and boys are quite small and today sex is a poor predictor of math and personality test scores.

C. Some aspects of gendered identity may be critical for achievement.
   1. Girls and boys have higher expectations for themselves for sex appropriate tasks.
      (a) SAT scores for boys are higher in math and girls outscore boys on verbal functioning.
      (b) Career choices are similarly influenced with women preferring to be teachers.
         (1) These career choices have a strong impact on future income and lifestyle.

D. Labor force participation by men and women is rapidly becoming very similar.
   1. Most young women expect to be full-time employees and mothers.
      (a) Gender norms dictate that men's work is more important than women's work.
         (1) These norms vary in regard to the importance of work and the type of work appropriate for men and women.

E. All societies view child care as a female responsibility; this is the major reason women are unequal with men.

1. The vast majority of women still marry, become parents and take on family responsibilities which are sharply gendered.
2. Most American women have (on the average) less than two children. This has created major role changes.
    (a) Now there is greater tolerance of childlessness.
    (b) Alternative roles in the economy and community are now possible.
    (c) While being a mother is often difficult, most women find the role rewarding.
3. Household production or domestic work is still mostly the responsibility of women.

F. Getting married and having children continues to be a powerful force for differentiating male and female behavior.

III. Who Benefits? Social Inequities Between Men and Women

A. Structural inequities exist between women and men.

B. Full-time, full-year female workers earn 65 percent as much as men.
    1. Sex segregation in the workplace is caused by gendered jobs, different qualifications and outright discrimination.
        (a) Gendered jobs segregate the workplace into women's work and men's work.
            (1) Few men or women feel comfortable working where they are the wrong sex.
        (b) Women and men often get the same quantity of education, but sharp differences exist with men choosing the more lucrative fields.
            (1) Women drop out of work for childbearing and thus lose valuable experience that ultimately curtails their career advancement.
        (c) Discrimination against women is common in the workplace and is tied to employers stereotyping women.
            (1) Discrimination can occur in hiring, promotions and in the salary received.
            (2) Employers may also discriminate against those women that they fear will drop out of the work force for childbearing.

(3) Never married, long-divorced and non-mothers encounter less discrimination.

C   The subordination of women permeates all aspects of our society
from social institutions to daily interaction.
1.   In the family, church and politics gender norms dictate
stronger roles for men than for women.
2.   The lower status of some influences their patterns of interaction.
(a) Women smile more and interrupt less than males do in
conversation.

D.   Male power and status are enormous advantages.
1.   Conversely, men live shorter, more dangerous lives, have more
heart disease, alcoholism and commit more suicides than
women.
2.   Masculinity means men form fewer close relationships with
children, kin and friends.

E.   Women of color are particularly disadvantaged by both sexism and
racism.
1.   While combating racism to their economic advantage, doing so
may make them vulnerable to the charge that they have
abandoned the fight against sexism.

IV. Perspectives on Sex Stratification.

A.   Several theories explain the continuing inequities between women
and men. They also address the problems of change that are
occurring.

B.   Structural-functional theory is based upon the premise that a gender
based division of labor in the family is functional.
1.   This specialization should:
(a) increase the expertise of each sex,
(b) prevent damaging competition between men and women
and
(c) strengthen the family by creating interdependent roles.
2.   This division of labor advantages males and it is still popular
with conservatives and the religious right.

179

C   According to conflict theory, women's disadvantage is designed to benefit men in general and the capitalist class in particular.

     1.   The <u>segmented</u> <u>labor</u> <u>market</u> advantages men with better jobs while keeping women in the poorer ones.

        (a) Women also provide a cushion against employment cycles.

D.   Gender inequality is maintained through several processes. They are socialization, learned expectations and prejudice and discrimination.

     1.   Socialization into gender roles means that most men and women never consider changing traditional patterns of behavior.

        (a) This perpetuates personal and economic disadvantages for women.

     2.   <u>Expectation</u> <u>states</u> <u>theory</u> argues that status characteristics create expectations in others. By acting upon these expectations, the expectations are confirmed.

        (a) Males and females expect each other to act accordingly and act in ways to bring this about confirming gender inequalities.

        (b) This tends to perpetuate the customary gender behaviors.

     3.   The belief that men and women have biologically different capacities and that these form a legitimate basis for the subordination of some is called <u>sexism</u>.

        (a) Sexism can be seen as part of a general strategy of stratification through restricting access to scarce resources.

     4.   <u>Sexual</u> <u>harassment</u> constitutes unwelcome sexual advances, requests for sexual favors or other verbal or physical conduct of a sexual nature.

        (a) Sexual harassment is illegal as a term of employment, a basis for employment decisions or if it interferes with an individual's work.

           (1) Two typical forms are <u>quid</u> <u>pro</u> <u>quo</u> harassment and the creation of a <u>hostile</u> <u>environment</u>.

        (b) Both sexism and sexual harassment constitute discriminatory behavior and are an integral part of societal sex stratification.

     5.   A special case of sex stratification occurs with the combination of pornography and violence against women.

        (a) Those exposed to pornography become more callous toward women, sympathize less with rape victims and believe the rape myth.

   (b) The more violent the pornography the more marked the effect.

   (c) While no direct scientific evidence links these attitudes to actual violence against women, scientists, feminists and many women believe the connection exists.

      (1) This raises important questions for the formation of public policy.

V. Feminist Theories

   A. All feminists view gender inequality as socially structured and feel that it should be eliminated.

     1. Liberal feminism applies standard moral and political values equally to men and women.

     2. Socialist feminism uses a Marxist critique to argue that the elimination of all private property including the private ownership of children is necessary to create equality for women.

     3. Radical feminism sees men, not social institutions as the problem.

      (a) This view advocates the severing of all heterosexual relationships and the creation of a separate women's culture.

     4. Socialist and radical theories are a distinct minority.

VI. Prospects for Change

   A. Traditional gender roles are thoroughly institutionalized, yet the last fifteen years have seen important changes.

     1. These changes have increased alternatives for women, eroded some male power and made men and women compete more between each other.

     2. Changes have increased role strain in that both men and women must add new roles.

   B. Despite some stress and change, traditional gender roles still dominate in the home.

CHAPTER 11

     C.   Women's low fertility and high education will help to erode traditional gender roles.
         1.   As gender roles become less differentiated, more equality will emerge between men and women.

MATCHING

A.   Household production

B.   Sexual harassment

C.   Sexism

D.   Socialist feminism

E.   Radical feminism

F.   Male gender role

G.   Expectation states theory

H.   Gendered characteristics

I.   Gender roles

J.   Liberal feminism

K.   Gender

L.   Sex

____ 1.   Creating a separate women's culture.

____ 2.   Rights and obligations assigned by sex.

____ 3.   Biological characteristic, male or female.

____ 4.   Certain behaviors suitable only for men or women.

____ 5.   Unwelcome sexual advances,

____ 6.   Expected dispositions assigned by culture to each sex.

____ 7.   Biological differences are a legitimate basis for discrimination.

____ 8.   Woman's work.

____ 9.   Hypertension, suicide and alcoholism.

____ 10.   Equality for women through abolishing private property.

FILL IN THE BLANK QUESTIONS

1.   Even within a culture ____ ____ vary by race, class and subculture.

2. It is estimated that ninety percent of American women born expect to have ____.

3. There are three primary reasons why women and men have different jobs: ____ ____ , ____ ____ and ____ .

4. ____ interrupt ____ more often.

5. Because of family responsibilities, women are more likely to end up working in ____ , ____ - ____ firms.

6. Women who were full-time, full year workers earned ____ percent as much as men.

7. Women's subordinate position is built into most ____ ____ .

8. Structural-functional theories of sex stratification are popular among ____ and ____ ____ factions of the public.

9. The major studies on violent pornography ____ but do not ____ a link between pornography and some aspects of violence toward women.

10. Conflict theory emphasizes the ____ ____ ____ which bribes working-class men into working against working-class women.

11. ____ is the public policy issue with the largest gender gap.

12. Radical feminists want to sever all heterosexual relationships and create a women's culture based upon ____ , ____ and ____ .

13. ____ ____ ____ is an extension of the self-fulfilling prophecy.

14. Submitting to unwelcome sexual advances in order to keep your job is called ____ ____ ____ harassment.

15. In the short run, the increasing demands upon men and women will create ____ ____ .

CHAPTER 11

MULTIPLE CHOICE

1. This term refers to rights, duties and obligations assigned to people in every society:

    a. sex.
    b. gender roles.
    c. life chances.
    d. conventional achievements.

2. Which is NOT a characteristic of gender roles?

    a. noncompliance leads to sanctions.
    b. are internalized.
    c. can lead to guilt when people fail to comply.
    d. easily changed by facts and rational thought.

3. Differences in rewards, rights, opportunities, status and income are aspects of this system:

    a. sex roles.
    b. sexual stratification.
    c. gender.
    d. life chances.

4. A special form of discrimination that is especially problematic for female workers and students:

    a. sexual harassment.
    b. denial of access to professional jobs.
    c. the educational gap.
    d. higher levels of unemployment.

5. This perspective holds that status characteristics create expectations in others about males and females:

    a. socialization.
    b. expectation state theory.
    c. prejudice.
    d. feminism.

6. Because of historical circumstances, many jobs in today's labor market are regarded as either "women's work" or "men's work." ____ is operating here.

    a. sexual harassment.
    b. gendered jobs.
    c. different qualifications
    d. discrimination.

7. Which is NOT true about how parents socialize their children?

    a. give sex-appropriate toys.
    b. punish children who play with cross-sex toys.
    c. encourage girls to be active and aggressive.
    d. punish boys more for exhibiting cross-sex behaviors.

8. John disagrees with his parents who always ask him to mow the yard and wash the car and his sister to help prepare dinner and take care of their small brother. Sometimes John would like to switch responsibilities with his sister. John is critical of:

    a. gender norms.
    b. his gender.
    c. his sister's poor work.
    d. his parents.

9. Many jobs are still sex segregated. Women are most likely to be employed in ____ and least likely to be employed in ____.

    a. clerical, professions.
    b. professions, blue collar.
    c. clerical, blue collar.
    d. professions, clerical.

10. The typical male in this class compared with the typical female can expect to:

    a.   earn less money.
    b.   have greater difficulty gaining access to a profession.
    c.   have less political power.
    d.   live fewer years.

11. These people wish to apply standard moral and political values to gender inequality:

    a.   liberal feminists.
    b.   socialist feminists.
    c.   radical feminists.
    d.   all feminists.

12. Which of the following statements reflects the highest degree of consensus between both men and women today?

    a.   best for the man to be the achiever.
    b.   prefer to work for a woman.
    c.   approve of a married woman earning money in business.
    d.   most of the important decisions in a family should be made by the woman of the house.

13. Studies show that girls are somewhat more likely than boys to have:

    a.   good verbal skills.
    b.   behavioral problems.
    c.   spatial skills.
    d.   independence.

14. Evidence of the impact of differential socialization is provided by:

    a.   unequal salaries for males and females.
    b.   the greater strength of boys.
    c.   different aspiration levels of girls.
    d.   discrimination by employers.

15. This theory of sex stratification is based on the premise of benefits for society from a division of labor:

    a. conflict.
    b. structural-functional.
    c. split labor market.
    d. radical feminism.

16. This belief encourages people to think that men and women have biologically different capacities and that these form a legitimate basis for the subordination of women:

    a. Marxism.
    b. sexism.
    c. functionalism.
    d. feminism.

17. Socialist feminism uses this framework to explain differences between the status of men and women:

    a. standard moral and political values.
    b. blaming men, not institutions.
    c. biological determinism.
    d. Marxist.

18. ____ theory maintains that women's lower status benefits capitalists because of the development of segmented labor markets.

    a. structural functional.
    b. conflict.
    c. symbolic interaction.
    d. expectation state.

19. Women have the highest status in:

    a. agricultural societies.
    b. industrial societies.
    c. Eastern societies.
    d. simple horticultural societies.

20. Which is true today about labor force participation for those aged 25-54?

    a. most men and women work.
    b. equal percentages of men and women work.
    c. less than half of women work.
    d. only about half of men and women work.

21. In terms of life chances, which is NOT true for females in the U.S. today?

    a. have fewer children.
    b. longer life expectancy than males.
    c. educational achievement increased faster than for males.
    d. elimination of the salary gap between males and females.

22. A comparison of SAT scores show that:

    a. boys and girls have equal scores.
    b. girls have better math skills.
    c. boys have better verbal skills.
    d. boys outnumber girls 13 to 1 among those scoring 700 or more on the quantitative test.

23. Which is cultural universal in terms of roles assigned to men and women?

    a. men raise crops and tend livestock.
    b. men are aggressive.
    c. men have more power than women.
    d. women wear make-up and spend hours preening.

24. Which situation best illustrates "quid pro quo harassment?"

    a. a male annoys a female at work.
    b. the male's behavior creates a hostile environment.
    c. submission to unwelcome conduct becomes an explicit condition of employment.
    d. A male who has been rejected asks for a date the second time.

25. A cross-cultural review of genders and sex roles indicates that:

   a.   sex is distinct, but gender roles may vary.
   b.   both gender and sex roles are distinct.
   c.   neither gender nor sex roles are distinct.
   d.   neither gender nor sex roles vary.

26. Which is NOT a key factor in determining women's status in a society?

   a.   degree they are tied to home by children.
   b.   intelligence and motivation.
   c.   degree economic activities are compatible with staying at home and caring for children.
   d.   the physical strength needed to carry on subsistence activities.

27. Looking to the 1990s and the next century, which is the best prediction about labor force participation?

   a.   most males and most females will work.
   b.   most males and about one-fourth of females will work.
   c.   participation rates will fall for males and females.
   d.   relatively fewer males will work.

28. A major cost paid by males because of traditional sex roles:

   a.   higher levels of mental illness.
   b.   greater incidence of poverty.
   c.   less political power.
   d.   less intimacy and affiliation with children.

29. Looking to the future, it may be that within this institution gender-role stereotypes may be the most resistant to change:

   a.   schools.
   b.   economy.
   c.   families.
   d.   politics.

30. ____ unites nearly all feminists.

      a.   women are seen as proletarians at work.
      b.   belief that all people are created equal.
      c.   defense of legal abortion.
      d.   the desire to create a revolution.

ESSAY QUESTIONS

1. What is a gendered identity and how is it obtained?

2. Discuss the impact of marriage and parenthood on women.

3. Discuss how expectation states theory constitutes a self-fulfilling prophecy for both men and women.

4. If sexual stratification is all pervasive and structured into society, how can it be eliminated or reduced?

5. What is sex stratification and how is it maintained over time?

Chapter 12

Age Differentiation and Inequalities

LEARNING OBJECTIVES

1. Briefly outline the aspects of aging that interest sociologists.

2. Define the concept of life course and discuss how age-related transitions are a product of social structure.

3. Outline the age norms for the following categories: children, adolescents, young adults, middle age and those over 65.

4. Discuss how the young are legally and economically disadvantaged.

5. List the characteristics of a youth subculture.

6. Discuss the relationship between crime, employment opportunities and the school performance of the young.

7. Carefully outline the advantages and disadvantages for those 65 and over.

8. To what extent are the young and old tied to their kin?

9. Note who is most likely to work until age 65, who will try to retire early and who is most likely to return to work after first retiring.

CHAPTER 12

10. Describe the changing age distribution of the U.S. and note the impact upon public policy for today and for the future.

11. Use the structural-functional and conflict perspectives to explain age stratification.

12. Use modernization theory to account for the impact of the industrial revolution on the power of the elderly in society.

13. Describe how age, gender and race can contribute to double or triple jeopardy.

14. What is ageism and how does it function in society both legally and illegally?

15. Briefly outline a life course and follow a cohort through time noting key transitions and appropriate rites of passage.

CHAPTER OUTLINE

I. Age Differentiation

 A. All societies assign different roles according to age.
  1. Sociologists are primarily interested in the norms and roles that structure different age categories.
   (a) Concern is also focused upon socially structured inequities.

 B. Aging and age expectations are an important part of social structure.
  1. Critical ages are 6, 16, 18 or 21 and 65. These are products of culture, not biology.
   (a) Bureaucracies reinforce these age norms by requiring schooling and retirement.
  2. Age-related transitions that are socially created, socially recognized and shared are referred to as the life course.
   (a) A cohort is a category of individuals who share a particular experience at the same point in time.
    (1) Each age category or cohort will experience aging differently because of their unique experiences over the life course.

II. Age Norms

A. Age norms refer to the attitudes and behavior expected when one "acts their age."
   1. Age norms are general and have few sanctions associated with them.

B. Norms of childhood establish a rather clear set of rights and responsibilities.
   1. Legal rights guarantee health, education, and protection.
   2. Obligations include playing and accomplishing developmental tasks.
   (a) Children can be objects of abuse.
   3. Increasingly more children are being raised in single parent households.

C. Adolescence is a period of irresponsibility.
   1. Four basic obligations are to:
   (a) become independent of their parents.
   (b) test and experiment with new roles.
   (c) to acquire adult skills.
   (d) to have fun.
   2. Adolescence is a period of great stress due to a lack of expectations.

D. The role of adult carries more burdens and more benefits.
   1. A rite of passage is a formal ritual marking the end of one status and the beginning of another.
   (a) There is no clear demarcation of the adult role.
      (1) Normally finishing school, becoming employed, married and a parent suffice.
      (2) The order and timing of these transitions has varied considerably in recent decades.
      (3) Adult roles impact men and women differently.
   2. Middle age (45 to 65) is usually a quieter and more prosperous period than the first 25 years of adult life.
   (a) Fewer role strains and conflicts occur.
   (b) It is a period of consolidation and assessment.
      (1) Some experience a mid-life crisis and reorganize their priorities.

3.   Adults over 65 should be independent, yet nonproductive, nonaggressive and noncompetitive.
     (a) Retirement is usually a positive stage in the life course despite negative stereotypes of older adults.
         (1) Life satisfaction is correlated with good health, adequate income and a good family life.

III.   Life Chances and Inequalities

A.   Adults between 30 and 65 control society thus creating inequities for young and old alike.

B.   Young people are not considered responsible and have few legal rights.
     1.   Societal beliefs hold that age is a measure of competency and lacking age, the young may be legally discriminated against.
        (a) The lower status of youth is institutionalized into the culture.
     2.   Most American youth earn the minimum wage or are unemployed.
        (a) Youthful minorities and young families are most often the victims of these economic practices.
        (b) The young are not fully integrated into society and are overrepresented in crime and accident statistics.
           (1) Youthful crime rates are tied to the availability of work for juveniles and the quality of work for young adults.
        (c) Educational roles are critical for structuring experiences for the young.
           (1) The best predictor of adolescence self-esteem is school performance, with those being rewarded in school being the most likely to stay out of trouble.
     3.   A youth subculture exists that emphasizes passive escape and style.
        (a) Style is based upon image, demeanor and argot.
           (1) Mastery of style enhances one's self-esteem.
        (b) The youth subculture is basically a leisure time activity.

C   Those over 65 are not particularly disadvantaged if they are healthy.

1. The average life expectancy at 65 is sixteen additional years.
   (a) The "young old" have lost physical stamina and cannot effectively care for their homes or themselves.
2. Social Security, private pensions and government programs have significantly increased the income of the elderly in the last three decades.
   (a) Adequate retirement benefits have lowered the number of people over age 65 who work.
       (1) Working-class jobs characterized by physical demands, poor worker health and no mental rewards create pressures for early retirement.
       (2) Those mentally challenged on the job retire later.
       (3) An increasing number of retirees return to work.
   (b) Older people have fewer expenses and most now survive adequately with the reduced income of retirement.
       (1) Those living closest to poverty before retirement find that poverty awaits them in retirement.
       (2) Single women and minorities are the most disadvantaged.
3. Few older people are forced into retirement, and most look happily forward to retiring.
   (a) Age discrimination in the form of <u>ageism</u> works to the disadvantage of middle-aged persons seeking employment.
       (1) Ageism is reinforced by the negative stereotypes of older persons.
4. The Elderly vote more so than any other age group.
   (a) Consensus is not reached due to the cleavages created by race, class and gender.
       (1) Older people tend to feel politically powerless.
5. Despite the advantages of age and retirement, most older persons are accorded reduced levels of honor and esteem.
   (a) Reductions in vigor, attractiveness and productivity mean less prestige.
       (1) Historically the elderly have suffered the same indignities.
6. Social integration into society declines with the age related loss of roles.
   (a) Ties with friends and relatives are still critically important although some family roles may force the older person to be dependent upon their children.

(1) Longevity has led to the creation of a "generation squeeze."

IV.   The Changing Balance of Youth and Age

A.   America is rapidly becoming a society of older adults.
1.   The proportion of the elderly is increasing as the proportion of the young declines.
(a) Low fertility and increased longevity account for the changes in age distribution.

B.   Younger people are effectively disenfranchised and adults control the contest for scarce public resources.
1.   Recent federal budget cutbacks have seriously disadvantaged youth while the elderly remain unscathed.
(a) Poverty has increased among children and decreased among the elderly.
(1) This reflects the belief that children are the responsibility of their families while the elderly are the responsibility of the government.
(2) Illegitimacy and divorce compound this problem.

V.   Explanations for Age Stratification

A.   The young and the old lack status because they are less competent and less productive.

B.   Structural-Functional theory sees age stratification as functional.
1.   The young are afforded time to learn and the old are allowed to disengage.
2.   Disengagement theory is a functionalist theory that argues that the elderly voluntarily disengage themselves from active social participation.
(a) Disengagement allows for the orderly transition from one generation to the next while reducing the stigma of declining productivity attributed to older workers.
(1) It is argued that a consensus exists that disengagement is a benefit to all.
3.   Conflict theory sees age stratification as arising from competition over scarce resources, namely jobs.

(a) Excluding youth and highly paid older workers benefits workers between 20 and 65 as well as their employers.
(b) Mandatory retirement achieves this end.

4. Current values argue that retirement suits both the aging worker and the economic system.
(a) Conflict may emerge again as fewer young people exist to support an increasing population of the elderly.

5. Modernization theory (Cowgill) argues that industrialization reduces the power of the elderly by reducing the value of their traditional resources: land, labor and experience.
(a) As occupations displace land as the basis for income and prestige, the elderly lose control of the power associated with inherited land.
(b) Modern productivity robs the elderly and children of a valuable economic role.
(c) Rapid change makes the experience of older adults outmoded.

6. All three theories account for the current status of the young while only disengagement theory seems applicable to today's elderly.

VI. Cross-Cutting Statuses: Age, Gender and Race

A. A person low on two or more of these dimensions of stratification is said to be in double or triple jeopardy.
1. Aging and gender are especially problematic for women.
(a) Women outlive men and will spend their last years alone and uncared for.
(1) Husbands typically die first at home in the care of their wives.
(b) Men who widow remarry easily while most older women are seldom able to find a new spouse.
2. Government programs, higher esteem in ethnic communities and closer family ties may aid the older minority individual.
3. Minorities still experience major economic dislocations with age and are less likely than anglos to reach retirement.

VII. Some methodological considerations

A. Research on aging often relies upon cross-sectional data which cannot adequately assess the difference between <u>age effects</u> and <u>cohort effects</u>.

1. Cohort effects or generational differences in experience may be confused with age effects.

    (a) The interpretation of these effects rests upon the particcular theory being utilized.

MATCHING

A. Cohort

B. Middle age

C. Modernization theory

D. Generation gap

E. Conflict theory

F. Ageism

G. Role theory

H. Disengagement theory

I. Youth subculture

J. Life course

K. Empty nest

L. Rites of passage

M. Adolescence

N. Honeymoon

O. Double or triple jeopardy

____ 1. Age legitimizes unequal treatment.

____ 2. Age-related transitions that are socially created, recognized, etc.

____ 3. A period of great role stress.

____ 4. Industrialization reduces the value of land, labor and experience.

____ 5. A period of assessment.

____ 6. All those born in 1965.

____ 7. Formal rituals marking transitions.

____ 8. Functionalist theory of aging.

____ 9. An emphasis on passive escape.

____ 10. Low status on 2 or more dimensions of stratification.

FILL IN THE BLANK QUESTIONS

1. Aging and age expectations are in large part products of ____ ____.

2. A ____ is a category of individuals who share a particular experience at the same point in time.

3. Current estimates indicate that one out of ____ girls will experience sexual abuse by their parents.

4. The most common transition sequence into adult status is to finish school, getting a ____, ____ and ____ - ____.

5. Some claim that retirement is a ____ role due to the ____ of rights and duties.

6. As long as the elderly remain ____ they generally report higher levels of life satisfaction.

7. Discrimination against ____ may be legally approved inequality.

8. Style in the youth subculture consists of ____, ____ and ____.

9. The average person reaching 65 can expect to live an additional ____ years.

10. The ____ are more likely to vote than any other age group.

11. The "old old" are disproportionately ____ and ____.

12. Data has shown that poverty has increased among ____ and decreased among the ____.

13. On the average women outlive men by ____ years.

14. The availability of ____ for juveniles and ____ ____ for young adults are strongly tied to the crime rate.

15. The kind of work experienced by the ____-class creates pressures to retire early.

CHAPTER 12

MULTIPLE CHOICE

1. A category of people who share a particular experience at the same point in time:

   a. family.
   b. cohort.
   c. group.
   d. society.

2. These serve as the "road map" that structures us on the life course:

   a. age norms.
   b. biological characteristics.
   c. chronological ages.
   d. gender norms.

3. Carries with it more rights and responsibilities than any other age role:

   a. childhood.
   b. adolescence.
   c. old age.
   d. adulthood.

4. Persons thought to have a "roleless role:"

   a. over 65.
   b. adolescents.
   c. children.
   d. middle-aged.

5. A set of patterned responses to some problems that are unique to a particular group:

   a. age expectations.
   b. life chances.
   c. rites of passage.
   d. subculture.

6. These mark the passage from one age status to another:

    a. age norms.
    b. rites of passage.
    c. life course.
    d. life chances.

7. Age differentiation differs from other bases of differentiation in that:

    a. it is less severe.
    b. it is more severe.
    c. it is independent or prejudice.
    d. other bases tend to be mutually exclusive.

8. Not of primary interest to sociologists who study age:

    a. systematic physical and psychological changes.
    b. social norms.
    c. roles that structure behavior.
    d. relationship between privileges and inequality.

9. A sociologists completes a study of people of a given age who have had unique experiences. This is a study of:

    a. life course perspective.
    b. age structure.
    c. age norms.
    d. cohort perspective.

10. The description of a situation in which the middle generation experiences demands from their children and parents:

    a. lack of integration.
    b. roleless role.
    c. generation gap.
    d. generation squeeze.

11. Which group of people is NOT caught in a situation of double jeopardy?

    a. white adolescents.
    b. black adolescents.
    c. aged women.
    d. black women.

12. This seems to explain why our society does not provide as much aid to children to escape poverty as it does for the aged:

    a. lack of knowledge about causes of poverty.
    b. decrease in poverty rates for children since 1970.
    c. belief that parents should care for children.
    d. increase in poverty for the aged since 1970.

13. Ageism is thought to be correlated with:

    a. job discrimination.
    b. forced retirement.
    c. loss of physical strength.
    d. long life.

14. Generalizing from the results of the last century, a society could anticipate an increased proportion of older people if:

    a. fertility falls.
    b. fertility rises.
    c. mortality falls.
    d. mortality rises.

15. The theory is supported by the existence of mandatory retirement rules:

    a. physiological.
    b. disengagement.
    c. conflict.
    d. modernization.

16. Which conclusion is associated with a modernization explanation of age stratification?

    a. youths excluded so others will benefit.
    b. reduced social participation of aged good for the aged and society.
    c. elderly excluded so others will benefit.
    d. decreased status for elderly because of erosion of power bases.

17. In everyday usage, most people rely upon this theory of age stratification:

    a. conflict.
    b. physiological.
    c. disengagement.
    d. modernization.

18. Which theory suggests that the aged voluntarily severe social relations and decrease active social participation?

    a. conflict.
    b. disengagement.
    c. modernization.
    d. symbolic interaction.

19. Not a critical point in the age distribution for Americans:

    a. 6.
    b. 18 or 21.
    c. 65.
    d. 2.

20. About what percent of children born in the 1980s will live in a single-parent household at some time before they are 18?

    a. 5 percent.
    b. 20 percent.
    c. 90 percent.
    d. 60 percent.

21. By the year 2030, there will be only ____ earners for every person over age 65 which may threaten the financial soundness of our Social Security System.

    a.   5.
    b.   10.
    c.   2.
    d.   15.

22. In law, people under 18 are called:

    a.   children.
    b.   infants.
    c.   adolescents.
    d.   young adults.

23. These people are most likely to suffer unemployment:

    a.   black youth.
    b.   white youth.
    c.   white adults.
    d.   black adults.

24. When men of middle age remarry, they usually marry women who are:

    a.   of their same age.
    b.   women who are 10-15 years older.
    c.   women who are 10-15 years younger.
    d.   women who will not live as long as they will.

25. In contrast to sex norms, age norms:

    a.   are less specific.
    b.   generate more sanctions.
    c.   guide the behavior of few people.
    d.   affect only a few people.

26. The normative transition sequence in the U.S.

    a.   finish school, job, children, spouse.
    b.   job, finish school, children, spouse.
    c.   finish school, job, spouse, children.
    d.   spouse, job, finish school, children.

27. If one's parents are typical they least expect an adolescent to:

    a.   become independent.
    b.   be responsible.
    c.   experiment with new roles.
    d.   have fun.

28. This variable is NOT correlated with life satisfaction among those over age 65.

    a.   meaningful work.
    b.   good health.
    c.   adequate money.
    d.   satisfying family life.

29. These are the most structurally disadvantaged:

    a.   youth and adults.
    b.   youth and middle-aged.
    c.   youth and those over 65.
    d.   youth and those over 40.

30. Which can society expect to see if trends in the "feminization" of poverty and sex differences in mortality continue?

    a.   more males than females above age 75.
    b.   heterosexual contacts will decrease.
    c.   more elderly will marry again.
    d.   male-headed households will be poorer.

CHAPTER 12

ESSAY QUESTIONS

1. How adequately do structural-functional and conflict theories account for the position of today's elderly?

2. Discuss how children are more greatly disadvantaged than the elderly by age stratification.

3. Discuss how the role of the retired can be seen as a roleless role.

4. Explain how those between 30 and 65 control society.

5. Explore the implications of the phenomenon of the feminization of the elderly.

Chapter 13
The
Family

LEARNING OBJECTIVES

1. Outline the six universal functions/responsibilities of the family noted by Murdock.

2. Differentiate between the following concepts: institution, family, kin group and marriage.

3. Define each of the following terms and note those that are typical of modern society: nuclear family, extended family, neolocal, matrilocal, patrilocal, monogamy, ploygyny, polyandry, polygamy, patriarchal, matriarchal and egalitarianism.

4. What are the key characteristics of the contemporary American family?

5. Explain how the divorce rate is calculated and indicate the current trends in divorce.

6. Describe how the dating game operates and specify the role played by propiniquity, homogamy, physical attractiveness and the love filters.

7. Discuss the complications introduced by increasing sexual permissiveness and note the role sex plays in marriage.

8. Describe the correlates of marital happiness and the correlates of divorce.

9. Note how the characteristics of African American and Hispanic families differ from affluent white families.

10. Describe how voluntary singles and homosexuals are both included and excluded by the family institution.

11. Differentiate between the various forms of family violence and briefly note how these patterns might be eliminated or reduced.

12. Discuss the impact of divorce, who are the winners and who are the losers?

13. Compare and contrast the rewards and liabilities of having and raising children for both mothers and fathers.

14. Use the conflict, structural-functional and symbolic interactionist approaches to highlight current problems in the family.

15. Note the structural changes in the American family and indicate the consequences of these changes, include in your answer the following terms: courtship, marriage, parenting and intergenerational ties.

CHAPTER OUTLINE

I. Marriage, Family and Kinship: Basic Institutions of Society

   A. Murdock contends that the major responsibilities of families are: replacement through reproduction, regulation of sexual behavior, economic responsibility for dependents, socialization of the young, ascription of status and the provision of intimacy.
      1. Every society provides some institutional structure to meet these responsibilities called the family.
         (a) The family is a relatively permanent group of persons linked together in social roles by ties of blood, marriage or adoption who live together and cooperate economically and in the rearing of children.
         (b) The family is usually embedded in a larger set of relatives - the kin group.
         (c) Marriage is an institutionalized social structure providing

an enduring framework for the regulation of sexual behavior and for child bearing.

(1) While some family ties are biological, marriage is a key concept in understanding the family as a social group whereby society controls the formation of new family units, kinship relationships and inheritance. This ensures continuity in the existing patterns of stratification, etc.

2. Families universally regulate sexual behavior, provide care for dependents and offer emotional and financial security. In doing so, many cultural variations occur.

(a) Family patterns include the <u>nuclear family</u> where the married pair establish an independent household and the <u>extended family</u> where the parents live with other kin.

(b) Residence patterns also vary with the nuclear family living by itself in the <u>neolocal</u> pattern. Other patterns include the <u>matrilocal</u> and <u>patrilocal</u> forms.

(c) Courtship patterns are a reflection of social values and economic interests.

(1) Arranged marriages are typical where prestige and property are involved with the parents playing a major role in selecting the mates.

(2) When the economic interests of the parents are not directly involved and the young have freedom there is a decrease in familial involvement and control.

(3) Parents still exert strong indirect control through their selection of neighborhood and schools.

(d) Marriage patterns vary from <u>monogamy</u> to <u>polygamy</u> and even <u>polygyny</u>.

(1) Viewed cross-culturally polygyny has been the most popular marriage form while the vast majority of the world population practices monogamy.

(e) Authority patterns in western society are typically <u>egalitarian</u> where the spouses share equally in decision making, control of family resources and childrearing. Alternative forms include <u>patriarchal</u> and <u>matriarchal</u> patterns.

CHAPTER 13

II.   The American Family Over the Life Course

    A.   There have been many changes in the American family over the
last few decades.

    B.   Generally all young people are expected to date; it is an obligatory
form of social behavior.
        1.   Because of divorce, delayed first marriages and remarriages,
many more people are engaged in the courtships process.
        2.   The choice of a marriage partner is influenced by several
factors.
           (a) Original attraction will be strongly influenced by the
spatial nearness   of potential partners (propinquity),
social similarity (homogamy) and physical attractiveness.
           (b) Dating may progress toward a serious consideration of
marriage as the respective partners pass a series of
barriers or filters.
               (1) The filters include propinquity, social background,
attractiveness, compatibility and a final assessment
called a balance sheet filter.
           (c) The dating game can be viewed as a shopping trip where
one is evaluating the goods and searching for the best
bargain.
        3.   Important norms concerning dating center upon the appro-
riate degree of sexual contact.   Norms range from abstinence
to total permissiveness.
           (a) Within the U.S. two major sexual revolutions have occur-
red; one in the 1920's that saw a sharp increase in
premarital sexual intercourse and a second in the late
1960's which featured an increase in permissiveness and
the decline of the double standard.
           (b) For the majority of Americans dating involves sex.
               (1) Young people take great risks with sex by not using
appropriate   contraception.
               (2) Between one third and one half of all women between
the ages of 15 to 19 become pregnant.
               (3) Almost all of these pregnancies are unwanted.
           (c) With sexual activity beginning earlier and marriage being
delayed, the number of years of non-marital sexual activity is increasing.

          (1) This increases the risk of <u>S.T.D.</u> or sexually transmitted diseases.

      (d) <u>Cohabitation</u> occurs when couples live together without legal marriage.

          (1) Cohabitation rates have increased dramatically in the past two decades and are linked to the rising age of marriage.

          (2) Sociologists view cohabitation as an additional stage in the courtship process rather than an alternative to marriage.

          (3) Cohabitation is quite ineffective as a trial marriage, those who cohabit have higher divorce rates.

C. A majority of American spend most of their adult lives married.

    1. Marriage is a sharply gendered relationship, both normatively and in reality.

      (a) Norms require that the husband ought to work and be the provider.

      (b) Norms also specify that the wife should do the housework.

          (1) Working wives often experience role overload.

      (c) Families with both parents working cope by lowering standards of household cleanliness and eating out more often.

    2. Norms recommend egalitarian authority patterns which are seldom realized.

      (a) Husbands still have more power than their wives.

    3. Sexual activity has changed little in the last thirty years except for increased acceptance of oral sex and that men and women are just about as likely to have an extramarital affair.

      (a) The importance of sex declines rapidly in marriage but a satisfactory sex life is still essential to a good marriage.

    4. Two-thirds of married couples claim that they are very satisfied in marriage.

      (a) The two best predictors of satisfaction are length of marriage and gender role agreement.

      (b) Marital happiness also declines with time.

D. The link between marriage and parenthood is being broken by non-marital births and delayed childbearing.

    1. Nearly one quarter of all births in the U.S. are to unmarried

women.

2. Fertility rates continue to drop as more women work in addition to desiring more personal freedom and economic security.

   (a) If divorce rates and women's labor force participation remain high, fertility rates will decline even further.

3. Children are emotionally and financially costly and require massive commitments of time, energy and money.

4. The central question for today's family is childcare.

   (a) The majority of mothers of all types work with their children being cared for by their father, other relatives or some type of daycare.

      (1) Shift work is a common response to the cost of day care.

   (b) Expectations for fathers to take greater responsibility in child care are increasing.

   (c) Single parents are becoming more prevalent, most are mothers.

      (1) Child support and contact by the other parent are episodic.

      (2) Single parent families often live in poverty.

   (d) Stepparenting is becoming more frequent with divorce and remarriage in our society. Unfortunately stepparenting is an especially stressful experience for the children and the stepparent involved.

      (1) Encouraging teenagers to leave the home reduces this stress as does the ultimate act -- another divorce.

      (2) The divorce rate for families with stepchildren is twice the rate for families without them.

5. The empty nest is that period in the marriage when all the children have left home. With fewer children and increasing longevity the empty nest typically can last up to 30 years.

   (a) Most parents adjust nicely to the empty nest.

   (b) Most parents want and have frequent contact with their adult children.

   (c) The empty nest may be delayed due to delaying marriage or the continuing education of the children.

E   Family ties, especially across generations, remain very important.

   1. A majority of adults contact their parents weekly, siblings stay

in touch and the parent-child tie remains the strongest among relatives.

    2.   Women are <u>kinkeepers</u> with female relatives being closer to each other than their male counterparts.

F.   African American and Hispanic families are characterized by higher rates of female headship and higher reliance upon an extended kin network.

    1.   43 percent of black and 23 percent of Hispanic families are female headed as opposed to 13 percent for whites.

        (a) Increasingly the extended kin network is not working very well.

        (b) Female headship occurs due to high rates of male unemployment, divorce and low marriage rates.

            (1) Female headship results in spiraling disadvantages for minority families.

G.   The never married and homosexuals must find alternatives to the institutionalized family structures.

    1.   Both may turn to their extended family for support.

III.   Problems of the American Family

A.   Child abuse, spouse abuse and parent abuse are not new.

    1.   The actual incidence is hard to measure but estimates place all of these at about four percent.

        (a) Violence is correlated with multiple problem families, especially those in the lower class.

    2.   New explicit laws about abuse may clarify the fuzzy norms that now exist.

B.   The <u>annual</u> <u>divorce</u> <u>rate</u> is 22 or 2.2 percent of the married women in the U.S.

    1.   The <u>lifetime</u> <u>divorce</u> <u>probability</u> indicates that nearly two thirds of all marriages in the last decade will end in divorce.

    2.   Six factors correlate strongly with divorce, they are: age at marriage, parental divorce, premarital childbeaing, education, race and bad behavior.

    3.   While divorce can have positive outcomes, it is closely linked with poverty.

(a) Poor families are the most likely to divorce; divorce reduces the family income and less than half of the non-custodial parents pay regular child support.

(b) Rising divorce rates contribute to increasing female head-ship which in turn leads to rising rates of poverty among women and children.

(c) The problems of divorce and poverty cannot be solved until the deeper issue of gender-based division of labor in the family is solved.

4. The increase in the probability in divorce during this century reflects important structural changes in society.

(a) With a shift from agriculture and industrialization to a service economy, economic assets like education and experience are not tied to the family.

(1) Opportunities in the economy are readily available outside of marriage--especially for women.

(2) Marriages thus have less institutional support than before.

C   Theoretical Approaches to the Problems of the Family

1. Perceptions of family problems and solutions are directly influenced by a given theoretical framework.

(a) Structual-Functionalists see the emphasis on self, happiness and growth as eroding the commitment to marriage.

(1) As fathers and mothers voluntarily leave families, the major task of childrearing is being undermined. This is seen as being dysfunctional.

(2) The increasing number of women and children in poverty reflects this problem.

(b) Conflict theorists still see the family as oppressive for both women and children who are exploited and often abused.

(1) Equality opportunity for women and state enforced support for children would ease the problems.

(c) Symbolic interactionists see the family instability as having a potentially harmful effect upon one's personal identity.

2. The family continues to perform vital functions for society and individual alike.

(a) Positive signs are the enduring mother and child bond, high remarriage rates, intergenerational help patterns and the continuation of stepparenting.

MATCHING

A. Nuclear family

B. Polygyny

C. Gender-based division of labor.

D. Homogamy

E. Cohabitation

F. Neolocal

G. Women

H. Propinquity

I. Dating

J. Extramarital sex

K. Legislated child support

L. Polygamy

M. Parents divorced

N. Age at marriage

O. Male single parents

____ 1. An obligatory form of social behavior.

____ 2. The nuclear family lives by itself.

____ 3. Kinkeepers.

____ 4. Marriage to more than one spouse at a time.

____ 5. 2.3 million couples are doing it.

____ 6. Married pair forms an independent household.

____ 7. Best predictor of divorce.

____ 8. Moral victory, not a solution.

____ 9. Spacial nearness.

____ 10. Root cause of women's and children's poverty.

CHAPTER 13

FILL IN THE BLANK QUESTIONS

1.   The ____ is a subset for a larger set of relatives called the ____ ____.

2.   ____ is an institutionalized social structure that provides an enduring framework for regulating sexual behavior and child bearing.

3.   Thus the key to strengthening minority families lies in changing the structure of ____ ____.

4.   The average woman desire more ____ ____ and ____ ____, both of which are adversely affected by taking time out for childbearing.

5.   Nearly one quarter of all births were to an ____ mother.

6.   When parent work alternate shifts, it usually involves both day care and ____ ____.

7.   Never married women are usually ____ ____ to their families.

8.   Increasingly ____ is viewed as an additional stage in the courtship process rather than as an alternative to marriage.

9.   American gender norms now specify an ____ authority pattern.

10. After the first year of marriage, ____ is of decreasing importance to most people.

11. Violence is most typical in families with ____ ____.

12. ____ is really the biggest gamble most married people will ever make.

13. ____ ____ ____ and years married seem to be the key to happy marriages.

14. Empirical data shows a considerable link between ____ and poverty.

15. Women are paid less because they ____ more.

MULTIPLE CHOICE

1.   A key concept in understanding the family as a social rather than a
     biological unit:

     a.   marriage.
     b.   birth of children.
     c.   economic activities carried out in families.
     d.   the care of children.

2.   All cultures discourage:

     a.   homosexuality.
     b.   extramarital relationships.
     c.   premarital relationships.
     d.   childbearing outside of marriage.

3.   A married pair and their children that have formed an independent house-
     hold living apart from other kin:

     a.   extended family.
     b.   nuclear family.
     c.   kin structure.
     d.   kinship.

4.   The kind of residence when the nuclear family lives by itself:

     a.   martrilocal.
     b.   patrilocal.
     c.   neolocal.
     d.   complex residence pattern.

5.   The kind of family form practiced by Mormons in the 19th century:

     a.   monogamy.
     b.   polyandry.
     c.   polygamy.
     d.   polygyny.

6. Which describes a pattern of authority with males dominant?

    a. matriarchal.
    b. patriarchal.
    c. egalitarian.
    d. polygyny.

7. Which does NOT qualify as a family:

    a. mother living alone with her child.
    b. a couple with no children.
    c. a man living with several wives.
    d. a person living alone.

8. Juan is a student from another country. There, he lives with his parents, and sometimes aunts and uncles live with them, too. This is an example of:

    a. a nuclear family.
    b. an extended family.
    c. kin structure.
    d. group marriage.

9. John believes that it is allright for him to play around but he expects his wife to be a virgin at marriage. This means that John believes in:

    a. a double standard.
    b. polyandry.
    c. the solocal family.
    d. romantic love.

10. Susan was attracted to Tim because they had so much in common in the way of religion, social class, age and interests. What factor was in operation with Susan and Tim?

    a. propinquity.
    b. homogamy.
    c. opposites attract.
    d. physical attractiveness.

11. Harold looks forward to marriage and having children. If Harold is typical, what do results from recent surveys of parents tell us about the values that Harold and his spouse will hold regarding their employment?

    a.   he should be employed and she should not.
    b.   he and she should both be employed.
    c.   he should be employed and she may be employed.
    d.   either he or she may be employed.

12. Western societies are coming to accept this pattern of authority:

    a.   egalitarian.
    b.   patriarchal.
    c.   matriarchal.
    d.   polyandry.

13. What proportion of unmarried women have had sexual intercourse by the time they reach their early 20's?
    a.   30%.
    b.   75%.
    c.   99%.
    d.   50%.

14. Based upon existing research findings, the best prediction is that marital satisfaction is a correlate of:

    a.   income, education.
    b.   education, number of children.
    c.   years married, agreement on gender roles.
    d.   income, years married.

15.   Theory suggests that as more and more women work for income outside of the home relationships between husband and wives will change, too. With regard to sex roles in marriage, which is true about the changing script?

   a.   the frequency of sexual activity has increased during the past 30 years.
   b.   women have reached parity with men in their probability of having an affair.
   c.   the double standard persists.
   d.   about 50% of all husbands but only about 10% of all wives have had an affair.

16.   A great deal of theory and considerable research has focused upon marital satisfaction. Which of these factors has been found to increase the marital satisfaction of couples?

   a.   the empty nest.
   b.   marrying young before age. 20.
   c.   couples with low incomes.
   d.   a wife's employment.

17.   Theory suggests that mate selection is processual, with people moving through filters in this sequence:

   a.   attractiveness, propinquity, compatibility.
   b.   attractiveness, compatibility, propinquity.
   c.   propinquity, attractiveness, compatibility.
   d.   compatibility, propinquity, attractiveness.

18.   ____ is the best predictor of divorce from a first marriage.

   a.   being white.
   b.   30+ at age of marriage.
   c.   12 years of education.
   d.   children before marriage.

19.   In colonial America, the family's primary responsibility was for:

       a.   replacement through reproduction and care of dependent children.
       b.   regulation of sexual behavior.
       c.   socialization of the young.
       d.   ascription of status.

20.   This function has taken on increased importance as a dimension of marital relationships in recent decades:

       a.   socialization of the young.
       b.   provision of intimacy.
       c.   economic responsibilities for dependents.
       d.   replacement through reproduction.

21.   For couples marrying in 1970 or later, the chances of a divorce are:

       a.   75 percent.
       b.   64 percent.
       c.   25 percent.
       d.   100 percent.

22.   About what percent of children in the U.S. live with both parents?

       a.   1%.
       b.   10%.
       c.   80%.
       d.   58%.

23.   By age 40, nearly ____% of Americans end up married at least once:

       a.   50.
       b.   70.
       c.   80.
       d.   95.

CHAPTER 13

24. Recent estimates suggest that it may cost as much as $____ to raise a middle-class child to adulthood.

   a. $10,000.
   b. $1,000,000.
   c. $150,000.
   d. $500,000.

25. Parents and kin are likely to control the activities leading up to marriage when:

   a. dowries or bride prices are exchanged.
   b. when the new spouse will not move in with the family.
   c. when prestige is not related to family ties.
   d. when the kin group's economic interests are not affected by the young people's choices.

26. Viewed cross-culturally, this has been the most popular marriage pattern:

   a. monogamy.
   b. polygamy.
   c. polygyny.
   d. polyandry.

27. There are no societies in which the cultural norms specify:

   a. patriarchal authority.
   b. egalitarianism.
   c. matriarchal authority.
   d. equality of authority.

28. Which is true about the divorce rate in the U.S.?

   a. the divorce rate has risen steadily in the post-World War II period.
   b. the divorce rate is about 10.0 at present.
   c. of persons in the 1890s, the proportion ending in divorce was about 40%.
   d. for couples marrying in 1970, the proportion expected to be divorced in their lifetime is about 80%.

29.   Which is true about cohabitation in the U.S.?

    a.   increasingly viewed as an additional stage in courtship.
    b.   occurs with same frequency in urban and suburban areas.
    c.   limited to those with low incomes and educations.
    d.   the majority are people who have been married before.

30.   Which is true about child care arrangements for children whose mothers are employed?

    a.   most children will be in day care.
    b.   about one quarter of all children will be cared for by relatives.
    c.   about one fifth of all children are cared for by fathers.
    d.   most single parenting will be done by fathers.

ESSAY QUESTIONS

1.   How has the American family changed in the last three decades?

2.   Discuss in detail how the American family can be seen as an institution.

3.   What are the correlates of divorce and what is their relationship to social class?

4.   Describe in detail the problems confronting the minority female headed family in poverty.

5.   What has been the impact of changing male and female gender roles on the structure of the American family?

Chapter 14
Education

LEARNING OBJECTIVES

1. Briefly recount the history of American education noting the values and factors that have led to our current system of education.

2. What are the micro and macro factors in education and how do they operate to reproduce inequality?

3. Describe the different attitudes and skills that middle, working and lower-class families bring from their homes into the classroom and the school system.

4. Outline the strengths and weaknesses of tracking.

5. Discuss what makes some schools better than others.

6. Discuss how being a racial minority causes difficulties for some students and serves to help others.

7. Summarize the current trends in educational attainment for whites, minorities and women.

8. Outline the consequences for the operation of junior colleges.

9. Indicate, for the individual, the consequences of completing a college education. Include the impact on income, occupation and values.

10. Compare and contrast the Japanese and American educational system.

11. Outline the functional model of education noting the manifest functions, latent functions and the dysfunctions of our educational system.

12. Use the conflict approach to explain the relationship between social class and credentialism in American education.

13. What inequities exist in American education and what will it take to eliminate them?

14. Differentiate between the concepts of mass education and elite education.

15. Critique the use of I.Q. test in education.

16. Describe why we are a nation at risk.

CHAPTER OUTLINE

I. Development of U.S. Education

    A. Prior to the 19th century there was no consensus on education and the forms varied greatly.
        1. In the 19th century consensus emerged among all classes that free, mandatory education was a necessity.
           (a) Parents demanded that their children acquire basic intellectual skills.
           (b) Labor unions saw education as a source of mobility for their children.
           (c) Compulsory attendance was seen as a means of social control for certain youth and for the acculturation of immigrants.
               (1) The educational system is an arena for conflict over whose values will prevail, the elites or others.

    B. Mass elementary school education was in place by 1900 with an emphasis on high school emerging in the 1930's and a virtual explosion of colleges in the post world war two era.
        1. Several wars, the "G.I. Bill" and fear of being drafted increased

the demand for college educations.

2.   Minorities also gained access to public education with blacks, Hispanics and Native Americans encountering difficulties.

(a) Inferior education, segregation and mandatory deculturation have hindered their progress.

(b) Slightly more than half of all blacks, Hispanics and Native Americans over age 25 have completed high school.

II.   Inequality and the Schools

A.   Sociologists are more concerned with the link between education and stratification. Their concerns are for both macro and micro level factors.

1.   Social class is an important variable in that children raised in middle class homes arrive at school with values better suited to success than do children from the lower socioeconomic classes.

(a) Parents' social class also influences what neighborhoods the children grow up in as well as the quality of the school attended.

(b) Middle class parents provide help, support and resources for the most part unattainable by the lower classes.

(c) Children of affluent families also acquire <u>cultural capital</u> through preschool and home experiences.

(1) This capital enhances one's self-concept.

2.   Two important processes in schooling have a critical effect upon the quality of the output. They are cognitive development and tracking.

(a) Children undergo a process where their mental skills grow and expand called <u>cognitive development</u>.

(1) Cognitive development is enhanced by complex and demanding work without close supervision and by high teacher expectations.

(2) Lower class and minority classrooms often are highly authoritarian and structured thus impeding development.

(3) Development processes in schooling are seldom reinforced in the lower class and minority home.

(b) <u>Tracking</u> occurs when evaluations relatively early in a child's career determine the educational programs the child will be encouraged to follow. By having classes geared to their level, bright and slow learners should benefit from increased teacher attention.

(1) Research shows tracking becomes a self-fulfilling prophecy where bright students benefit and the lowest groups decline in performance.

(2) One aspect of tracking is the use of so-called standardized tests that claim to measure mental ability. They have strong cultural biases including reasoning, knowledge, competitiveness, familiarity with testing and achievement aspiration, all of which depend upon prior experiences.

(3) Given their inherent biases they might be better suited as measures of cultural deprivation rather than as measures of natural ability.

(c) Track assignment is directly related to social class and thus tracking replicates social class rather than combating it.

(1) Tracking can help those minorities with high college aspirations.

(2) Once segregated into the upper track some working class children can get college preparatory training.

(d) Despite perpetuating inequality, tracking seems bureaucratically justifiable and functional.

B. Social class is a better predictor of school performance than school characteristics like per pupil expenditures. Some school characteristics do have an impact on performance.

1. Catholic schools have a demanding curriculum, high expectations and strong parental involvement.

(a) Parental involvement seems to be the best indicator of performance.

2. Schools with a large black majority often do a poorer job because the students are both racially and socio-economically segregated.

(a) All students suffer when discipline and control become more important than teaching.

3. Many schools, including those in the inner city are excellent. These effective schools are characterized by a strong basic core, discipline and order, smaller size, committed teachers and a positive climate.

III. College

A. Two thirds of all high school graduates do not attend college.
   1. Parental S.E.S. is the best indicator of college attendance.
       (a) These families value education and can afford it.
   2. Half of all college enrollments are in junior colleges. These schools often mix college preparation with vocational training.
       (a) Students starting at two year schools are much less likely to graduate than are students of comparable ability at four year schools.
           (1) Junior college students generally are poorly prepared, have lower aspirations, self confidence and receive less support.
           (2) These students are not integrated into a college community and have less attachment to the institution.
       (b) Those transferring to four year colleges face stiffer competition and have high drop-out rates.
       (c) Conflict theorists see junior colleges as another form of tracking while functionalists prefer to stress the success experienced by some of the students.
   3. Minority enrollments have soared in the past few decades.
       (a) Enrollment of black and Hispanic women still is growing slightly, but at a slower rate than whites.
           (1) Black male enrollment has dropped significantly.

B. College graduates earn considerably more than high school graduates.
   1. Female college graduates still earn less than high school male graduates.
   2. Black college male graduates reap the largest relative gains.

C. The bottom line for a college graduate is that a college degree is a rewarding and valuable experience.
   1. College graduates are more knowledgeable, more tolerant, less prejudiced, more active socially and politically and they are more open to ideas.

IV. Models of Education

A. American schools have come under strong criticism as the quality of the students has declined especially in comparison to the Japanese.

B. The Japanese model of education features more schooling, more explicit tracking and closer links to jobs than does the American model.
1. Japanese students spend 240 days a year in school, attend special cramming schools and do much more homework than U.S. students.
2. Students are tracked rigorously through a rigid system of national testing and placement.
3. Japanese schools often have direct ties to employers which in turn is tied to good student performance and the need for good evaluations.

C. The American system is less demanding, more flexible and more forgiving than the Japanese.

D. A structural-functional model of American education stresses the consequences of educational institutions for the maintenance of society.
1. The manifest functions of education have been designed to meet multiple needs.
(a) Cultural reproduction occurs when schools transmit society's culture from one generation to the next.
(b) Social control occurs with the socializing of the young into patterns of conformity.
(c) Assimilation is achieved by exposing students from diverse backgrounds to a common curriculum which helps to create and maintain a common cultural base.
(d) Training and development entails teaching specific, socially valued skills.
(e) Selection and allocation occurs as schools sift, cull and sort students into those that will be allowed to go on and those which will not.
(f) Promotion of change is accomplished by aiming new knowledge and technology at children and by encouraging critical and analytic skills and skepticism.
2. Latent functions and dysfunctions happen in which the conse-

quences are either unintended or actually negative.

    (a) A <u>generation gap</u> occurs when the knowledge imparted by schools drives a wedge between generations by contradicting values held by parents.

    (b) <u>Custodial care</u> is an important consequence of compulsory education that enables elders to command higher wages in the market place and allows parents to forego their responsibility of supervising children.

    (c) A <u>youth culture</u> is created by isolating young people from the larger society and confining them to the company of others their own age.

    (d) Schools function to <u>perpetuate inequality</u> by distributing educational resources inequitably especially for minorities and disadvantaged students. Education therefore functions to maintain and reinforce the existing social class hierarchy.

E.   Conflict theory offers a crucial perspective on the relationship between education and the social class system arguing that modern education serves the interests of the elite.

    1.   Capitalism needs a steady supply of skilled, productive workers who are obedient, punctual and loyal and who accept the ideology that inequalities result from merit and achievement rather than coercion.

        (a) A <u>hidden curriculum</u> socializes young people into obedience and conformity.

        (b) Most scholars are skeptical regarding the claims made by conflict theory arguing that education represents core values, not those imposed by an elite.

    2.   The elites further maintain their advantages by fostering the educational practice of <u>credentialism</u> or the use of educational degrees as job requirements to ward off any encroachment of the lower classes upon upper class jobs.

        (a) Credentialism is a way of manipulating the system for the benefit of the well-off.

        (b) Credential inflation favors the elite who can easily afford more education.

F.   Reducing inequality in education is most difficult because those that benefit from it will seek to perpetuate it - namely the middle and upper-middle classes.

1.   These parents are trying to protect their children and their schools and usually oppose redistricting and untracking.

    (a) Most Americans are willing to raise their taxes to support better schools and headstart programs.

2.   Schools help the middle-class maintain its advantages while magnifying the disadvantages of poorer children.

3.   A national commission on education declared that we are a "Nation at Risk" due to our poor educational system.

    (a) In order to achieve excellence more demand on basic studies were urged as were higher standards and a longer school year.

        (1) Most students benefiting from these changes would be the better students.

        (2) A latent dysfunction of an emphasis on excellence is an increased drop-out rate.

    (b) Combating drop-outs requires three separate steps.

        (1) Have teachers raise expectations.

        (2) Reduce the size of schools.

        (3) Make a flexible education to include youth who work, bear children and marry.

MATCHING

A.	Content of education.	___ 1.	A major dysfunction of education.
B.	Keep student options open	___ 2.	Schools should ensure the best use of the best minds.
C.	Middle class families		
D.	Selection and allocation	___ 3.	Cultural capital.
E.	Hierarchies of authority	___ 4.	Plays a crucial role in reproducing social class.
F.	Credentialism	___ 5.	Committed teachers, positive climate.
G.	Lower socioeconomic classes		
H.	Effective schools	___ 6.	Single best predictor of attending college.
I.	Parent's SES	___ 7.	American model for education.
J.	Coleman report		
K.	Over education	___ 8.	Does school structure affect learning?
L.	Hidden curriculum	___ 9.	A surrogate for social-class background.
M.	Macro level		
N.	Tracking	___ 10.	Socialize the young into obedience and conformity.
O.	Perpetuation of inequality		

FILL IN THE BLANK QUESTIONS

1. Three major factors driving the growth of public schools in the 19th century are ___ demand, ___ demand and ___ ___.

2. The success of Catholic schools appears to rest primarily upon ___ ___.

3. Working-class parents pay more attention to being quiet and polite and less attention to ____ ____ than do middle-class parents.

4. Conflict theory offers a critical perspective by arguing that education serves to perpetuate ____.

5. The ____ prepares young people for life in the industrial working class by teaching them obedience and conformity.

6. Research on tracking shows that performance ____ for those in the top group and that performance ____ for those in the lowest group.

7. It is recommended that I.Q. tests be used not as a measure of ____ ____ but as a measure of ____ ____.

8. Middle class children have more ____ ____ for their education rather than

9. The average ____ college graduate who works full time earns less than a ____ high school graduate.

10. Those that benefit most from the educational system will try to protect it, in most cases this will be the ____ -class.

11. College graduates are generally more ____ and less ____ and ____ active in public and community affairs.

12. Historically, capitalists wanted ____ training for students and labor wanted an ____ curriculum.

13. An increased emphasis on academic ____ could increase the ____ rate.

14. Raising ____ ____ raises attendance, and the performance levels of both good and poor students.

15. The use of educational credentials to measure social origins and social status is called ____ .

MULTIPLE CHOICE

1.   The two main criticisms of education are equity, and ____:

    a.   cost.
    b.   quality.
    c.   emphasis on athletics.
    d.   too bureaucratic.

2.   Which was NOT a force encouraging the growth of schools in the 19th century?

    a.   religious demand.
    b.   parental demand.
    c.   labor demand.
    d.   social control.

3.   At the micro level, sociologists are interested in knowing about:

    a.   the adequacy of school budgets.
    b.   how the school experiences of the working class and middle class differ.
    c.   trends in SAT scores.
    d.   prayer in the schools.

4.   This term is used to describe how schools evaluate, sort, and select students on the basis of achievement and competition:

    a.   testing.
    b.   counseling.
    c.   teaching.
    d.   tracking.

5.   I.Q. tests are supposed to measure:

    a.   what has been learned.
    b.   interests held.
    c.   innate capacity to learn.
    d.   motivation level.

6. Consider the functions of American education. ____ means that the schools transit society's culture from one generation to another.

    a. Selection and allocation.
    b. Cultural reproduction.
    c. Assimilation.
    d. Promotion of change.

7. In the <u>early</u> colonies, parents wanted schools to stress:

    a. humanities.
    b. military training.
    c. basic skills
    d. political theory.

8. This has been called a surrogate for social-class background:

    a. family name.
    b. tuition grants.
    c. credentialism.
    d. I.Q.

9. The concept "social-class gap" refers to:

    a. difference between teacher's and student's class.
    b. class student aspires to.
    c. class of student's parents.
    d. inadequacies of school attended.

10. Which is a characteristic of "effective schools?"

    a. strong, basic core.
    b. large size.
    c. less concern for discipline.
    d. excellent athletic teams.

11. Which is NOT true about the Japanese model of education?

    a.   more school days per year.
    b.   more explicit tracking.
    c.   stronger link between school performance and jobs.
    d.   most children aged 15-17 do not attend school.

12. Latent functions of education are unintended consequences. Those critical of racial and class stratification are concerned about:

    a.   the generation gap.
    b.   youth culture.
    c.   perpetuation of inequality.
    d.   social control.

13. John's parents have not encouraged him in school, and he has fallen behind. What process is deficient in this example?

    a.   social development.
    b.   emotional development.
    c.   physical development.
    d.   cognitive development.

14. According to cognitive development theory, what factor must be present for maximum development in students?
    a.   intelligence.
    b.   highly paid teachers.
    c.   demanding work and high teacher expectations.
    d.   social class gap.

15. This structural factor is thought to dilute the effect of social class on education:

    a.   relatively higher aspirations of minorities.
    b.   sex.
    c.   age.
    d.   income.

16.   Conflict theorists argue that modern education primarily serves the interest of:

a.   teachers.
b.   the elite.
c.   students.
d.   coaches and fans.

17.   Which assessment of 2-year colleges is most likely to be made by a structural-functionalist?

a.   offer limited programs and facilities.
b.   another level of the tracking process.
c.   academic climate is less supporting.
d.   an effective democratizing agent.

18.   Conflict theorists point to the schools' ____, which socializes young people into obedience and conformity.

a.   high value placed on athletics.
b.   preference for tracking.
c.   emphasis on credentialism.
d.   hidden curriculum.

19.   The expansion of secondary and college education largely took place:

a.   after World War II.
b.   1776-1800.
c.   1864-1900.
d.   1914-1930.

20.   The expansion of education has been uneven, and today only about ____ of minority adults over age 25 have completed high school.

a.   80-90%.
b.   10-20%.
c.   50-60%.
d.   70-80%.

21. The best bet when predicting who will go to college is to look to students who:

    a. have high grades.
    b. have aspirations and money.
    c. are the most deserving.
    d. work while attending high school.

22. The average white female college graduate who works full time earns:

    a. as much as comparable males.
    b. less than white male high school graduates.
    c. more than comparable males.
    d. less than minority females.

23. This includes social assets, such as familiarity with elite culture:

    a. formal education.
    b. cultural capital.
    c. income.
    d. education.

24. In a 1989 interview, President Bush stated that ____ was one of his most memorable undergraduate courses.

    a. math.
    b. English.
    c. philosophy.
    d. sociology.

25. It has been concluded that this is a latent function of public education:

    a. social control.
    b. youth culture.
    c. training and development.
    d. selection and allocation.

26.   Evidence indicates that tracking benefits these students most:

    a.   bright students.
    b.   slow learners.
    c.   average students.
    d.   bright students and slow learners.

27.   Based upon what is known about tracking, which will be the most likely result if tracking is introduced in a school?

    a.   gifted students will be penalized.
    b.   low ability students will be taught less.
    c.   low ability students will receive more rewards for their efforts.
    d.   gifted students will learn less.

28.   This parental characteristic determines the neighborhoods in which children are raised and the types of schools in which they enroll:

    a.   social class.
    b.   race.
    c.   home environment.
    d.   family composition.

29.   The correct sequence from low to high dropout rates is?

    a.   blacks, whites, Hispanics.
    b.   Hispanics, whites, blacks.
    c.   whites, blacks, Hispanics.
    d.   whites, Hispanics, blacks.

30.   Which is most likely if the conflict perspective of education is correct?

    a.   the capitalist will scheme to keep down the masses.
    b.   credentialism will fade away.
    c.   those who benefit from education will seek to perpetuate it.
    d.   lower-class parents will benefit most.

ESSAY QUESTIONS

1. What is the value of a college degree in light of credentialism?

2. Discuss how the disadvantages of race, class and gender are compounded by the American educational system.

3. Critique the use of "I.Q." tests.

4. Which theory of education do you favor and why?

5. Discuss why Americans would resist the imposition of the Japanese model of education on their children.

Chapter 15
Political
Institutions

LEARNING OBJECTIVES

1. Differentiate between power, authority, coercion and influence.

2. Describe each of Weber's authority types and the circumstances under which each is most likely to be found.

3. Differentiate between political institutions and the state.

4. Indicate the difference between authoritarianism and democracy and then specify the conditions that exist in order for democracy to flourish.

5. Describe the difficulties that the U.S.S.R. would face should democracy occur.

6. Discuss the conditions that are conducive to the maintenance of a two-party system.

7. Describe the conditions that undermine the voting solidarity of the working classes.

8. Outline the characteristics of the pluralist, elite, conflict and state autonomy models of American government.

9. Describe single issue voting and discuss why it is on the increase.

10. Describe who governs America and who the government really represents. How did this happen?

11. Differentiate between individuals, publics, interest groups and PACs.

12. Describe the patterns of political affiliation and individual participation in American politics.

13. Outline how political participation varies by age, class, race and ethnicity.

14. Use social choice theory to explain political alienation and low voter turnout.

CHAPTER OUTLINE

I. Power

    A. Power is the ability to direct others' behavior even against their wishes.
        1. Coercion is the exercise of power through force or the threat of force.
        2. Authority is power supported by norms and values that legitimates its use.
           (a) Authority based upon the sanctity of time-honored routines or a reverence for the past is called traditional authority.
           (b) Authority derived from the perceived extraordinary personal characteristics of the individual is charismatic authority.
               (1) Charisma may be powerful but it is also inherently unstable because it resides in the individual and is thus mortal. Charismatic authority may evolve into traditional authority.
           (c) Unequal authority based upon rationally established rules constitutes rational-legal authority.
               (1) Rational-legal authority has gradually supplanted traditional authority and is seen as being more flexible and changeable.
           (d) In practice, authority is usually a combination of two or

more types.

     (1) In that authority rests upon norms and values, it can usually be exercised without conflict. It ultimately rests upon the legitimation of coercion.

  3. Influence occurs when a person must rely on persuasion and individual personal appeals based upon personal or ideological grounds and not upon social structure. Influence and power often exist side by side.

B.   Power does not exist randomly, it is socially structured. Political institutions are concerned with the social structure of power.

II. The State

A.   The state is a social structure that successfully claims a monopoly on the legitimate use of coercion and physical force within a territory.

  1. States are responsible for gathering resources, arbitrating relationships and maintaining ties with other societies.

  2. The state has jurisdiction for legitimate decision making for society as a whole and maintains control through three types of coercion: police power, taxation and the maintenance of armed forces.

    (a) The legitimate use of coercion has declined in other institutions like the home and the school and has been   · strengthened in the state.

    (b) Taxation is legitimated confiscation.

III. Democratic vs. Authoritarian Systems

A.   Democracy is a political system that provides regular, constitutional opportunities for a change in leadership according to the will of the majority.

  1. Where income inequality is low and class differences are small the political climate is seen as legitimate.

    (a) High income inequality leads people to see the system as unjust and to demand drastic changes.

  2. Competing interest groups will aid in the maintenance of democratic systems when each group is a minority. Tiny and factionalized groups do not work well in sustaining democracy.

  3. The absence of fundamental cleavages means that interest

groups have basically compatible values.
(a) Deep and bitter divisions preclude cooperation.

B. <u>Authoritarianism</u> is a political system in which the leadership is not selected by the people and legally cannot be changed by them.
1. Many different forms and degrees of authoritarian governments exist.

C. Three general conditions must be met before democracy can flourish. There must be competing interest groups, an absence of fundamental cleavages, and a high level of economic development.

D. The Soviet Union is slipping toward democracy; applying the three criteria of democracy shows some strengths and weaknesses.
1. Low income inequality and competing interest groups exist under favorable conditions.
2. Fundamental cleavages characterize the Soviet Union and make the appearance of democracy unlikely.
3. Historically, the Soviet Union lacks the discipline of self governance. The patience and tolerance required for democracy is not likely to survive the immediate need for change.

IV. American Political Parties

A. The two party system is focused upon an extra legal practice of the <u>political</u> <u>party</u> or an association specifically organized to win elections and secure access to the power of the state.
1. Parties use nonviolent means and are both gracious winners and losers.
(a) They are voluntary associations with open recruitment.
2. A unique aspect of American parties is the winner-take-all rule that requires a party to win fifty percent or more of the votes to hold office.
(a) In a heterogeneous society, majority backing requires a program that combines and balances the interests of many smaller groups.
(b) Stability in American parties is based upon an appeal to diverse groups and the lack of well-defined class boundaries or ideology.
(c) Working class solidarity is undercut by the heterogeneity

of its composition, abundance in the economy and the American dream.

(1) Consequently there is no major workers party in the U.S.

B. Philosophical differences between the two American parties lead to different patterns of affiliation.
1. The Democratic party is seen as being more oriented to the needs of the poor and the working class. It attracts those with high education and liberal values. Minority voters and nonwhites also vote Democratic.
2. Republicans are seen as more interested in economic growth and attract the more conservative voter with a higher income.
3. In recent years there has been a switch to issue voting and voters who call themselves independent.

V. Who Governs? Models of American Democracy

A. Politics is like a pyramid where the state occupies the top, political parties are below and under them are interest groups and publics.
1. Individuals sharing unique interests belong to publics.
    (a) Power requires organization. To become effective, publics must become self-conscious interest groups.
        (1) Interest groups vary from voluntary associations to PACs.
        (2) Interest groups attempt to influence our public officials by lobbying or providing funds through PACs.
        (3) PACs have proven to be highly effective.

B. The pluralist model of power sees a continual process of coalition and competition among many organized groups, none of which is consistently a winner.
1. Pluralism depends upon the existence of shifting allegiances.
2. Critics say that the real exercise of power occurs in higher circles.

C   The power elite model (Mills, 1956) contends that there is a higher level of decision making where an elite makes all the major decisions in its own interest.
1. The power elite consists of the people who occupy the top positions in three key bureaucracies: the military, industry

and the executive branch of government.
  (a) Additional factors solidifying the power of the elite lies in their similarity and interchangeability.
    (1) The upper class is highly overrepresented in the power elite.

D. The conflict/dialectic model is based upon Marxian conflict theory in which there is an elite consisting of those who control production. It stands in opposition to a subordinate class easily awakened by the rise of class consciousness and class action.
  1. The dialectic stresses the conflict that arises over changing economic and political conditions.
    (a) Both sides struggle for their vested interests.
      (1) Conflict may also occur between elites.
  2. The conflict model differs from the power elite model in that a much smaller elite dominates and that the elite can experience internal tension and aggressive competition.
    (a) Conflict can also exist between the elite and the non-elite.

E. The state autonomy model views the federal bureaucracy as a powerful, independent political force.
  1. The state plays off elites against publics and enhances the voice of non-elites through its powerful mediating role.
  2. Federal agencies will act to maintain and enhance their own existence and power.

F. All models of American government stress one fundamental point: organized entities have power, individuals do not.

VI. Individual Participation in American Government

A. The average citizen is not politically oriented or active, thus some groups have more influence than others. Voters differ from nonvoters on social class, race and age.
  1. Political participation of any sort is strongly related to social class, people with more education, more income and more prestigious jobs are more likely to be politically active.
  2. The differences between minority and white political participation are due almost entirely to social class differences. In fact, controlling for social class reveals that African

Americans have increased voter participation.
- (a) Low participation of minorities and the working class can be in part attributed to the absence of a political party that directly represents their interest.
3. There is a steady increase in political interest, knowledge, opinion and participation with age.
4. Overall, elected officials tend to be white men from the professional classes.

B. Social choice theory argues that individual decisions (like voting) are based on cost/benefit calculations.
1. Increasingly people find the costs of voting outweigh the benefits.
- (a) Parties with centrist platforms that are often quite similar inhibit effective choice and ultimately voting.
  - (1) Voters often identify self-interest with political party.

C. Political alienation affects those who cynically believe that voting is a useless exercise that has no influence on decision-making. They are not politically active.
1. Alienation among voters has increased substantially since the 1960's.

D. The strong correlation between social class and political participation means that government is not representative.
1. The poor and undereducated are particularly disadvantaged.

CHAPTER 15

MATCHING

A. Social choice theory

B. American Dream

C. Charismatic authority

D. Totalitarianism

E. Power elite

F. Authority

G. Coercion

H. State

I. Political parties

J. Abortion

K. Traditional authority

L. Alienation

M. pluralist model

N. The business class

O. Influence

____ 1. A positional theory of power.

____ 2. Legitimate power.

____ 3. Voluntary associations with open recruitment

____ 4. Perceived extraordinary personal characteristics.

____ 5. Processes of coalition and competition.

____ 6. Sanctity of time-honored routines.

____ 7. Cost benefit calculation.

____ 8. A reliance upon persuasion and personal appeals.

____ 9. Undercuts working class solidarity.

____ 10. Most powerful interest group in the U.S.

FILL IN THE BLANK QUESTIONS

1. ____ is the ability to get others to do something against their wishes and ____ entails the threat or use of force.

2. In order for a ____ to become an ____ ____, it must become organized.

3. The ___ ___ ___ sees government as a powerful and independent actor in political decisions.

4. The state is the unit that has the ___ for legitimate decision-making and it controls the use of ___ in society..

5. Government can be seen as having the form of a___ .

6. All ___ share constitutional procedures for changing leaders and these changes reflect the will of the majority.

7. Under___, leadership is not selected by the people and legally cannot be changed by them.

8. An important characteristic virtually unique to American democracy is the ___ ___ ___ ___.

9. The ___ ___ model is based upon three key factors: control of vast bureaucracies, similar interests and background.

10. The ___/___ model sees underlying tensions between the elite and the non-elite.

11. Political participation is no longer related to ___ .

12. There is a steady increase in political interest, knowledge, opinion and participation with ___ .

13. It is not wealth that predicts successful democracy, but ___ ___ .

14. ___ are so efficient that no interest group can afford to be without one.

15. Russia will have great difficulty in becoming a democracy chiefly because of deep ___ ___ .

CHAPTER 15

MULTIPLE CHOICE

1. The institution most concerned with the social structure of power:

   a. family.
   b. religion.
   c. state.
   d. education.

2. The exercise of power through force or the threat of force:

   a. influence.
   b. will.
   c. coercion.
   d. authority.

3. Decision-making power that is based on the sanctity of time-honored routines:

   a. coercion.
   b. traditional authority.
   c. charismatic authority.
   d. rational-legal authority.

4. A characteristic virtually unique to the American brand of democracy:

   a. existence of political parties.
   b. winner-take-all-rule.
   c. a constitution.
   d. presence of coalitions.

5. C. Wright Mills coined this term for the people who occupy the top positions in three bureaucracies:

   a. leaders.
   b. power elite.
   c. generals.
   d. administrators.

6. ____ is the ability to direct others' behavior, even against their wishes.

    a. Coercion.
    b. Authority.
    c. Power.
    d. Influence.

7. Universities and other organizations sometimes recruit retired generals or other famous people to help with their fund raising. When they do this they are emphasizing:

    a. traditional authority.
    b. charismatic authority.
    c. rational-legal authority.
    d. coercion.

8. When researchers study local communities in order to find out who has informal power they are focusing upon people with:

    a. influence.
    b. rational-legal authority.
    c. coercive power.
    d. traditional authority.

9. Which is NOT an example of a socially structured power relationship?

    a. student/teacher.
    b. parent/child.
    c. officer/soldier.
    d. two friends.

10. When people respond favorably to political leaders because of their personal characteristics, they are responding to:

    a. charismatic authority.
    b. traditional authority.
    c. legal authority.
    d. influence.

11. This may mean that democracy will be virtually impossible in the Soviet Union:

    a. weak army.
    b. lack of trust between republics.
    c. absence of income inequality.
    d. absence of interest groups.

12. In his analysis, Muller found that only countries with ____ survived as democracies.

    a. a western European heritage.
    b. large rural populations.
    c. high standards of living.
    d. low levels of income inequality.

13. Theory suggests that three conditions must be present before stable democratic governments can exist. The conditions are:

    a. competing groups, absence of fundamental cleavages, and low income inequality.
    b. mass media, public education, and competing groups.
    c. competing groups, economic development, and mass media.
    d. competing groups, strong military, and public education.

14. A vital part of the pluralist model of power:

    a. importance of the dialectic.
    b. class consciousness.
    c. shifting coalitions.
    d. a power elite.

15. Those who identify with a conflict/dialectic model of power think that the working class can gain power by emphasizing this resource:

    a. economic wealth.
    b. alliances with corporate leaders.
    c. class consciousness.
    d. the revolving door principle.

16. In the context of the strip-mine example in the text, the conflict/dialectic model would assume:

    a.   that the elite is divided.
    b.   competition among various interest groups.
    c.   that each affected groups would seek allies among peripherally affected groups.
    d.   a cohesive group of business and other leaders.

17. Based upon the gun control issue, one can predict that to influence politics you must:

    a.   above all, influence public opinion.
    b.   avoid interest group tactics.
    c.   get organized.
    d.   be dispassionate.

18. This model suggests that the state maintains its power by playing elites off against publics and interest groups.

    a.   state autonomy model.
    b.   conflict model.
    c.   power-elite model.
    d.   pluralist model.

19. The state uses three primary types of coercion. Which of these is NOT one of the primary types:

    a.   police power.
    b.   mass media.
    c.   taxation.
    d.   maintain an armed force.

20. The age group LEAST likely to be registered to vote:

   a.   35-44.
   b.   45-64.
   c.   65+.
   d.   18-24.

21. This factor helps to explain why political participation is relatively low in the U.S. compared to other democracies:

   a.   absence of clear wages.
   b.   lack of effective choice.
   c.   lower income.
   d.   lack of tradition.

22. What percent of those eligible vote in local elections?

   a.   90 - 100%.
   b.   80 - 90%.
   c.   50 - 75%.
   d.   25% or less.

23. Studies show that voters differ from non-voters. Non-voters are more likely to be:

   a.   less well educated.
   b.   male.
   c.   white.
   d.   older.

24. The federal government spends about $____ each year.

   a.   one hundred million.
   b.   five hundred million.
   c.   two hundred million.
   d.   one trillion.

25. The state claims a monopoly on the legitimate use of:

    a.   influence.
    b.   coercion.
    c.   media.
    d.   charismatic authority.

26. Based on trends since the 1960s, one can predict that political alienation will:

    a.   remain high and perhaps even increase.
    b.   continue to fall slowly.
    c.   continue to be unrelated to self interest and voting.
    d.   cease to be a topic of interest to social scientists.

27. Which is true about governments?

    a.   most societies have lacked the conditions for democracy.
    b.   most people in most times have lived under democracies.
    c.   authoritarian governments are very uniform in the extent to which they control peoples' lives.
    d.   no authoritarian governments have governed through rational-legal authority.

28. With regard to the two major political parties in the U.S.:

    a.   both are centrist.
    b.   both are left wing.
    c.   both are right wing.
    d.   one is left and one is right wing.

29. A more varied group of people have been seeking political offices in recent years. These people still lag behind others in their office seeking:

    a.   women.
    b.   blacks.
    c.   Hispanics.
    d.   nonelites.

30. If current trends continue, one of the firmest findings in social science will be that political participation is strongly related to ____.

    a. race.
    b. age.
    c. region.
    d. social class.

ESSAY QUESTIONS

1. Describe the thing we call democracy and outline the factors that sustain it.

2. Discuss the factors that contribute to the perpetuation of the two party system.

3. Explain the lack of working class solidarity.

4. What are the consequences for low levels of political participation?

5. Describe how social class is a major factor in political participation.

Chapter 16
Economic Institutions

LEARNING OBJECTIVES

1. Discuss what is meant by the term "economic institutions."

2. Outline the major characteristics and life style for preindustrial, industrial and post-industrial economic structures.

3. Differentiate between primary, secondary and tertiary productions.

4. Compare and contrast capitalism and socialism.

5. Describe the nature of a political economy for both capitalism and socialism.

6. Demonstrate how America has a mixed economy.

7. Describe the elements of the dual economy including the industrial core, the size of units, interdependence, the competitive sector, the segmented labor market and informal economies.

8. Note the benefits and problems attributed to multi-national corporations.

9. Who are the petty bourgeois and what role do they play in America.

10. Describe the differences between professional, blue collar, white collar and pink collar work.

11. Discuss the problems of employment and unemployment.

12. Discuss the impact of unemployment on the individual.

13. Explain the nature and origins of alienation on the job.

14. Describe the conditions that produce work satisfaction and note the role played by intrinsic and extrinsic rewards.

15. Discuss the impact of de-industrialization and de-laborization on the economy, communities and the individual.

CHAPTER OUTLINE

I. Economic Institutions

    A. Sociologists focus on the enduring pattern of norms, roles and statuses at both the macroeconomic and microeconomic levels that make up the economic system.

    B. There are three types of economic institutions. They are:
      1. Preindustrial economic structures are characterized by small settlements, small production units, the utilization of human and animal energy sources and a labor force engaged in extracting raw materials from the environment or primary production.
      2. The industrial economic structure is characterized by a reliance upon new sources of energy, large, bureaucratically organized work units and secondary production or the processing of raw materials.
      3. Post-industrial economic structures rest upon tertiary production or the production of services like government, education, medical care, repairs, etc.
        (a) The tertiary sector has grown rapidly and has replaced blue collar workers with white collar and pink collar workers.
        (b) Post-industrial society creates enormous potential for deliberate social change.

II.   Modern Economic Systems

A.   <u>Capitalism</u> is the economic system in which most wealth is private property. Both the production and distribution of goods is for profit.
1.   Capitalism is based on competition and individual struggle. It assumes that everyone tries to maximize their own returns which in theory maximizes society's returns.

B.   <u>Socialism</u> is an economic system in which the group owns the means of production. Production and distribution are managed for the benefit of the group.
1.   Under <u>state</u> <u>socialism</u> private property is abolished and all decisions about production and distribution are made by government bureaucracies.
(a) The major purpose is not high productivity but equitable distribution.
(1)   An explicit goal is the elimination of unequal rewards as incentives.
(2)   Capitalism excludes those who cannot compete and socialism deliberately includes them.

C.   Most western economies represent a mixture of both capitalism and socialism.
1.   Many services and key industries have been nationalized.
2.   The United States has done the least of all western economies to create a mixed system, the one exception being human services.

D.   The concept of a political economy arises from the fact that any economic system is dependent upon a political system.
1.   State socialism has two major forms.
(a) Democratic socialism has been achieved with the support of the people.
(b) Communism is socialism grafted onto an authoritarian political system.
(c) State socialism in soviet bloc nations is undergoing rapid change as authoritarianism is being replaced by responsive economies. This is called <u>perestroika</u> in the U.S.S.R.
(1)   A shift in economic power means a corresponding shift in political power away from the bureaucrats to the factory managers.

2. The U.S. political economy is being constantly debated between those who see government controlling business and those who say government has been captured by pro-business interests.
   (a) The actual amount of intervention depends upon the level of government involved: federal, state or local.
3. <u>Multi-nationals</u> are large corporations that operate internationally.   Their vast power and resources have caused some worry because of their potential as political actors.

III. The U.S. Economic System

A. The U.S. has a <u>dual</u> <u>economy</u> composed of an industrial core and a set of small competitive organizations.
1. The industrial core consists of a large pool of capital and a series of industrial giants.
   (a) The size of each unit is quite large on the average with larger American corporations being among the largest in the world.
   (b) The American corporate unit is tied to others where common membership on boards of directors ties many companies together.
       (1) Size and interdependence have reduced some competition for markets thus making the capitalist class a potent political force.
2. The competitive sector consists mainly of small, family-owned businesses or partnerships.   They are mainly the <u>petty bourgeois.</u>
   (a) These businesses are characterized by few employees, low levels of bureaucratization, particularism in employment and economic uncertainty.
   (b) The self-employed are typically blue collar, do independent contracting, own franchises or beauty salons.   Many are on the edge of economic disaster, yet many more are thriving.
       (1) There is an <u>informal</u> <u>economy</u> that escapes record keeping and regulation.
   (c) The dual economy features a <u>segmented</u> <u>labor</u> <u>market</u> in which hiring, advancement, and benefits disproportionately favor the industrial core over the competitive sector.

IV. Work in the United States

    A.   Employment is characteristic of over two-thirds of the adult population in the labor force at any given time.
        1.   The <u>labor force</u> consists of the <u>unemployed</u> and the <u>employed</u>.

    B.   Minorities, especially blacks and Hispanics are overrepresented among the unemployed.
        1.   Employment determines one's status, income and structures lives.
        2.   Unemployment depends upon individual and structural factors.
            (a) Individual factors are education, race and skill.
            (b) The structural factor is which sector of the economy one is employed in.
                (1) Blue collar workers and minorities are the most vulnerable.
                (2) Unemployment and layoffs are typical of the industrial core while quitting, being fired and discrimination are found in the periphery.

    C.   Occupations may be classified as professional, white collar, blue collar or pink collar.
        1.   <u>Professions</u> are occupations that demand specialized skills and creative freedom. They are characterized by the production of unstandardized products, personality involvement, knowledge of specialized techniques, a sense of obligation, group identity and significant service to society.
        2.   <u>White collar</u> workers work with their "heads." <u>Blue collar workers</u> are employed in primary and secondary industry and work with their "hands."
            (a) Blue collar workers have lower incomes, status, security and suffer closer supervision and more routinized work.
            (b) Post-industrial economies use fewer blue collar workers, consequently problems lie ahead for the traditional working class.
            (c) <u>Pink collar</u> work is primarily in the service sector and features a nonexistent career ladder and minimum wage.
            (d) Employment in the future will be of two types; high education, high skill or no skill.

263

> (1) The skilled blue collar worker is the most likely victim of this shift in occupations.

V. The Meaning of Work

A. Work is a means to a livelihood, a major structural determinant of our lives and has a direct effect upon self-esteem and identity.
1. Work satisfaction may be <u>intrinsic</u> and arise from the process of work itself or it may be <u>extrinsic</u> in the form of tangible benefits like income and security. The learned professions are the most satisfied workers and auto assembly line workers the least satisfied.
2. <u>Alienation</u> is the degree to which workers have control over their work. Alienation can result from reducing work to simple, boring repetitive tasks, or binding people to regulations so as to rob them of personal judgment.
(a) Professional workers are low on alienation while clerical and blue collar workers have higher alienation scores.
(1) Alienation may be offset by adequate salaries and job security.
3. Self-direction in one's work affects satisfaction, alienation and our personalities.
(a) Job complexity, degree of supervision and the degree of routinization are the components of self-direction.
(1) Low routine, low supervision and high complexity provide the most benefits.
(2) High routine, high supervision and low complexity create alienation.

VI. Technology and the Future of Work

A. When technology is introduced to the job <u>deskilling</u> occurs, workers are displaced and management gains greater supervision over the worker.

B. Labor opposes these practices and argues that labor need not suffer with automation.
1. Management obviously opposes labor's agenda.
2. A radical critique of the situation argues for a different system

for the distribution of profit.

3. The issue is not particularly new, the <u>Luddite</u> movement in 1811 had similar concerns.

C. The economic changes of the last decade can be called a number of different names like post-industrialization, de-industrialization or even de-laborization.

1. The reconstruction of the economy has created a "hour glass" labor market, ample on the top and bottom and thin in the middle.

    (a) The short term effect has been de-laborization which impoverishes individuals and communities alike.

2. Policy options include conservative, liberal and social welfare approaches.

    (a) Conservatives want to reduce wages and benefits while liberals wish to protect communities and individual workers through government intervention.

    (b) Social welfare advocates want more programs to help those left behind by economic changes.

CHAPTER 16

MATCHING

A. Anti-automation   ___ 1. Maximize our rewards.

B. White collar   ___ 2. Luddites.

C. Professionals   ___ 3. Work with one's hands.

D. Tertiary production   ___ 4. Processing raw materials.

E. Labor force   ___ 5. Expected to think
                                     independently.

F. Petty bourgeois
                             ___ 6. Extracting raw materials.
G. Multi-nationals
                             ___ 7. Freedom from supervision.

H. Primary production   ___ 8. Production of services.

I. Blue collar   ___ 9. Small family owned
                                     businesses.
J. Capitalism
                             ___ 10. U.S. is least advanced in the
K. Socialism   West.

L. Mixed economies

M. Alienation

N. Pink collar

O. Secondary production

FILL IN THE BLANK QUESTIONS

1. In ___ economic structures, the children, the elderly and the sick   were
    the responsibility of the family.

2. The shift from ___ production to ___ production is characterized by

growing surpluses.

3. The ____ ____ has grown very rapidly while those employed in ____ production has been reduced to nil and the portion employed in ____ production has halved.

4. The ____ ____ is that part of the economy that escapes record keeping and regulation.

5. The explicit goal of ____ is to eliminate unequal reward as the major incentive to labor.

6. ____ was one of America's first socialized industries.

7. ____ is socialism grafted onto an authoritarian political system.

8. The result of shared ownership and control is that the capitalist class is increasingly ____ rather than ____.

9. A segmented labor market is one in which hiring, advancement, and benefits vary systematically between the ____ ____ and the ____.

10. It is little wonder that ____ is associated with high levels of alcoholism, violence and depression.

11. An important characteristic of ____ ____ workers is a short or non-existent career ladder coupled with minimum wages.

12. The shift to a post-industrial society means more unemployment or worse unemployment for the traditional ____ ____.

13. Marxists argue that being satisfied with a job that has no opportunity for individual control is an example of ____ ____ .

14. Two kinds of rewards are ____ which arise from the process of work and ____ which are more tangible benefits such as income and security.

15. The impact of new technology has been ____ , ____ workers and greater ____.

CHAPTER 16

MULTIPLE CHOICE

1.   An issue related to the production side of economic institutions:

     a.   a scarcity or abundance.
     b.   what proportion goes to workers versus the manager.
     c.   who is responsible for the support of non-workers.
     d.   how much of society's production is distributed on the basis of need
          rather than effort.

2.   This economic system is based upon competition:

     a.   capitalism.
     b.   socialism.
     c.   communism.
     d.   totalitarianism.

3.   Term used to show the close relationship between the economy and the
     political system:

     a.   power elite.
     b.   middle class.
     c.   political economy.
     d.   mixed economy.

4.   The most important reward all professionals have shared:

     a.   high income.
     b.   freedom from supervision.
     c.   prestige.
     d.   large amounts of time free for leisure.

5.   The condition where workers have no control over the work process or
     products of their labor:

     a.   unemployment.
     b.   alienation.
     c.   socialism.
     d.   blue-collar work.

6. ____ has three components: job complexity, degree of supervision, and degree of routinization.

   a. alienation.
   b. job satisfaction.
   c. self-direction.
   d. intrinsic rewards.

7. Sociologists interested in the economic institution focus upon:

   a. the federal reserve system.
   b. causes of inflation.
   c. enduring patterns of norms, roles and statuses.
   d. the national debt.

8. A production activity stressed in an industrial economic structure:

   a. fishing.
   b. farming.
   c. foresting.
   d. steel production.

9. Those who do not have required credentials may successfully find employment here:

   a. competitive sector.
   b. industrial core.
   c. professions.
   d. multinationals.

10. A socialized service in the U.S.:

   a. religion.
   b. agriculture.
   c. public schools.
   d. railroads.

11. Which is NOT a consequence of "de-laborization?"

    a.   the "hour glass" labor market.
    b.   entire communities impoverished.
    c.   U.S. exports raw materials and imports products.
    d.   jobs with more security for most people.

12. Jobs that provide the greatest rewards have:

    a.   high-routine, low-supervision, and high-complexity.
    b.   low-routine, low-supervision, and high-complexity.
    c.   low-routine, low-supervision, and low-complexity.
    d.   low-routine, high-supervision, and low-complexity.

13. Which is NOT a condition associated with the shift from primary to secondary production:

    a.   growing scarcity.
    b.   larger work groups.
    c.   new sources of power.
    d.   secondary production.

14. Development experts would predict that this economic activity would increase in a post-industrial economy:

    a.   primary production.
    b.   secondary production.
    c.   services.
    d.   manufacturing.

15. Not thought to be an advantage of socialism:

    a.   societal resources can be used for the benefit of society as whole.
    b.   central planning.
    c.   automatically makes adjustments in changing supplies and demands.
    d.   produces equitable distribution.

16. What is the expected production in socialist countries compared to capitalist ones?

    a.   production higher in socialist.
    b.   production higher in capitalist.
    c.   production the same in socialist and in capitalist.
    d.   no relationship between form of economy and production.

17. Those most vulnerable to unemployment:

    a.   adult women.
    b.   young men.
    c.   young women.
    d.   minorities.

18. What impact does theory suggest that increased technology will have on the future of work?

    a.   increase the skill needed for jobs.
    b.   increase the scope required of individual judgment.
    c.   greater supervision
    d.   creation of many jobs.

19. An example of an intrinsic reward from work:

    a.   pride felt in creativity.
    b.   income.
    c.   security.
    d.   benefits.

20. Those workers most likely to consider new technology as a boon:

    a.   service.
    b.   less skilled.
    c.   professionals.
    d.   blue collar.

21.	Communism is the combination of:

	a.	socialism and authoritarianism.
	b.	socialism and democracy.
	c.	capitalism and authoritarianism.
	d.	capitalism and democracy.

22.	This country has done the least among major Western powers in creating a mixed economy:

	a.	France.
	b.	United States.
	c.	Great Britain.
	d.	West Germany.

23.	Which is NOT true about multi-national corporations?

	a.	mostly European in origin.
	b.	owe no allegiance to any particular country.
	c.	they dwarf many national governments in size.
	d.	must also be seen as political actors.

24.	The conservative free-market policy approach to post industrialization calls for:

	a.	increase wages and benefits.
	b.	decrease wages and benefits.
	c.	state investment in industries.
	d.	six-month notification of plant closings.

25.	Not a characteristic of preindustrial economic structures:

	a.	small production units.
	b.	reliance upon human and animal power.
	c.	bureaucratically organized work units.
	d.	emphasis on primary production.

26. An undesirable transformation associated with industrialization:

    a.   long life.
    b.   greater education.
    c.   population growth.
    d.   reduction of intolerance.

27. Post-industrial development rests on this stage of productivity:

    a.   primary.
    b.   tertiary.
    c.   secondary.
    d.   a combination of primary and tertiary.

28. Opportunities during the 1980s to 1990s are expected to decline for:

    a.   paralegals.
    b.   medical assistants.
    c.   stenographers.
    d.   nurses.

29. The competitive sector of the American economy is largely made up of:

    a.   the petit bourgeois.
    b.   large businesses.
    c.   home offices of multi-national corporations.
    d.   labor unions.

30. If present trends continue, the primary losers in the transformation of the labor market will likely be:

    a.   the professions.
    b.   white collar workers.
    c.   pink collar workers.
    d.   skilled manual labor.

CHAPTER 16

ESSAY QUESTIONS

1. What is your view? Are corporate capitalism and government too close?

2. Briefly describe the benefits and problems arising from the existence of political economies.

3. Summarize the blue collar woes.

4. Explain the origins of alienation on the job.

5. Who are the winners and the losers in the American process of de-industrialization?

Sports:
An Emerging
Institution?

FILL IN THE BLANK QUESTIONS

1.   Sports are probably a ____ aspect of human society.

2.   Sports are an important part of life at both the ____ and ____ level.

3.   Conflict theorists say that sports reproduce class relationships and thus act to support both ____ and ____.

4.   Sports probably have a lasting effect upon your ____ ____ and ____ ____.

5.   Sports are an important mechanism for teaching and reinforcing central social norms of ____ and ____.

6.   ____ ____ and ____ students are directed toward athletics, not academics.

7.   The average professional athletic career only lasts ____ years.

8.   Sports are an important, but ____ ____.

9.   Like the ____ of the Middle ages, our modern ____ symbolize what our society holds dear.

10. For most of us, sports duplicates functions that are served by other ____.

MULTIPLE CHOICE

1. Which doesn't describe sports in this country?

    a.   wide participation by the young.
    b.   introduction to sports while young.
    c.   a reason to spend money.
    d.   trivial.

2. A functional analysis suggests that the critical question to answer about sports is:

    a.   Do sports endure for generations?
    b.   Does it include a complex set of statuses, roles, norms, and values?
    c.   Does it meet a basic human need?
    d.   Do we have enough leisure time to enjoy sports?

3. Which is NOT a micro contribution or sports?

    a.   enjoyment as a spectator.
    b.   a major contribution to our national economy.
    c.   an impact on one's self concept.
    d.   helped some individual children stay out of trouble.

4. Which is NOT true about sports?

    a.   communist countries encourage sports.
    b.   capitalist countries encourage sports.
    c.   democracies encourage sports.
    d.   dictatorships discourage sports.

5. The statement that "There is no I in team" refers to which value that is reinforced by sports?

    a.   individuality.
    b.   fitness.
    c.   teamwork.
    d.   competition.

276

6. Which function of sports is the focus of conflict sociologists?

   a. reinforces norms important for society.
   b. reproduces inequality.
   c. the value of competition.
   d. helping to integrate society.

7. Which function of sports would be supported most by a structural functionalist and not by a conflict sociologist?

   a. reproduces social class relations.
   b. supports racism.
   c. supports sexism.
   d. channels aggression and hostility.

8. Conflict sociologists note that athletics as a form of tracking mostly:

   a. encourages athletics over academics.
   b. encourages academics.
   c. encourages athletics and academics.
   d. impacts all children equally.

9. About ____ of 12,000 high school athletes will earn money as a professional athlete.

   a. one hundred.
   b. one.
   c. five hundred.
   c. two hundred.

10. Life-threatening injuries occur every year. These are most common in:

    a. gymnastics and football.
    b. wrestling.
    c. outdoor track.
    d. basketball.

Chapter 17
Religion

LEARNING OBJECTIVES

1. Define what is meant by the concept of religion and note the aspects of religion that interest sociologists.

2. Carefully outline Durkheim's and Weber's approach to religion.

3. Explain how conflict theory interprets religion's role in society.

4. Spell out Weber's main argument in the Protestant Ethic and the Spirit of Capitalism.

5. Use the concept of tension between religion and society to differentiate between the church-like religions (ecclesiae and denominations) and the sect-like religions (established sects, sects and cults).

6. Discuss the structure and functions of church-like and sect-like religions using the Amish and the People's Temple as examples.

7. Explain the difference between a cult and a sect.

8. Define the term "liberation theology" and note where and by whom it is practiced.

9. Summarize the correlates of religiosity and commitment.

10. Identify the consequences of religiosity and religious affiliations.

11. Discuss the current practice of electronic religion and its impact on the contemporary religious scene.

12. Outline the changes in American religious behavior over the last two decades paying special attention to fundamentalism, civil religion and secularization.

13. Describe how the religious institution can have an impact on other institutions in society.

CHAPTER OUTLINE

I. The Scientific Study of Religion

    A. <u>Religion</u> is a system of beliefs and practices related to sacred things that unites believers into a moral community.

    B. Sociologists treat religion as a set of values and examine the ways in which culture, society, and class relationships affect religion and the ways in which religion affects individuals and social structure.

II. Why Religion?

    A. Durkheim identified three universal aspects of religion called the elementary forms of religion.
        1. The elementary forms of religion include a distinction between the <u>sacred</u> and the <u>profane</u>.
           (a) The process of transferring an idea or event from the sacred to the profane is called <u>secularization</u>.
        2. Another universal aspect of religion is a set of beliefs, myths and creeds about the supernatural.
        3. The third universal aspect is the expression through ritual of the things that are held sacred.
        4. Durkheim believed that religion was functional for individuals and for society as a whole.

(a) Religion offers the individual support, consolation and reconciliation.
(b) The major function of religion for society is that religion gives values and norms credence making them sacred. Religion gives tradition a moral imperative.

B. To Weber, the essence of religion is a search for knowledge about the unknown that may challenge the status quo as well as support it.
   1. Weber saw the major source of religion as lying in the charisma of extraordinary individuals.
   2. The Protestant Ethic and the Spirit of Capitalism thesis asserts that the Protestant Reformation paved the way for bourgeois capitalism.
      (a) The moral values that came to embody Protestantism became the values of early capitalism.
         (1) These values are hard work, duty, individualism and rationalism.
         (2) The latent function of these values was to get rich.
   3. Weber believed that religion could support the status quo or that it could be an active agent of social change.

C. Conflict theory as interpreted by Marx saw religion as a delusion deliberately fostered by the elite to distract workers from their state of oppression.

III. The Tension Between Religion and Society

A. Each religion is confronted with the tendency to compromise with the world and the tendency to reject the world. The resolution of this dilemma affects the form and structure of the religion.
   1. Churches are religious organizations that have become institutionalized. They have endured for generations and are supported by society's norms and values, and have become an active part of society.
      (a) Ecclesia are churchlike religious organizations that automatically include every member of society.
      (b) Denominations are churchlike religious organizations that have accommodated to society and to other religions.
      (c) Ecclesiae and denominations tend to be formal bureaucratic structures with hierarchal positions, specialization and

official creeds. Leadership is by professionals who received formal training at specialized schools.

2. <u>Sects</u> are religious groups that reject the social environment in which they exist.

  (a) A <u>cult</u> is a sectlike religious organization that is independent of the religious traditions of society. They challenge established religions.

    (1) Cults experience a high degree of tension with the environment and arise in times of rapid social change.

  (b) Sects typically seek to preserve their spiritual purity by remaining apart from the world.

    (1) Sects view themselves as restoring true faith and preserving religious tradition by cleansing the church of its secular associations.

  (c) An <u>established</u> <u>sect</u> is a sect that has adapted to the institutional environment.

    (1) In general, sect members prefer to withdraw from the world while established sect members attempt to influence the world.

  (d) All sects and cults are opposed to some basic societal institution and the appeal of the sect-like religions is focused upon those who are left out of or estranged from society: the poor, alienated or handicapped.

    (1) Leaders have no formal training and the services are informal.

    (2) Sects and cults are like primary groups: small, informal and loyal.

    (3) Close control exerted over members enhances identity and fosters cohesion.

3. Liberation theology aims at the creation of a democratic, Christian socialism that eliminates poverty, inequality and political oppression.

  (a) The moral community created by religion has often been the foundation for political action and social change.

4. Government protection is generally given to those religions that consensus places in the mainstream of American life.

IV. Religion in the United States

  A. Religiosity or one's degree of religious commitment is an important

American characteristic with the majority of Americans defining religion as being very important to their lives.

1. Older people and women are among the most religious with younger people and males being less involved.
2. High status individuals predominate among the church-like religions while those of low status seek the sect-like religions.
3. Adult religious involvement is strongly associated with community involvement and conventional values.
   (a) The young and the liberal participate less.

B. Civil religion is the set of institutionalized rituals, beliefs and symbols sacred to the American nation.

1. For many Americans civil religion and regular religion are inseparable.

C. Secularization or the decline of religion in social life appears to be characteristic of western society.

1. It has three dimensions:
   (a) the growing isolation of the church from other institutions,
   (b) increasing accommodation to secular life and
   (c) the reduced importance of religion to individuals.
2. While church attendance and general identification with religion remain high, the proportion who say religion is very important to their own lives has dropped significantly. Along with a moddest decline in church attendance, there is a decrease in the proportion of people believing that the Bible is the actual word of God.

D. Fundamentalism is a movement to restore original religious principles. Fundamentalism has been growing.

1. Fundamentalism occurs in all religions and the common aim is to bring the church back into tension with society.
2. The growth of fundamentalism is attributed to the fact that it does a better job of meeting the functions of religion for individuals.
   (a) It provides its members with common activities, a group identity and a sense of community.

E. The new Christian Right is a loose fundamentalist coalition that believes American government and social institutions must operate

according to Christian principles.
1.   There is a Christian obligation to be politically active.
      (a) This is a political rather than a religious movement and has
          attracted more publicity than power.

F.   Electronic religion allows people to enjoy religious participation with-
      out leaving home.
      1.   People using media religion are older, female, poorer, poorly
            educated, Protestant and usually come from the southern and
            mid-western regions.
      2.   Televangelism has created national controversy over the money
            raised.
            (a) Critics argue that money raised is for the evangelist and not
                for their religious activities.
                (1) Recent scandals lend support to these views.
            (b) Other critics say that this form of religion fails to bring
                people together in a moral community.

MATCHING

A.	Weber	____	1.	Things held in awe or respect.
B.	Ecclesia	____	2.	Religion is a delusion deliberately fostered by the elite.
C.	Established sect	____	3.	Religious group independent of the religious traditions of society.
D.	Durkheim			
E.	Amish	____	4.	Democratic Christian socialism.
F.	Sect	____	5.	The most institutionalized of all religious structures.
G.	Profane	____	6.	Things known and familiar.
H.	Secularization			
I.	Denomination	____	7.	Religious groups that have accommodated to society.
J.	Political movement	____	8.	Religion gives tradition a moral imperative.
K.	Ritual			
L.	Sacred	____	9.	A desire to spread the word and make converts.
M.	Liberation theology	____	10.	Peculiar people.
N.	Cult			
O.	Marx			

FILL IN THE BLANK QUESTIONS

1. According to Durkheim, all religions share a distinction between the ____ and the ____, a set of _____ and a set of ____.

2. Weber's major contribution was the notion that religion could be an important source of ____ in society.

3. In the Protestant ethic, ___ was an unintended consequence of behavior that was directed by religious motives.

4. ___ differed from ___ in that he saw religious support for tradition in a negative light.

5. ___ are religious organizations that are the most institutionalized while ___ are religious organizations that reject the social environment in which they live.

6. In ___ religions, congregations often function more as audiences than as active participants.

7. The ___ represents the successful compromisers and the ___ represents the virtuous outsiders.

8. The values of hard work, duty, individualism and rationalism were called by Weber the ___ ___.

9. Higher-status people are more often members of ___ religions whereas lower-status people are more often members of ___ and ___.

10. The decline in religion in social life is called ___.

11. ___ ___ provides a sacred context for understanding the nation's history and current responsibilities.

12. ___ can be found in all religions.

13. Since 1950 there has been a ___ in outward religious observance in America.

14. The ___ ___ is best understood as a political rather than a religious movement.

15. The televangelism scandals of the late 1980s have had a strong negative effect only only those people who already held ___ ___.

MULTIPLE CHOICE

1. The system of shared beliefs and practices including belief systems by which people invoke supernatural forces as explanations of earthly struggles:

    a. Marxism.
    b. religion.
    c. Church.
    d. fundamentalism.

2. The process of transferring things or ideas from the sacred to the profane:

    a. religion.
    b. science.
    c. secularization.
    d. religiosity.

3. Which is NOT a practice or emphasis of American civil religion?

    a. the Pledge of Allegiance.
    b. regular attendance at a church.
    c. folding and displaying the flag.
    d. rituals for folding and displaying the flag.

4. Fundamentalism is a grass roots conservative movement in the U.S. Which of these statements is NOT true about fundamentalism?

    a. found only in the Protestant church.
    b. aim is to bring the church back to its trends within religion.
    c. began as a countermovement to liberal trends within religion.
    d. favor a requirement that the Genesis story be taught along with or instead of evolutionary theory.

5. The New Christian Right is best understood as:

    a. a religious movement.
    b. a rebirth of the Protestant Ethic.
    c. a political movement.
    d. body of homogeneous conviction.

6. ____ is the most serious criticism raised against televangelism.

    a. Spreading the gospel.
    b. Bilking naive people.
    c. Failing to bring people together into a moral community.
    d. Increasing religious participation for those who are shut off from participation.

7. Which statement is NOT true about the place of religion in society?

    a. important only in capitalistic societies.
    b. helps people face personal dilemmas.
    c. an explanation for incomprehensive events.
    d. provides a familiar and comforting context even when rituals fail to solve immediate problems.

8. What do these historical figures have in common that is important for a sociological explanation of their success - Christ, Muhammad, Joseph Smith and Jim Jones?

    a. all were men.
    b. all were upper-middle class.
    c. all had charisma.
    d. all were religious.

9. Not included in the Protestant Ethic described by Weber:

    a. hard work.
    b. enjoyment of luxuries.
    c. rationalism.
    d. plain living.

10. This Sect developed from Protestant reformers who moved to Pennsylvania in 1827:

   a.   Old Order Amish.
   b.   Baptists.
   c.   Mormons.
   d.   Christian Scientists.

11. Sometimes referred to as "the church of the disinherited":

   a.   ecclesia.
   b.   denomination.
   c.   civil religions.
   d.   sects.

12. Fundamentalist religious leaders say that their primary mission is to:

   a.   bring people to Jesus.
   b.   picket for just causes.
   c.   organize the poor.
   d.   portray the Genesis story as a parable.

13. Which question correctly illustrates the sociological perspective on religion?

   a.   Does God exist?
   b.   Are these religious values good?
   c.   What are the origins of religious values and what are their consequences?
   d.   Which is the best religion?

14. Not included as one of Durkheim's three fundamental elements in all religion:

   a.   charismatic figures.
   b.   distinction between sacred and profane.
   c.   set of beliefs.
   d.   set of rituals.

15. Marx, unlike Durkheim or Weber, saw religion:

a. as a mechanism for economic change.
b. as a delusion deliberately fostered by the elite.
c. from a strict value-free position.
d. from a scientific perspective.

16. From the functionalist perspective, the worship of God is a barely disguised worship of:

a. man.
b. nature.
c. society.
d. the unknown.

17. Televangelists relatively infrequently reach and appeal to these people:

a. well educated.
b. Protestants.
c. females.
d. older persons.

18. Theory suggests that if sects become more like churches they will emphasize:

a. charismatic leaders.
b. greater in informality.
c. greater bureaucratization.
d. their appeal to the alienated.

19. The Jonestown "cult" headed by Jim Jones was different from other sects with links to Christianity in that:

a. it was a religion of the disinherited.
b. Jones abandoned Christianity and the Bible's God.
c. its membership formed a strong primary group.
d. rigid adherence to norms reminded the members of their common situation.

20. Approximately what percent of adults interviewed in the U.S. state that they believe in God?

    a. 10%.
    b. 20%.
    c. 50%.
    d. 94%.

21. The approximate percent of the U.S. population that belonged to a church in 1800?

    a. 95% or more.
    b. between 50 and 75%.
    c. about 25%.
    d. less than 10%.

22. A characteristic of those Americans who do NOT attend a church or synagogue on a regular basis:

    a. 50 or older.
    b. Catholic.
    c. male.
    d. Midwesterners.

23. Religious group with most members in the U.S.:

    a. Catholic.
    b. Jewish.
    c. Protestant.
    d. none.

24. The ____ are a classic example of an established sect.

    a. Catholics.
    b. Mormons.
    c. Lutherans.
    d. Methodists.

25. Which is a characteristic of sects but not of ecclesia or denominations?

    a.   emphasis upon a hierarchy of positions.
    b.   informality.
    c.   specialization.
    d.   official creeds.

26. Which is the correct ordering of religious from most to least tensions with society?

    a.   sects, cults, churches, established sects.
    a.   churches, cults, sects, established sects.
    c.   cults, churches, established sects, sects.
    d.   cults, sects, established sects, churches.

27. If current trends continue, religion in the 1990s will be characterized by:

    a.   continued growth of fundamental churches.
    b.   large decrease in church membership.
    c.   the rejection of the Old Testament.
    d.   government's outlawing of civil religion.

28. These people report greater attachment to religion than do other Americans:

    a.   Easterners and Westerners.
    b.   older people and women.
    c.   males and better educated people.
    d.   young adults.

29. The broadest issue with regard to state support for religion arise when we look at:

    a.   creationism.
    b.   prayer in the schools.
    c.   which religions the state supports.
    d.   legality of passing out pamphlets.

30. Which is true about the relationship between church and sect?

    a.   many churches start out as sects.
    b.   most sects started out as cults.
    c.   more and more churches are becoming ecclesia.
    d.   many established sects become cults.

ESSAY QUESTIONS

1. Discuss the text's definition of religion and note the aspects of religion of interest to sociologists.

2. Briefly summarize the current practice of electronic religion and its impact on the contemporary religious scene.

3. Under what conditions do cults and sects flourish and why?

4. Discuss the changes in American religious behavior over the last two decades.

5. Describe the consequences of religiosity and religious affiliation for the individual.

Chapter 18
Health
and
Medicine

LEARNING OBJECTIVES

1. Discuss how mental and physical health are both achieved statuses and how they are socially constructed.

2. Describe the sick role noting both the rights and obligations associated with it.

3. Use the notion of labeling theory and the sick role to explain how illness can be negotiated and why this might happen.

4. Note the consequences for society and the individual when deviance becomes medicalized.

5. Define the term epidemiology and explain how gender and minority status influence health.

6. Fully discuss the complex relationship between social class and life expectancy.

7. Describe the steps necessary to create a healthy lifestyle for all Americans.

8. List the characteristics of a profession and apply them to the profession of medicine.

9. Explain the high status and income of physicians and note how this is changing.

10. Describe the awkward, gendered role of nurses in the health care system and comment on the state of the current job market for nurses.

11. List all of the parts of the medical-industrial complex and note now these parts have contributed to the spiraling cost of health care.

12. Discuss the strengths and weaknesses of implementing a single national health insurance program managed by the government.

13. Differentiate between STD, HIV and AIDS and note who gets AIDS and what can be done about it.

14. Describe how the technology of organ transplants has created a social problem.

CHAPTER OUTLINE

I. The Social Construction of Health and Sickness

    A.   Symbolic interactionism views physical and mental health as statuses that are socially constructed, negotiated and achieved.

    B.   Our physical self and our attitudes towards it have consequences for how we interact in the social world.
        1.   The sick role entitles one to:
            (a) Be exempt from normal social roles and to be relieved of the responsibility for one's condition.
            (b) It also requires that one seek competent help and try to get well.
            (c) Being granted the sick role depends on the visibility of the problem and the degree to which one's own actions contributed to the problem.
        2.   Illness like deviance is relative. It may also be seen as a

labeling process that depends on symptoms, individual characteristics and other circumstances.

(a) The medicalization of deviance has operated to label deviant behavior like alcoholism as a medical problem.

(1) Other problems like homosexuality have been "de-medicalized."

II. Health and Social Structure

A. Studying how social statuses relate to the distribution of illness and mortality is called social epidemiology.

1. Class, race and gender are significantly related to ill health and mortality.

(a) Gender roles lead men into risky behavior while providing inadequate guidelines for coping with stress. Consequently, mortality is higher for men than women.

(1) Men have poorer coping mechanisms and social support structures for dealing with stress.

(b) Social class influences standard of living, stress levels and education. These factors lead to poor coping strategies which produce poor health and higher mortality.

(1) Free health care does not reduce class differentials in mortality.

(c) Racial minorities have significantly higher rates of mortality.

(1) Income differences by race contribute to a higher risk of physical and psychological stress.

B. Sociologically speaking, a healthy lifestyle is one that includes satisfying social roles, some control over one's social environment and integration into one's community.

1. These factors are also closely correlated with social class.

III. Health Care Professions

A. The medical institution is directly influenced by the structure of the medical professions.

1. Professionals are characterized by: specialized knowledge, a sense of obligation to one's field, service to society, a strong feeling of identity with others in one's field, high personal involvement in one's work and an unstandardized product.

       (a) The pressure of learning medicine forces doctors to depersonalize their patients and GROP.

       (b) Practicing physicians quickly leave these practices behind and practice more humane medicine that incorporates biological, psychological and social factors into patient care.

         (1) The structure of the medical profession does not directly reward personal patient care.

2. There are several explanations why physicians enjoy high status and incomes.

       (a) Functionalists follow Davis and Moore arguing that high rewards (income and status) must be offered to motivate the few capable to do the work.

       (b) Conflict theorists are not so forgiving, instead physicians' use of power in their self-interest explains their status and income.

       (c) The AMA is a powerful professional association committed to maintaining the individual physician as the independent provider of medical care in a capitalist system.

3. The status and autonomy of physicians has declined as the government and the insurance industry have forced more physicians into bureaucratically run group practices.

       (a) Patients today are more critical and selective in their choice of medical provider.

4. Nurses have little independence, short career ladders and very stressful careers.

       (a) The nursing profession is controlled by physicians with income and power differentials paralleling sex differences in other institutions.

       (b) Standards and income have increased with income.

         (1) The problems of the profession have created a nursing shortage.

IV. The Medical-Industrial Complex

    A. There are three basic types of hospitals: proprietary, non-profit and state run.

       1. Each is under intense financial pressure which affects their operation.

       2. Hospitals are characterized by a dual authority structure composed of professional administrators and doctors who are not

hospital employees.

3. Medical costs are rapidly increasing due to the development of expensive, high technology diagnostic and treatment procedures, competition among providers and high consumer demand.

    (a) The threat of malpractice suits encourages physicians to practice defensive medicine and pay large insurance fees.

4. Payment for health care can be by private payment, insurance or government program.

    (a) Most individuals are forced to rely on private insurance or government programs.

        (1) Insurance programs are available to many workers, but not all workers.

        (2) The government sponsors two main programs: <u>Medicare</u> and <u>Medicaid</u>.

    (b) At least 14 percent of the population has no medical coverage.

        (1) These are mostly unemployed adults and the working poor.

B. The U.S. is the only major industrial nation to not provide financial coverage for medical care for the majority of its citizens.

1. A national health scheme might be able to balance off the high cost services against the lower ones.

    (a) Currently the private sector has captured the profitable cases while the government covers the costly ones.

    (b) Critics claim that the government is inefficient and that the private sector provider is more efficient.

2. Failure to have a national health plan may be related to the lack of a large scale workers or socialist political party.

V. Generally there are three strategies for improving America's health.

A. Encouraging healthy lifestyles assumes that individual bad habits can be altered by legislation and education.

1. This is a popular and cheap policy that will not alter the fundamental inequalities in class and race that contribute to mortality differentials.

B. Universal health care is very desirable but very costly and it will not eliminate the root causes of mortality differentials.

C   The most radical and costly program would attack class and racial inequities to eliminate the disadvantages that contribute to mortality differentials.

    1.   This will require structural changes in our major institutions.

VI. AIDS presents both a medical and social problem to all parts of the health care system.

    A.   The epidemiology of AIDS shows that it is an STD transmitted primarily by having multiple sexual partners.

        1.   Chief among these are homosexual/bisexual men, intravenous drug users and their children.

           (a) Current trends show increasing rates among blacks and Hispanics.

    B.   Because of lifestyle choices, AIDS victims are often denied access to the sick role.

        1.   Increasing incidence of AIDS among heterosexuals and children is changing this.

           (a) The stigma of dealing with death by AIDS makes the negotiation of an identity particularly difficult.

        2.   The health care system is encountering two major problems with AIDS.

           (a) The first is the cost of care and the other is how to protect medical workers from contracting the disease.

    C   Several steps are needed to cope with AIDS.

        1.   More research funds are needed to develop the technology to stop HIV from becoming AIDS.

        2.   The spread of AIDS to new populations must be stopped.

        3.   Safe sex practices are also required.

        4.   Other basic health policies noted earlier could also help to develop better lifestyles, health care, education and to attack basic social and economic inequities.

VII. The medical technology for organ transplants has led to a series of related social and economic issues.

    A.   Medical technology and ethics collide when deciding who should

receive the rare organ available for transplant.
1. A system of silent triage is usually used.
   (a) Medical experts decide using the patient's psychological stability, probable length of survival and the quality of life after surgery.
    (1) Social class and lifestyle directly influence these factors.

CHAPTER 18

MATCHING

A. Micro level

B. Homicide

C. Primary Health Care

D. Registered Nurses

E. Achieved statuses

F. GROP

G. Social epidemiology

H. Defensive medicine

I. Hospitals

J. AIDS

K. Physicians

L. AMA

M. Macro Level

_____ 1. Emphasis on accessible caregivers over well-trained caregivers.

_____ 2. Mental and physical health.

_____ 3. Distribution of illness and mortality.

_____ 4. Single largest racial differential.

_____ 5. Meaning of health and illness.

_____ 6. Specialized skills and creative freedom.

_____ 7. Awkward dual authority.

_____ 8. Largest category of health care employees.

_____ 9. Capitalist model of medical care.

_____ 10. Rational physicians.

FILL IN THE BLANK QUESTIONS

1. Approximately _____ percent of Americans are uninsured.

2. To the extent that AIDS results from individual choices, many people think that AIDS victims are not entitled to the _____ _____.

3. To a significant extent, _____ is relative rather than absolute; it depends upon

the social situation.

4. Relabeling alcoholism from deviance to sickness is an example of the ____ of deviance.

5. The labeling of illness depends partially on the symptoms, but also on ____ ____ and on socio-historical circumstances.

6. In 1976 the American Psychological Association ____ homosexuality.

7. On the average ____ live seven years longer than ____.

8. Men are more vulnerable to stress because of different ____ ____ ____.

9. In the fifty years of free health care in Britain ____ ____ ____ in mortality have not changed.

10. In the late 1980's there was a ____ in black mortality.

11. Conflict theorists argue that the cause of disadvantage in health is in the ____ ____ in social structure.

12. The sociological imagination suggests that improvements in the nation's health will require changes in ____ ____.

13. Nowhere in the medical profession does the structure of rewards encourage ____ ____.

14. ____ is the government program for the elderly and ____ is the government program for the poor.

15. The fastest growing categories of AIDS victims are ____ and ____.

MULTIPLE CHOICE

1. A symbolic interaction view of our physical self:

    a. bestowed upon persons by structure.
    b. socially constructed.
    c. unrelated to self identity.
    d. unrelated to role behavior.

2. Sociologically, being granted the sick role means that you:

    a. are labeled deviant.
    b. are absolved of the responsibility for meeting your usual role obligations.
    c. no longer have rights.
    d. are completely dependent.

3. This concept has to do with how social statuses relate to the distribution of illness and mortality in a population:

    a. social epidemiology.
    b. role strain.
    c. deviance.
    d. luck.

4. This gender role factor appears to account for the disadvantage that men have in mortality:

    a. biological inferiority.
    b. normative approval for aggression and risk taking.
    c. inferior medical care.
    d. occupational roles.

5. The concept healthy lifestyle is getting considerable attention. Which is NOT included in a consideration of healthy lifestyle?

   a. hours of sleep.
   b. nutrition.
   c. marriage.
   d. smoking and alcohol.

6. Which is NOT true about health as an institution?

   a. complex.
   b. enduring status network.
   c. actors guided by shared norms.
   d. relatively few statuses.

7. Social epidemiology focuses upon the distribution of illness. With regard to this, it is interesting to observe that life expectancy in this country increased from about age ____ in 1900 to about age ____ now.

   a. 30, 90.
   b. 50, 72.
   c. 40, 60.
   d. 50, 60.

8. Structural factors are correlated with differences in life expectancy and death rates. The cause of death demonstrating the single largest racial differential is:

   a. homicide.
   b. cancer.
   c. heart disease.
   d. stroke.

9.   One's lifestyle may include behavior that can have a negative impact on health.   Which is true about the lifestyle of the average male compared to the average female?

   a.   males less likely to drink alcohol and smoke.
   b.   females more likely to skip breakfast.
   c.   males more likely to sleep less.
   d.   females more likely to snack.

10.   The public sometimes criticizes physicians because of their relatively high incomes and the tendency of some physicians to run their practices "too much like a business."   This criticism means that the physician thus violates which characteristic of a professional?

   a.   specialized knowledge.
   b.   identity with others in the field.
   c.   high personal involvement in one's work.
   d.   service to society.

11.   As part of their training, medical interns and residents learn to "GROP" which means to:

   a.   pay dues to the AMA on time.
   b.   willing treat charity patients.
   c.   get rid of patients.
   d.   grant respect to official policies.

12.   The awkward dual authority structure in hospitals often leads to this group being caught in the middle:

   a.   physicians.
   b.   administrators.
   c.   nurses.
   d.   patients.

13. Theory suggests that this factor may account for some people not being sympathetic toward people with AIDS:

    a. too few cases to worry about.
    b. no medical treatment possible.
    c. treatment costs are high.
    d. belief that persons brought trouble on themselves.

14. The labeling perspective on health and illness is useful for understanding:

    a. illness, like deviance, is relative.
    b. illness is always interpreted the same way at all times.
    c. ill people are treated the same regardless of their age.
    d. ill people play no role in the labeling process.

15. Generalizing from what we know about health and mortality for men in this society, which is the best prediction?

    a. the lower one's stress, the less likely to die of heart attacks.
    b. one's occupation is the major determinant of health.
    c. coping skills and a network of intimates reduces health risks.
    d. the impact of stress is the same for men and women.

16. In the theoretical model of poverty and illness presented, poverty is thought to have a direct effect on:

    a. coping.
    b. stress and indirect effect on coping.
    c. low education and on poor health.
    d. coping.

17. This theoretical perspective regards the emphasis on lifestyle as more "blaming the victim:"

    a. structural-functional theory.
    b. conflict theory.
    c. symbolic interaction.
    d. epidemiology.

CHAPTER 18

18. The most radical health-care policy that could be enacted to combat socially structured inequalities would be to:

   a.   increase the number of nurses.
   b.   enact Medicare and Medicaid legislation.
   c.   encourage people to quit smoking.
   d.   equalize life chances.

19. The largest single specialty within sociology:

   a.   sociology of sport.
   b.   criminology.
   c.   family.
   d.   sociology of medicine.

20. About what percent have accepted the medicalization of alcoholism and think that it is a disease?

   a.   60%.
   b.   10%.
   c.   90%.
   d.   30%.

21. By simply taking a vote, the American Psychological Association "demedicalized" this form of deviance in 1976:

   a.   alcoholism.
   b.   homosexuality.
   c.   having AIDS.
   d.   mental illness.

22. About what percent of people who seek treatment for mental illness have adopted an aligning action and voluntarily adopt the label "mentally ill?"

   a.   almost none.
   b.   10%.
   c.   more than 50%.
   d.   30%.

23. Thanks to Medicare, nearly 100% of this group has health insurance:

    a. over age 65.
    b. minorities.
    c. unemployed.
    d. children.

24. About ___% of Americans are covered by private health insurance plans, most of which are provided by their employers.

    a. 25.
    b. 75.
    c. 10.
    d. 50.

25. Which is true about our physical self?

    a. people with the same handicaps react to them the same way.
    b. redefinition of self is a necessary consequence of changes in one's physical condition.
    c. some develop positive self redefinitions following changes to their bodies.
    d. the physical, and not the symbolic meaning of health, counts most.

26. Which is true about life expectancy and death rates in this country?

    a. relatively more whites die of cancer.
    b. relatively more whites die of heart disease.
    c. black males outlive black females.
    d. males experience higher cancer and heart disease rates.

27. In general, people who are disadvantaged in terms of mortality tend to be disadvantaged in illness. The one exception is:

    a. sex.
    b. social class.
    c. minorities.
    d. region.

28. The only industrialized country in the world that does not provide financial coverage for medical care for a majority of its citizens:

    a. United States.
    b. Soviet Union.
    c. West Germany.
    d. Japan.

29. The fastest growing categories of victims of AIDS:

    a. homosexuals.
    b. homosexuals with intravenous drug use.
    c. intravenous drug users.
    d. heterosexuals and children.

30. The sociological imagination suggests that changes are needed to improve the nation's health and most of these changes will have to occur:

    a. in medical and other professional schools.
    b. in hospitals.
    c. in individuals who accept responsibility for their own health.
    d. outside of the medical institution.

ESSAY QUESTIONS

1. Discuss how becoming ill is very much a social process.

2. Why would some individuals gladly seek out the sick role?

3. How has medicine changed from the horse and buggy days?

4. Discuss the social and economic factors behind rising medical costs.

5. Who in American society is at risk and what can be done about it?

Chapter 19
Population

LEARNING OBJECTIVES

1. Define the following: crude birthrate, crude death rate, natural growth rate, fertility, mortality, life expectancy and demography.

2. Fully describe the process called the demographic transition.

3. Compare the West (Europe and America) to the emerging nations of the world regarding the operation of the demographic transition.

4. Recount how the bubonic plague altered economic relationships in feudal society.

5. Discuss the effects of social structure on fertility and on mortality, then discuss the effects of fertility and mortality on social structure.

6. Briefly describe the relationship between population and social structure for Kenya, Europe and China.

7. Differentiate between pronatalism and antinatalism and note the circumstances contributing to each.

CHAPTER 19

8. Explain the vicious circle formed by the interaction of population, the environment and poverty.

9. Outline the three approaches to the problem of population and poverty.

10. Discuss the problem posed by momentum and differentiate between zero population growth and replacement level fertility.

11. Describe current patterns of fertility and mortality in the U.S.

12. Identify the problem posed by immigration in America and note the particular problem posed by Hispanic immigration.

CHAPTER OUTLINE

I.   The Demographic Transition

    A.   Students of <u>demography</u> calculate the world population in 1990 as 5.03 billion and growing rapidly. Since 1950 the world population has doubled leaving millions in poverty. Malnutrition and under-education abound while the world economic system strains toward bankruptcy.

        1.   Three measures of population are important in understanding demographic changes. They are the <u>crude birthrate</u>, <u>crude deathrate</u> and the <u>natural growth rate</u>.

    B.   For most of history, especially the preindustrial era, <u>fertility</u> (childbearing) was barely able to keep up with <u>mortality</u> (death), <u>life expectancy</u> was low and the population grew little or not at all.

        1.   A birthrate of 50 per 1,000 means a lifetime of childbearing for the average woman and precludes any participation in social structures outside the family.

        2.   A mortality rate equally high would mean that a high proportion of the population dies in infancy and death is a frequent visitor to the household.

    C   The <u>demographic transition</u> is the process of reducing birthrates and deathrates set in motion by the industrial revolution. During the transition fertility exceeds mortality and the population growth occurs.

D. In the nations of the west, improvements in nutrition were the first major cause of the decline in mortality. A second major cause centered upon a general increase in the standard of living.

E. Europe and America experienced a long period of population growth.
  1. This rapid growth was offset by technological changes that increased the standard of living, the opening of colonies and the dampening effect of a slowly declining death rate.
  2. The third world nations also grew after World War II when mortality fell and fertility lagged behind.
    (a) Life expectancy has soared with technological and medical advances.
    (b) Additional improvements await changes in the standard of living.

II. Fertility, Mortality and Social Structure

A. The effects of social structure is reflected in the fact that the level of fertility in a society is strongly related to the roles of women. When the family is the source of security, income, social interaction, and even salvation, fertility is high.

B. Fertility also affects the role of women in that the smaller the number of children, the more likely she is to have any involvement outside the family in social, political and economic roles.
  1. Fertility influences age structure. A high fertility rate produces a young population.
  2. Mortality also influences family structure and composition. A high mortality rate produces a fractured family of stepmothers, half-sisters and stepbrothers.

III. Population and Social Structure: Three Examples

A. Kenya is a society with traditional social structures that encourage high fertility.
  1. Kenyan society has several pronatalist, or socially structured,

pressures for childbearing.

2.   A new effective birth control program has had a significant impact on educated urban women who find contraceptives acceptable and available.

(a) Rural areas still reject the <u>antinatalist</u> pressures.

B.   European fertility is too low and Europe as a whole will begin losing population over the next few generations.

1.   There are fears of "population suicide," i.e. an age structure with too many old people and labor force shortages.

2.   Factors influencing fertility include: changed gender roles, reduced importance of the family, low marriage rates and increased dependence upon government support programs.

3.   Pronatalist policies are being used as incentives to encourage fertility. These include paid maternity leave and cheap day care.

(a) These programs are seldom successful.

C   China, with a population of one billion has an aggressive and effective <u>antinatalist</u> policy of structured disincentives for childbearing.

1.   Low fertility will offset the effects of periodic food shortages and free more women to enter the work force, reduce education costs and free more funds for development.

2.   A woman's esteem, security and income depend on the state and the community. Her self-interest lies in her work, not in having children.

3.   In 1986 the birthrate rose slightly reflecting a relaxation of policies.

(a) Enforcing the antinatalist policy was difficult and fear of an older age structure led to a more flexible policy.

IV. The Population Problem: Dilemmas and Approaches

A.   Environmental devastation often exists in combination with high population growth and poverty.

1.   Individuals and nations often destroy the environment to feed the hungry mouths of their children.

2.   Reduced population growth is desirable in combination with social and economic reforms to reduce rural poverty and improve farming. Reducing overconsumption by the affluent

nations and the reduction of third world debt are also essential.

B. High population growth and high poverty levels characterize third world nations.
    1. High birth rates are synonymous with poverty and the lack of economic development.

C. Reducing fertility will ease some problems but not solve them.
    1. Declining fertility is still desirable and necessary.
        (a) Family planning programs bring modern birth control technology to aid many poor nations.
        (b) Economic development also reduces fertility.

D. World fertility has steadily declined since 1970 but the high fertility nations have a population of children or future parents that is much higher than the current generation of parents. This situation is referred to as momentum.
    1. Zero population growth means that the number of births is the same as the number of deaths and results in no population growth.
    2. Replacement level fertility requires that each woman have approximately two children, a replacement for herself and her husband. This insures that each generation will remain the same size.

V. Population in the United States

    A. While our problems are not of the magnitude of some nations, fertility, mortality and migration still influence social structure.

    B. Fertility trends are toward the two-child family with an increasing number of families stopping at one child or remaining childless.
        1. Two other trends are emerging, the first is voluntary childlessness and the other is the rapid increase in non-marital births.

    C. Mortality declined spectacularly during this century. As the mortality rates level off, race and class differences are declining.

    D. Migration is a major factor in American population growth with nearly one-third of our growth coming from <u>immigration</u> instead of <u>natural</u> <u>increase</u>.

1. Most immigrants come legally or illegally from Mexico and Latin America.

2. To stop illegal immigration means closing our borders and deporting the illegal aliens. This is quite difficult to do without offending our own self-image, alienating Mexico and harassing legal Hispanic residents.

3. By 2030 immigration will be the only source of U.S. population growth.

   (a) New government policies are aimed at limiting "chain migration" and giving the government more control over immigration.

MATCHING

A.	Demographic transition	____	1. Studies of population
B.	Bubonic plague	____	2. Fertility
C.	Childbearing	____	3. One measure of society's age structure.
D.	Pronatalist pressures	____	4. Aggressive antinatalist policies.
E.	Death		
F.	Demography	____	5. Primary cause of mortality declines in the west.
G.	Planned Parenthood	____	6. Basis for the fertility decline in Europe.
H.	Role of women	____	7. Kenya.
I.	Crude birthrate		
J.	Withdrawal	____	8. Mortality.
K.	Nutrition	____	9. The fertility level in society.
L.	Anglos	____	10. Majority of illegal immigrants.
M.	Dependency ration		
N.	China		
O.	Hispanics		

FILL IN THE BLANK QUESTIONS

1. Almost all the world population growth in the next few decades will be in the ____ developed nations.

2. The major cause of the decline of fertility in the west was in response to

changed ____ and ____ triggered by the whole transformation of life.

3.   In the west the second most important factor influencing mortality is an increase in the ____ ____ ____.

4.   The higher the fertility, the ____ the population.

5.   Historical data indicates that three-generational families constituted a ____ percentage of all families.

6.   In Kenya a decision to have a child is rational on the ____ level and ultimately irrational on the ____ level.

7.   In Europe, incentive plans to increase the birth rate have had a ____ effect.

8.   The major reasons for declining fertility in Europe are changed ____ ____ and the reduced importance of the ____.

9.   In Europe, it is increasingly evident that people believe that one child provides a reasonable balance of ____ and ____.

10. Twenty-five percent of the next generation will start life in a ____ home.

11. By 1988 fully ____ percent of the women in peak childbearing years were childless.

12. The cycle of environmental destruction is characteristic of high population growth in combination with ____.

13. At the end of the 20th century, the ____ ____ was nearly complete in the West.

14. The main reason for past legal migration exceeding projections was the practice of ____ ____.

15. It is estimated that by 2030 that the only source of population growth will be ____.

MULTIPLE CHOICE

1. The transformation of population since the Industrial Revolution is called:

    a.   demography.
    b.   natural growth rate.
    c.   fertility.
    d.   demographic transition.

2. This measure of population is obtained by dividing the number of births per year by the total population and multiplying by 1000:

    a.   crude birth rate.
    b.   crude death rate.
    c.   fertility.
    d.   natural growth rate.

3. Zero population growth (ZPG) means that:

    a.   births equal deaths.
    b.   no births are allowed.
    c.   each woman is encouraged to have two children.
    d.   the number of deaths are greater than the number of births.

4. The demographic transition in the Third World was different than the earlier transition in the West in that:

    a.   the birth rate fell before mortality.
    b.   mortality rates fell suddenly.
    c.   both birth and mortality fell suddenly.
    d.   the death rate fell, then fertility declined.

5. Immigrants are those who move from one country to another. Which people were favored by immigration policies in the U.S. prior to 1965?

    a.. Hispanics.
    b.   Asians.
    c.   Africans.
    d.   Western and Northern Europeans.

6. Replacement-level fertility requires women to bear approximately _____ children.

    a.   two.
    b.   four.
    c.   five.
    d.   one.

7. A crude birth rate of 50 per 1000 population really means that there are really about 153 potential mothers.   By age 45, each woman will bear _____ children:

    a.   2.
    b.   3.
    c.   6-10.
    d.   5.

8. A crude death rate of 50 per 100 population means that:

    a.   the society has many older people.
    b.   the average life expectancy is about 75 years.
    c.   many people die in infancy.
    d.   one is old at 35.

9. What was the major factor contributing to the first major cause of mortality decline in the West?

    a.   better medicine.
    b.   improvements in nutrition.
    c.   general increase in the standard of living.
    d.   changes in hygiene.

10. A dependency ratio of 1.0 means that:

    a.   there are ten producers for each dependent.
    b.   there is one producer for each dependent.
    c.   there are ten dependents for each producer.
    d.   there is one dependent for every two producers.

11. Kenya has the highest crude birth rate in the world at this time (52) and a crude death rate of 12. This means that its natural growth rate is:

   a. 64.
   b. 4.0.
   c. 12.
   d. 40.

12. "Chain migration" is illustrated by:

   a. moves from small cities to larger ones.
   b. slaves brought to this country against their wishes.
   c. new citizens bringing relatives to this country.
   d. citizens of the U.S. moving to other countries.

13. A number of hypotheses have developed about the decline in the death rate, the decline in fertility, and the development of industrialization. What is considered to be the main and direct cause of the fertility reduction in the West?

   a. reduced mortality.
   b. greater industrialization.
   c. changed values and aspirations.
   d. government intervention.

14. It has been strongly suggested that meaningful reductions in the birth rate are not possible without modern contraceptives. Which of these methods was primarily responsible for the decline in fertility in Europe?

   a. coitus interruptus.
   b. condoms.
   c. diaphragms.
   d. delaying the age of marriage.

15. Your text says that when the family is the major source of security and interaction,

    a.   mortality is high.
    b.   mortality is low.
    c.   fertility is low.
    d.   fertility is high.

16. What is the relationship between high fertility and poverty in the developing countries today?

    a.   high fertility causes poverty.
    b.   poverty causes high fertility.
    c.   no simple cause and affect relationship.
    d.   there is no relationship between these concepts.

17. What does the Kenya case study suggest about the likely impact of high fertility in the Third World?

    a.   positive for women and society.
    b.   negative for women and society.
    c.   positive for society, negative for women.
    d.   positive for women, negative for society.

18. The key to understanding the high birth rate in Kenya lies in the fact that:

    a.   mothers gain status through continual childbearing.
    b.   fathers are considered more masculine if their wives get pregnant.
    c.   children are an economic asset.
    d.   families gain status by having many daughters.

19. The present world population is about 5 billion. By the time this generation of college students reaches reaches retirement age, the world population will be about:

    a. 1 billion.
    b. 9 billion.
    c. 20 billion.
    d. 30 billion.

20. For the world as a whole in 1990, the crude birth rate and crude death rate were approximately:

    a. 28 and 10.
    b. 10 and 10.
    c. 10 and 20.
    d. 20 and 20.

21. A population increase of 1.8 percent per year doesn't seem like very much. If the population of the world does grow at this rate, it would double every:

    a. 100 years.
    b. 500 years.
    c. 5 years.
    d. 39 years.

22. These people became the scapegoat and received blame for the plague that swept the world during the 14th century:

    a. religious leaders.
    b. Jews.
    c. blacks.
    d. academics and scientists.

23.   What is the "good news" and the "bad news" with regard to current population trends in the world?

      a.   fertility is declining but the momentum is still bad.
      b.   fertility is declining most among nations that have made the least steps toward development.
      c.   fertility is still increasing at alarming rates but may soon begin to decline.
      d.   fertility is still high but the death rates will soon fall dramatically.

24.   At the present time, the population of the People's Republic of China is about:

      a.   five hundred million.
      b.   one hundred million.
      c.   two hundred and fifty million.
      d.   one billion.

25.   The natural growth rate for the world's population in 1990 continues to alarm some people.   The highest rate is found in:

      a.   Europe.
      b.   North America.
      c.   Africa.
      d.   Asia.

26.   If current trends continue, immigrants to this country will continue to come mainly from:

      a.   Western Europe.
      b.   Eastern Europe.
      c.   Asia.
      d.   Central America or Mexico.

27. The demographic transition in the Non-West began when the crude death rate fell in a very dramatic fashion. About when did this occur?

    a. 1750.
    b. 1850.
    c. 1900.
    d. 1940.

28. What is the official population policy today in Europe and in China?

    a. pronatalism for both.
    b. antinatalism for both.
    c. pronatalism for Europe and antinatalism for China.
    d. pronatalism for China and antinatalism for Europe.

29. Which strategies have been used in successful programs like China's?

    a. family planning.
    b. economic development.
    c. manipulation of incentives.
    d. family planning, economic development, and manipulation of incentives.

30. The People's Republic of China enacted a one-child per family policy after the communists came to power in 1949. Looking to the future, it is likely that:

    a. families will continue to have but one child.
    b. rural families will continue to oppose the policy.
    c. population policy will become less important.
    d. policy makers will forget population policy and concentrate on economic growth.

ESSAY QUESTIONS

1. Describe the effect of the bubonic plague on economic relationships in Feudal society.

2. Explain the vicious circle formed by the interaction of poverty and

population.

3. Account for the long term fertility decline in the U.S. population.

4. Discuss the relationship between fertility and social structure in Europe.

5. Describe the relationship between declining fertility and momentum in the U.S.

Chapter 20
Urban
Living

LEARNING OBJECTIVES

1. Recount the factors associated with the development of the preindustrial, industrial and late-industrial city.

2. Use the concentric zone and multiple nuclei theories to depict the patterns of urban growth.

3. Discuss how changes in communication and transportation have influenced the shape of the city.

4. Differentiate between metropolitan and nonmetropolitan.

5. Contrast western urban centers with third world cities.

6. Describe how Tonnies, Durkheim and Weber characterized urbanization.

7. Compare Wirth's "Urbanism as a Way of Life" with the compositional and subcultural views.

8. Discuss the consequences of urban living on the personal integration of family, friends and neighbors, and upon life satisfaction.

9.   Explain what is meant by the term suburbanism and note its role in metropolitan decline, nonmetropolitan resurgence and the move to the sun belt.

10. Describe how rural and urban areas differ by reference to the stereotypes of each.

11. Describe the impact on the city of poverty, racial segregation and a declining tax base.

12. Contrast the past World War II suburban life styles to the suburbs of today.

13. What is urban revitalization and what problems arise when it occurs?

14. Describe how political decisions in business and government contributed to the decline of the central city and gave rise to suburbs.

15. Discuss how the principle of independent political control has led to major problems in American cities.

16. Note the processes by which urban revitalization can occur.

CHAPTER OUTLINE

I.   Urban Growth and Change

     A.   Urban growth began in earnest in the last century and has resulted in over one-half of the U.S. population and one-quarter of the world population being urban.

     B.   The preindustrial city is dominated by primary production with the emerging cities being largely trading and administrative centers.
          1.   The preindustrial city was quite small with a concentration of life into crowded, teeming squares. Segregation was not between business and family but between kinds of businesses.
          2.   The city was a dominant force in the development of art and culture while also being a crowded, filthy and dangerous place.

C. The <u>industrial city</u> was a result of industrial production in urban factories that occurred in the 19th century.

  1. The density of these cities occurred as cities grew around urban factories where the majority still walked to work. There was a dense crowding of working class housing around the factories.

  2. A lack of transportation and communication facilities led to the development of the central business district that became the hub of the city.

  3. Spatial analysis of early urban growth indicated that cities grew in a series of expanding rings or concentric zones.

D. The <u>late-industrial city</u> was shaped by the greater ease of transportation and communication, the change of tertiary production and the rise of single unit housing.

  1. The contemporary central city is dominated by white collar industries, services and retail trade.

    (a) The shift to tertiary production has eliminated the industries that shaped the development of the 20th century U.S. city.

    (b) Modern telecommunications allow for even greater geographic dispersion of activities.

  2. Modern cities are most likely to be characterized by the <u>multiple nuclei</u> model.

    (a) Cities arising after 1950 easily adapt to this model while older cities suffer major declines in the C.B.D.

      (1) These older cities face the vexing issues of urban revitalization.

E. A <u>metropolitan area</u> is a county that has a city of 50,000 or more in it plus any neighboring counties that are significantly linked, economically or socially with the core county.

  1. A <u>nonmetropolitan area</u> is a county that has no major city in it and is not closely tied to a county that does have such a city.

  2. Three-fourths of Americans live in metropolitan areas, with most living in suburban rings.

    (a) Most recent metropolitan growth has occurred in the Sunbelt while the Northwest and the Midwest have lost population.

      (1) Most nonmetropolitan residents live in the Midwest

or the South.

3. Progressive urbanization occurred in the U.S. until the decade of 1970.
    (a) Urbanization has returned as the dominant pattern in the 1980's with the most rapid growth occurring in the South and West.

F. Third world cities are predominantly trade and administrative centers which are growing at staggering rates as rural residents migrate to find greater economic opportunities.

II. Urban Life in the United States

A. Urbanization is the process of population concentration and is distinct from the unique mode of life developed in cities called urbanism.

B. Western theoretical views of urban life are strongly anti-urban with classic and contemporary theorists believing that the quality of life in the cities is significantly worse.
    1. Early writers developed analytical typologies of urban and rural differences.
        (a) Tonnies use the terms gemeinschaft and gesellschaft to differentiate between rural primary group ties and urban secondary relationships.
        (b) Weber saw a parallel shift from tradition to rationalism.
        (c) Durkheim saw the social cohesion of rural society arising from the similarity of the residents while urban solidarity was based more upon a high division of labor and interdependence.
    2. Wirth's "Urbanism as a Way of Life" was the classic negative statement about the consequences of urban living. Wirth argued that the size, heterogeneity and density of urban life led to a breakdown of norms and morality.
    3. Compositional theorists see the city as a mosaic of small worlds that are manageable and knowable for the individual.
    4. The subcultural view argues that the size of the urban center allows for the formation of a critical mass of people who share an uncommon set of norms.

C. Evidence on the personal integration in urban settings indicates that urbanites are no more lonely, alienated or estranged from their family and friends than others.

   1. The neighborhood is a weak group because urban dwellers have been freed from the necessity of liking the people they live next to.

     (a) Urban people do have intimates but they are unlikely to live in the same neighborhood with them.

   2. Urban living offers the availability of quality services, entertainment, culture, etc. These constitute important incentives to many who prefer to live in urban centers.

     (a) Noise, crowding, fear of crime and expensive living act to deter many.

     (b) Most people prefer to live close to a large city, not in one.

     (c) Urbanites develop a cool indifference to nonintimates.

III. The Other Americans

A. Most Americans do not live in the massive urban centers like New York or San Francisco. They live in suburbs and small towns.

B. Suburbs are changing from bedroom communities to retail shopping centers and major manufacturing centers.

   1. Suburbia is becoming more crowded and less dominated by families with young children.

     (a) Suburban life styles now include singles, childless married couples and the elderly.

       (1) Townhouses, duplexes and apartments are often typical.

       (2) Older suburbs continue to deteriorate and renters are more frequent than before.

   2. Suburban living increasingly brings with it problems of high housing costs, fragmented local governments, transportation and crime.

   3. Most of today's rural and urban differences are more stereotypic than real.

C   The nonmetropolitan population of the U.S. continues to grow.
    1.   The young leave for urban employment while the elderly remain behind.
    2.   Community involvement, affordable housing, open space and low crime rates attract people to nonmetropolitan living.
        (a) Small town residents enjoy less crime, more conformity and greater social control.
            (1) Lifestyle options are often limited due to a lack of a critical mass of nonconformers.
    3.   The city is still the major source of innovation and change but modern transportation and telecommunications have greatly reduced rural-urban differences.

IV.   The Political Economy of Spatial Distribution.

    A.   Land is a critical form of capital and land owners manipulate economic and political processes to maximize their profit.
        1.   Zoning ordinances are political arrangements used to restrict land use and to protect property values.
        2.   Urban growth is fostered because it increases demand for property and increases property values.
            (a) Private interest groups favoring growth usually dominate.
                (1) Regulatory agencies and planning commissions are often captured by these interests.

    B.   Home owning is an important, if only modest, form of power.
        1.   Recently the U.S. has been characterized by suburban growth and decay in the central city.
            (a) Redlining is the process of not loaning money for home mortgages in some areas and making loans in other areas.
                (1) This leads to systematic disinvestment producing urban decay.
            (b) Government loan policies favor new home construction in the suburbs that favor working and middle-class white home owners.
            (c) Low income federal housing projects led to greater inner city segregation by race and class.
                (1) Working-class poor were displaced by these projects.

C. Political decisions have resulted in systematic disinvestment in central city housing.
  1. Poverty became concentrated in city centers.
  2. Central cities have increasingly become racially segregated as many people of color moved to the cities for work and suburbanization became an Anglo phenomenon.

D. The fragmented urban political jurisdictions were based upon the principle of independent (local) control.
  1. As a consequence, most urban centers lack a unifying authorrity structure.
   (a) City and suburban political boundaries limit the sharing of social resources and isolate the well-off from the poor.
   (b) Fragmentation benefits the affluent suburbs governed by local control.
    (1) They are able to escape a strong central authority and thus can protect their individual property values.
   (c) A centralized government and taxing authority could develop a unified tax plan balancing off affluent suburbs with inner city needs.

E. Some decaying urban centers are being revitalized through municipal development and gentrification.

MATCHING

A.   Post industrial city

B.   Subcultural view

C.   Multiple nuclei

D.   Redlining

E.   CBD

F.   Defensible space

G.   Automobile

H.   Gemeinschaft

I.   Urban revitalization

J.   Metropolitan County

K.   Gesellschaft

L.   Suburban segregation

M.   Trade and administrative centers

N.   Preindustrial city

O.   Compositional model

P.   Wirth

____ 1.   Classic statement of the negative consequences of urban life

____ 2.   Area of highest land values

____ 3.   Eliminated need for housing for the working poor.

____ 4.   Discrimination by insurance companies and mortgage lenders.

____ 5.   Urban sprawl or horizontal growth

____ 6.   The diminishing role of the central business district.

____ 7.   Rural society dominated by primary group ties.

____ 8.   Fragmented government.

____ 9.   Critical mass.

____ 10. Characteristics of third world cities.

FILL IN THE BLANK QUESTIONS

1. Urban growth and development is largely a story of the ___ century.

2. In preindustrial cities, living conditions were so poor that the ___ could not keep up with the ___.

3. The industrial city was a product of a ___ economy and a relatively ___ labor force.

4. Most of the current nonmetro growth in American cities is in the ___ or the ___.

5. Durkheim, Tonnies and Weber believed that the quality of human social life was significantly worse in the ___.

6. Compositional theorists envision the city as a mosaic of small worlds that are ___ and ___.

7. Compositional theory argues that deviants, etc., are ___ ___ the cities rather than ___ ___ them.

8. There is no evidence that urban people are disproportionately ___, ___ or ___ from family and friends.

9. Urban people do have intimates and they are ___ to live in the same neighborhood.

10. City and suburban ___ ___ limit the sharing of social resources and isolate the well-off from the poor.

11. Suburbanization was a disproportionately ___ phenomenon.

12. For the most part urban revitalization is aimed at ___ ___ neighborhoods.

13. By the year 2000, ___ ___ will be the largest city in the world.

14. Political decisions have been made that resulted in systematic ___ in central city housing.

CHAPTER 20

15.   Most people who ____ in the suburbs ____ in the suburbs.

MULTIPLE CHOICE

1.   Which is a characteristic of the industrial but not the preindustrial city?

      a.   a central business district.
      b.   largely trading and administrative centers.
      c.   most smaller than 300,000.
      d.   segregation based upon kinds of business.

2.   The industrial city, in contrast to the preindustrial and late-industrial city:

      a.   was safer with less crime.
      b.   had much more advanced transportation systems.
      c.   saw much more crowding.
      d.   had yet to develop a central business district (CBD).

3.   A metropolitan area in the U.S. is a county with a major city of at least:

      a.   100,000 population.
      b.   50,00 population.
      c.   10,000 population.
      d.   20,000 population.

4.   The term coined by Frederick Tonnies to mean dominated by a primary group ties:

      a.   primary group.
      b.   gemeinschaft.
      c.   gesellschaft.
      d.   rural.

5.   Which is true about neighbors and neighborhoods?

      a.   neighborhood is usually heterogeneous.
      b.   neighbors are seldom strangers.
      c.   city living requires that people like the people they live next to.
      d.   most feel free to ask neighbors for large favors.

6. According to surveys, ____ are the least preferred places to live in the U.S.

    a. suburbs.
    b. cities.
    c. rural communities.
    d. farms.

7. Spatial analysis of early industrial cities suggest that they approximated a series of rings or concentric zones. Zone 1 was the:

    a. low class residential district.
    b. central business district.
    c. wholesale and light manufacturing district.
    d. medium class residential district.

8. Mexico City has been cited in the text as the most dramatic example of third-world urbanization. Which of these statements is true about Mexico City?

    a. largest city in the world by the year 2000.
    b. most of its growth due to migration to the city.
    c. almost no standard housing.
    d. very adequate level of public services.

9. Which is NOT a characteristic of urban life as seen by Louis Wirth:

    a. greater conformity.
    b. cold and calculating personal styles.
    c. heightened awareness of subcultures.
    d. more crime.

10. Some stereotyping of urban and rural life does occur. Research does show that some differences are real. For example, urban people are less likely to:

   a. oppose labor unions.
   b. help a stranger in trouble.
   c. be opposed to abortions.
   d. disapprove of legalizing marijuana.

11. While many would like to move to the suburbs, some who do live there find it very inconvenient. A major inconvenience factor is the lack of:

   a. good schools.
   b. adequate fire and police protection.
   c. public transportation.
   d. desirable housing.

12. At present, suburbia as a concept in the U.S. includes:

   a. communities with virtually no problems.
   b. little major manufacturing and retail centers.
   c. increased diversity.
   d. suburbs as bedroom communities.

13. Urban theory suggests that the new cities are shaped more like a multiple nuclei than concentric zones or sectors. Which is NOT a characteristic of these new cities in contrast to older industrial cities:

   a. CBD vital as a retail trade center.
   b. less dominated by the CBD.
   c. vertical growth diminished.
   d. huge, climate-controlled, pedestrian-safe suburban malls.

14. This sociologist is given credit for developing the classic statement of the negative consequences of urban life for the individual and for social order:

   a. Louis Wirth.
   b. Frederick Tonnies.
   c. Max Weber.
   d. Emile Durkheim.

15. Emile Durkheim thought that social cohesion in urban centers would be provided by:

    a. similarity (mechanical solidarity).
    b. a shift from traditional to rationalism.
    c. an increase in gemeinschaft.
    d. division of labor (organic solidarity).

16. What factor does the subculture theory of urbanism emphasize?

    a. a critical mass of people is needed for subcultures to develop.
    b. population density.
    c. importance of primary groups.
    d. population size.

17. In his influential book Urbanism as a Way of Life, Louis Wirth proposed that a breakdown of the normative and moral fabric would be caused by:

    a. size.
    b. size and homogeneity.
    c. size, heterogeneity, and density.
    d. homogeneity and density.

18. Which is an emphasis of compositional theory:

    a. essential aspects of urban living include size and density.
    b. consequences include opportunity to develop subcultures.
    c. the city is a mosaic of small managable worlds.
    d. higher crime caused by normative confusion.

19. How does the urban population of the U.S. compare with that of the Third World?

    a. the U.S. is more urban than the rest of the world.
    b. the U.S. is less urban than the rest of the world.
    c. the U.S. and the rest of the world are equally urban.
    d. most of the U.S. population and most of the world's population live in cities of 100,000 or more.

20. Because of this problem, all areas of the industrial city were densely packed:

    a.   poor planning.
    b.   corrupt politicians.
    c.   inadequate transportation.
    d.   the desire to know one's neighbor.

21. Considerable research has been conducted to determine the actual effects of urban living on personal integration. The research indicates that living does:

    a.   narrow the kin group while expanding the number of non-kin intimates.
    b.   significantly reduce the number of intimate ties.
    c.   make people feel more lonely.
    d.   make people less likely to develop a hard shell against non-intimates.

22. The composition of many U.S. cities is changing. Included among those who are least likely to stay in the central cities are:

    a.   blacks.
    b.   white middle class.
    c.   elderly.
    d.   poor whites.

23. Since 1980, most of the population growth has been in the:

    a.   West.
    b.   South or West.
    c.   East.
    d.   North.

24. Surveys find that fear of crime is highest i

    a.   rural communities.
    b.   suburbs.
    c.   small cities.
    d.   cities over 1 million population.

25. Preindustrial cities can be compared to rural villages of the same period. Which is NOT a characteristic of preindustrial cities?

   a.   a major force for the development of art, culture and technology.
   b.   a crowded, filthy, and dangerous place.
   c.   lower death rates than rural areas.
   d.   human and animal waste turned streets into sewers.

26. Which is NOT an advantage of city life:

   a.   less expensive housing.
   b.   medical services.
   c.   entertainment.
   d.   culture.

27. A key difference between third world cities and their postindustrial counterparts is that:

   a.   postindustrial cities are growing more rapidly.
   b.   third world cities never were industrial centers.
   c.   postindustrial cities have large shadow labor forces.
   d.   only postindustrial cities provide working-class jobs.

28. What is the distinction, if any, between urbanization and urbanism?

   a.   both refer to population concentration.
   b.   both refer to a way of life.
   c.   the former refers to concentration and the latter to a way of life.
   d.   the former refers to a way of life and the latter to population concentration.

29. A popular conception of urban life held by persons in the Western world:

   a.   sophisticated and aware.
   b.   less inequity and vice.
   c.   little corruption of youth.
   d.   a good place to rear a family.

30.   In contemporary capitalism, ____ may be the critical class distinction.

   a.   large incomes from stocks and bonds.
   b.   important contacts with top government leaders.
   c.   home ownership.
   d.   being a white-collar worker.

ESSAY QUESTIONS

1.   Discuss how the quality of life in preindustrial and industrial cities differed from today's urban centers.

2.   Why are rural-urban differences declining?

3.   Discuss the process of urban revitalization, who wins and who loses?

4.   Explain how political decisions and the vested interests of land owners have significantly altered the face of the urban landscape.

5.   How do the patterns of urbanization in the U.S. differ in the emerging nations of the world?

Photo Essay:
Information
Technology

1. Three important aspects of the impact of information technology are
   ____ ____, ____ ____ and ____.

2. As a result of information technologies we are linked to the rest of the
   ____.

3. Improved communication will probably reduce regional and international
   ____ ____.

4. While information technology has vastly increased the number of people
   to whom we are linked, the content of our relationships is still determined
   by ____ ____.

5. One major consequence of information technology is an increased ability
   to ____ and ____.

6. In the electronic cottage ____ ____ ____ can be carried out at home.

7. Working at home may create family ____.

8. Working at home requires more ____ ____ and ____.

9. Many people get more work done, enjoy their work more and experience
   more self esteem when working at the ____ than from working at ____.

10. Some believe that home work will be another means to oppress ____.

1. The entire contents of the twenty-volume Oxford English Dictionary can be stored on:

    a.   ten CD-ROM disks.
    b.   one CD-ROM disk.
    c.   five CD-ROM disks.
    d.   twenty CD-ROM disks.

2. Which is NOT a contribution of computers and word processing?

    a.   ease of library research.
    b.   ease of moving sentences and sections in papers.
    b.   spelling checker.
    d.   doubles creativity.

3. About how many college students have access to information technology?

    a.   10%.
    b.   very large portion.
    c.   25%.
    d.   relatively few.

4. This enables one to send a paper and receive a corrected copy back from another person in as little as an hour:

    a.   SOCIOFILE.
    b.   spellcheck.
    c.   electronic mail.
    d.   thesaurus.

5. Your text says that one of the most important consequences of the new information technology is:

    a.   better marriages.
    b.   increased control and monitoring.
    c.   fairer taxes.
    d.   world peace.

6. Not included as a new kind of worry brought about by information technology:

    a.   new forms of crime.
    b.   realization that one can know too much.
    c.   new defense worries.
    d.   new inefficiencies.

7. The outcome of new technologies will depend primarily upon:

    a.   social institutions.
    b.   computer hardware.
    c.   computer software.
    d.   the physical environment.

8. Which is NOT promised as part of the "electronic cottage?"

    a.   be able to work at home.
    b.   more electric appliances for homes.
    c.   live in smaller communities.
    d.   more flexible working hours.

9. Which isn't an obstacle to the development of the "electronic cottage" in the near future?

    a.   inadequate technology.
    b.   people miss personal contacts at work.
    c.   children may be underfoot.
    d.   may create family stress.

10. Telecommuting is most likely to be a blessing to:

    a.   women.
    b.   blue collar workers.
    c.   upper-level white collar workers.
    d.   routine clerical workers such as data entry.

Chapter 21
Collective Behavior

LEARNING OBJECTIVES

1. Differentiate between collective actions and social movements.

2. Use the concepts of dominant emotion and organizational form to develop six categories of crowds.

3. Outline the key concepts of contagion, convergence and emergent norm theories.

4. Use the three theories of crowd behavior to analyze the British soccer tragedy and the 1967 Newark race riot.

5. Critique each of the theories of crowd behavior.

6. Identify the role played by the mass media in promoting collective action.

7. Compare and contrast relative deprivation theory with mobilization theory.

8. Differentiate between a sociial movement, a social movement organization (SMO), indigenous SMO's, professional SMO's, a conscience constituency and and countermovements.

9. Describe the kinds of people who tend to be members of social movements.

10. Discuss what is meant by the concept of frame alignment and note the tactics used by social movements.

11. Note the advantages of bloc mobilization as opposed to micro mobilization.

12. Recount the factors associated with social movement success and note why free riders are a problem.

13. Use the preceding terms and concepts to analyze the gay rights and environmental movements as SMO's.

CHAPTER OUTLINE

I. Collective behavior is nonroutine action by an emotionally aroused gathering of people who face an ambiguous situation.

    A. A crowd is a gathering of people who are reacting to a nonroutine event.
        1. Lofland divides crowds on dimensions of dominant emotion and organizational form.
            (a) The forms of dominant emotion are fear, hostility and joy.
            (b) The organizational forms are those of a crowd and a mass.

    B. Theories of crowd behavior include contagion theory, convergence theory and the emergent norm theory.
        1. Contagion theory stresses crowd situations that lead to the development of unamimous and intense feelings and behaviors that are at odds with the usual predispositions of the individual participants. It explains only one type of crowd behavior: the escalating response.
        2. Convergence theory contends that the cause, or triggering event, for crowd action selectively draws people who share a common set of predispositions.
            (a) The convergence of many like-minded people provides the critical mass for their predispositions to be put into action.

          (b) The major criticism against convergence theory is that it ignores the heterogeneity of most crowds.

3.   Emergent-norm theory suggests that each crowd is governed by norms developed and validated by group processes within the crowd. That is, the crowd develops a shared conviction that their behavior is appropriate to the situation.

          (a) The process is similar to the one used by which we negotiate encounters.

               (1) The crowd improvises an answer to the question "what is going on here?"

               (2) The crowd frames the encounter and decides upon appropriate action.

               (3) The crowd will act with unity as the members maintain the appearance of group conformity.

4.   Emergent norm theory enjoys great support because of its ability to explain a variety of crowd behaviors despite apparent differences especially in different historical and cultural contexts.

5.   Collective behavior theories can lend insight into such diverse occurrences as the 1983 Bedford gang rape, the 1967 Newark race riot or the tearing down of goal posts after a football game.

II.   A social movement is an ongoing, goal-directed effort to change social institutions from the outside.

    A.   Relative deprivation theory sees social movements arising when social change causes people to redefine their deprivation as illegitimate and fixable. It is also known as breakdown theory.

        1.   Deprivation is not absolute; instead, one is deprived relative to some other group or circumstance. Deprivation only leads to social movements when it is defined as illegitimate.

        2.   Criticisms point out that the theory fails to specify the conditions under which relative deprivation will lead to social movements.

          (a) Empirical evidence fails to clearly support the notion that deprivation leads to action.

    B.   Resource mobilization theory suggests that social movements

develop when organized groups are competing for scarce resources.
1.   Organization is thus the key to creating a social movement.
        (a) Social movements are rational attempts to change the
            distribution of societal resources.
            (1) The emphasis on organization leads some to call this
                solidarity theory.
2.   A major shortcoming is to overlook the role played by anger
        and spontaneity as triggers for social movements.

C   An integration of relative deprivation and resource mobilization
        theory allows for an emphasis on the emotional and spontaneous
        triggering events as well as the organization needed to sustain a
        social movement.
        1.   Resource mobilization theory is the dominant theoretical
                perspective.
                (a) If it is broadened to include emotionality, etc. it can be
                    a usefully complete model.

D.   A social movement entails many diverse organizations, each pur-
        suing the same general goal. These social movement organizations
        (SMO) can be divergent and also competitors.
        1.   Diversity is usually seen as being functional to the overall
                social movement.
                (a) Indigenous SMO's are characterized by volunteer staffing
                    while professional SMO's have paid staff.
                (b) Indigenous organizations maintain a sense of urgency and
                    generate publicity while professional organizations solicit
                    support from a conscience constituency.
                (c) Professional SMO's are more stable and better at coalition
                    building.
                (d) Indigenous SMO's maintain a sense of urgency which
                    propels the organization into more innovative tactics.
                (e) The environmental movement has gained strength from a
                    combination of professional and indigenous organizations.

E.   Mobilization is the process by which a unit gains significantly in the
        control of assets it previously did not control.
        1.   Micro-mobilization is the recruitment of individuals. It
                usually entails a process of frame alignment.

(a) The tactics of frame alignment are <u>frame</u> <u>bridging</u>, <u>frame</u> <u>amplification</u>, <u>frame</u> <u>extension</u> and <u>frame</u> <u>transformation</u>.

2. <u>Bloc</u> <u>Mobilization</u> is the recruitment of other organizations to the social movement.

3. Social movements are helpful when existing linkages exist between the aggrieved parties.

(a) Dense social networks are especially helpful.

4. Free riders rob the organization of needed support.

5. The gay rights movement is a typical SMO, complete with gender and class divisions.

(a) Despite the divisions, the organization has the goal of defining gay identities, establishing them as legal, achieving civil rights equality, securing family rights and challenging the ascription of gender roles in society.

(1) AIDS networks increase solidarity among gays and lesbians.

F. There are a number of success factors associated with social movements.

1. The demands of the movement must be consistent with the broader values of society.

2. The movement has the support of influential third parties or demonstrates that its demands benefit other groups as well.

3. The movement's demands are concrete and focused.

4. The movement can exert pressure on those responsible without harming third parties.

5. The movement adopts techniques the authorities are unfamiliar with.

6. Neutral third parties interested in restoring harmony are present.

7. The movement's demands are negotiable.

8. The movement's demands are reasonable in that they do not demand a fundamental redistribution of income and power.

9. The movement seeks to veto proposed policies rather than to implement new ones.

10. The moveement is large enough to organize for conflict, but is not perceived as a serious threat to the dominant group.

G. <u>Counter</u> <u>movements</u> seek to resist or reverse the change advocated by a social movement; they are defenders of the status quo.

III.   Social Movements are related to collective behavior in that instances of collective behavior keep the issues before the public and help maintain a sense of grievance.

IV.   The mass media contributes to nonroutine collective behavior by publicizing events, demonstrating techniques and providing rationales.

    A.   The mass media can also be vital to social movements by portraying dramatic events and providing authoritative sources.
       1.   SMO's can also plan events so that they coincide with news cycles (timing) and fit into established news nets.

MATCHING

A.	Contagion Theory	____ 1.	Crowds are moved to extremes and irrational behavior through a vicious cycle of exchange.
B.	Eco-terrorists		
C.	Resource mobilization theory	____ 2.	Seeks to maintain the status quo.
D.	Collective actions	____ 3.	Actions prompted by nonroutine events.
E.	Micro-Mobilization		
		____ 4.	A process by which SMO's recruit other organizations.
F.	Relative deprivation theory		
G.	Frame alignment	____ 5.	Another name for breakdown theory.
H.	Gay rights		
		____ 6.	An attempt to explain quiet as well as rowdy crowds.
I.	Counter movement		
J.	Social movements	____ 7.	Deliberate, organized attempts to change social institutions.
K.	Emergent Norm Theory		
		____ 8.	Another name for solidarity theory.
L.	Volunteers		
M.	Crowd	____ 9.	Best general theory of collective behavior.
N.	Bloc mobilization		
		____ 10.	Indigenous SMO.
O.	Convergence theory		

FILL IN THE BLANK QUESTIONS

1. ____ theory attempts to explain only one kind of crowd behavior: the

excalating response.

2. According to ____ theory, there is no process within crowds: nothing new develops.

3. The ____ ____ theory of crowd behavior is broader than either contagion or convergence theory.

4. The British soccer tragedy was best explained by reference to ____ theory.

5. Federal agencies have changed their environmental policies due to the ____ of the environmental constituency.

6. Bridging, amplification, extension and transformation are all tactics assoc-ated with ____ ____.

7. The mass media contributes to non-routine collective action by ____ ____, ____ ____ and ____ ____.

8. According to ____ ____ theory, the key to social movements is in the rela-tionship between expectations and rewards.

9. According to ____ ____ theory, solidarity rather than alienated, disenchan-ted individuals is the key to the formation of social movements.

10. ____ ____ are almost always right wing in orientation.

11. ____ theory is particularly appropriate for understanding counter movements.

12. ____ ____ is a vital mechanism through which resource poor organi-zations can generate public debate over their grievance.

13. The most important schism in the gay rights movement is between ____ and ____.

14. People who benefit from social movements but don't participate are called ____ ____.

15. Crowds may be categorized on two dimensions, they are: ___ ___ and ___ ___.

MULTIPLE CHOICE

1. Which is a characteristic of social movements?

    a.   spontaneous.
    b.   broad based.
    c.   short term.
    d.   confined to a particular place and time.

2. Collective behavior actions are episodes that are prompted by an ambiguous situation. Which of these should NOT be included as examples of collective actions?

    a.   temporary crowds.
    b.   the gay rights movement.
    c.   minor riots.
    d.   disorganized protests.

3. A kind of crowd in which hostility is the dominant emotion present:

    a.   riot.
    b.   reaction to a disaster.
    c.   religious revival meeting.
    d.   spring break riots.

4. An organized attempt to change social institutions which is carried on outside of legitimate channels:

    a.   mob.
    b.   riot.
    c.   social movement.
    d.   rumor.

5.   A relatively large number of people drawn to a common location by some non-routine event:

        a.   organization.
        b.   public.
        c.   crowd.
        d.   social movement.

6.   ____ refers to the procedure through which SMOs attract individual new members.

        a.   social movement.
        b.   micromobilization.
        c.   contagion.
        d.   bloc mobilization.

7.   Which is NOT a characteristic of collective behavior ?

        a.   ambiguous situations.
        b.   collective planning.
        c.   emotional arousal.
        d.   being limited to a specific time and place.

8.   The 1989 British soccer tragedy is cited in the text as an example of:

        a.   panic crowd.
        b.   race riot.
        c.   social movement.
        d.   crowd without emotion.

9.   Which is NOT an example of a social movement effort?

        a.   Affirmative Action hiring requirements.
        b.   gay rights demonstrations.
        c.   antinuclear protests.
        d.   antiabortion organizations.

10.   ____ is the process by which a unit gains significantly in the control of assets it previously did not control.

   a.   Contagion.
   b.   Social movement.
   c.   Mobilization.
   d.   Breakdown.

11.   Many men and women in the U.S. participate in the current gay movement. The major schism within this movement is between:

   a.   men and women.
   b.   whites and blacks.
   c.   lower-class and middle-class people.
   d.   charismatic leaders and rank-and-file members.

12.   "White-hot mobilization" is reached when:

   a.   almost everyone is totally dedicated to the movement.
   b.   when religious leaders assume command.
   c.   whites oppose minorities.
   d.   mobilization is just getting started.

13.   Contagion theory of crowds emphasizes:

   a.   extreme and irrational behavior caused by a vicious cycle of exchanges.
   b.   selective factors that draw people together who share common norms.
   c.   the convergence of like-minded people.
   d.   that crowds are governed by norms that emerge from within the crowd.

14. Which ISN'T true of convergence theory?

    a.   attempts to explain only rowdy crowds.
    b.   shows concern for triggering events.
    c.   ignores process within crowds.
    d.   concern for conformity of crowd behavior.

15. Which is true about emergent norm theory?

    a.   has its roots in group conformity.
    b.   ignores or downplays importance of interpersonal exchange processes.
    c.   completely ignores the role of contagion.
    d.   narrower than either contagion or convergence theory.

16. Which is true of the relative-deprivation theory of social movements?

    a.   often called "solidarity theory."
    b.   movements occur when conditions get better.
    c.   movements occur when conditions worsen.
    d.   emphasis is on intolerable gap between rewards and expectations.

17. In mobilization theory, the major independent variable or factor leading to a social movement is:

    a.   competition between organized groups.
    b.   social change.
    c.   discontent.
    d.   social disorganization.

18. In micromobilization theory, frame transformation:

    a.   is equivalent to a religious conversion.
    b.   targets people who have similar interests.
    c.   is equivalent to consciousness raising.
    d.   broadens the frame or scope of the social movement.

19. Recently, the male homosexual mvoement has been galvanized by:

    a. police brutality.
    b. AIDS.
    c. more frequent discrimination.
    d. action by the American Psychological Association.

20. The triggering event in the 1976 Newark riot:

    a. an assault on a white youth.
    b. arson in a white neighborhood.
    c. the rape of a white woman.
    d. police arresting a black cab driver.

21. Which is NOT a tactic of frame alignment in mobilization?

    a. frame bridging.
    b. frame amplification.
    c. frame destruction.
    d. frame extension.

22. The strategy pursued by professional SMOs of the environmental movement:

    a. in the courts and legislatures.
    b. sit-ins.
    c. "monkey wrenching."
    d. sabotage.

23. Counter social movements often develop when it begins to look like a controversial social movement mobilizes sufficiently to make it look at least possible that its goals will be realized. Most of the counter social movements in the U.S. today came from:

    a. mental health profession.
    b. academic community.
    c. corporate leadership.
    d. the rightwing.

24. Which was true of the anti-ERA movement?

   a. refused to engage in bloc mobilization.
   b. stated that it was opposed to equality as a societal goal.
   c. stated that it supported traditional values.
   d. closely tied to disadvantaged groups.

25. If you wanted to sabotage a social movement, theory suggests that you should:

   a. "stonewall" the issue and do nothing.
   b. encourage mobilization.
   c. encourage general, diffuse goals.
   d. eliminate poverty and injustice.

26. Explains how the black community in Newark first defined the riot as a protest and later as a white attack:

   a. emergent-norm theory.
   b. convergence theory.
   c. contagion theory.
   d. mobilization theory.

27. Research shows that the most effective social movements share these two characteristics:

   a. conservative ties, homogeneity.
   b. overlapping ties, little publicity.
   c. heterogeneity, overlapping ties.
   d. homogeneity, overlapping ties.

28. Indigenous SMOs are generally better than professional ones at:

   a. soliciting resources from outside disadvantaged groups.
   b. keeping aggrieved group supportive.
   c. coalition building.
   d. providing continuity.

29. Generalizing from relative deprivation theory, which condition is least likely to result in relative deprivation?

    a. level of living increases faster than expectations.
    b. level of living drops relative to expectations.
    c. both level of living and expectations are improving but expectations rise faster.
    d. expectations rise faster than level of living.

30. The gay rights movement began in Germany in the late 19th century and it began in the U.S. in the:

    a. 1940s.
    b. 1920s.
    c. 1960s.
    d. 1980s.

ESSAY QUESTIONS

1. Discuss how a social movement differs from a crowd.

2. Use convergence theory, contagion theory and emergent norm theory to analyze the Neward race riot.

3. Describe all of the factors associated with the success of the environmental movement.

4. Discuss the role played by the mass media in collective actions.

Chapter 22
Social Change: an International Perspective

363

9. Describe the impact on the U.S. for foreign capital penetration and the Third World debt crisis.

10. Define the terms of glasnost and peristroika and discuss their impact on the U.S.S.R. and their former satellites.

11. Outline the rationale for the sociological study of war and peace.

12. Describe the HSI and discuss the relationship between inequality and suffering.

CHAPTER OUTLINE

I. Inequality and Development

    A. Countries are classified on the basis of their position in a world of inequality.
        1. The <u>first world</u> consists of the core of wealthy nations who dominate the world system.
        2. The <u>second world</u> consists of the former European communist countries, their allies and dependents.
        3. The <u>third world</u> consists of the less developed nations characterized by poverty and political weakness.

    B. <u>Modernization theory</u> is a functionalist theory of development based upon Western experiences, and assumes that developing nations can follow the Western path to wealth through industrialization.
        1. Critics point out that the fortuitous circumstances of Western development are not present for the non-industrialized nations of today's world.

    C. <u>World systems theory</u> is a Marxist analysis of the relationship between developing and developed countries, and suggests that the economic dominance of core societies will prevent the progress of peripheral societies.
        1. <u>Core societies</u> are rich and powerful nations that are economically diversified and relatively free of outside control.
        2. <u>Peripheral societies</u> are poor and weak, with highly specialized economies over which they have little control.

3. The economic relationship becomes one of perpetual economic colonialism.

4. A major insight of world systems theory is that individual economies cannot be understood in isolation.

   (a) World wide economic activity is regulated only by market forces like supply and demand.

      (1) Western capitalist nations and multinational corporations continue their 200 year domination of the world economic system.

II. First World Prosperity and Third World Poverty

A. International inequality is the result of conflict and competition within an international capitalist economic system.

   1. Nations in the periphery have little control over their economies and quickly become dependent as alliances are formed between their weak governments, multinational corporations and local elites.

      (a) Three forms of dependency are industrial dependency, foreign capital dependency and the classic banana republic.

         (1) Often local governments must guarantee no unionization and grant major tax concessions to attract foreign investment.

      (b) The consequences of dependency are likely to be sectoral inequality, income inequality, growing authoritarianism and increasing conflict.

   2. The power of foreign capital penetration is so great that it can also increase poverty, inequality and political instability.

III. Three Case Studies

A. China was consistently isolated from the Western economic influences by national policies, wars and revolution.

   1. The communist victory in 1949 has produced a ruling communist party and an authoritarian government.

   2. In efforts to enhance development, equality and to solidify power important reforms were utilized. They are the <u>Great Leap Forward</u>, the <u>Great Proletarian Revolution</u> and the <u>Four Modernizations</u>.

(a) These revolutionary reforms are moving China toward the direction of free enterprise and economic development.

(b) China's large work force makes it an ideal target for foreign capital.

    (1) The strong government means a more equitable agreement with foreign investors than other weaker nations.

(c) The tension between strict Marxist-Leninism and capital investment is currently discouraging investment.

B.   Nicaragua spent most of this century under U.S. domination, both economic and military.

    1.   The Sandinista forces overthrew the U.S. backed military dictatorship of Somoza and established a less repressive and more participatory government.

    2.   Development strategies center upon independence from foreign investment and establishing secondary industries.

    3.   The U.S. attempted to overthrow the Sandinista government by supporting armed intervention in combination with economic sanctions.

    (a) This caused major economic and social difficulties.

    4.   Despite electing a new government, Nicaragua remains a dependent Third World nation.

    (a) Renewed investment will again only aid those in power.

C.   The Soviet Union dominates the second world.

    1.   As a communist nation, it sought to become a modern, efficient egalitarian society through the collective ownership of the means of production.

    (a) The government is highly authoritarian.

    (b) The Soviet Union combined strong defense industries with military domination of Eastern Europe and much of the Third world.

    (c) Glasnost and peristroika have brought major changes to the U.S.S.R. and its satellites.

        (1) Multiple political parties, democracy and elections are flourishing.

        (2) A decline in productivity and political order has also occurred which is calling into question the very future of the Soviet Union.

    2.   Economic development lags far behind the West and the Soviet Union is not a serious threat to the world capitalist system.

        (a) Major economic restructuring is required to make Soviet goods competitive on the world market.

D.   The U.S. emerged as the dominant capitalist nation through its participation in World War II.

    1.   The internationalization of our economy has led to a reduced manufacturing output and a smaller share of the world market.

    2.   Other core nations have increased their competitive edge and our dominance has weakened.

    3.   The U.S. has become a debtor nation, lost money on Third World loans and has become vulnerable to foreign capital penetration.

        (a) The U.S. must decide where to invest limited dollars.

            (1)   Should we invest in Eastern Europe or in the Third World nations?

        (b) The U.S. must also decide if it wishes to continue to use military intervention to maintain world markets.

I V. War, Peace and Sociology

A.   After 45 years the cold war is over and the threat of world war has diminished.

    1.   Smaller nations with nuclear arms, guerrilla warfare and limited regional conflicts now need more attention.

B.   Sociologists can contribute to world peace through studying the decision making and organizational cultures that lead to war.

    1.   Studies of programs to reduce inequality and data on volatile social movements can also help the peace effort.

CHAPTER 22

MATCHING

A.   Banana Republic

B.   First world

C.   Second world

D.   Third world

E.   Individual Responsibility
     System

F.   Predictions

G.   Diffusion

H.   HSI

I.   Development

J.   Glasnost

K.   Conflict functionalism

L.   Sectoral inequality

M.   World systems theory

N.   Modernization theory

O.   Iron Rice Bowl

____ 1. Excessive investment in urban industrialization.

____ 2. Development is a natural, evolutionary process.

____ 3. Sees the international economic system through Marxist eyes.

____ 4. United States and Western Europe.

____ 5. Poverty and political weakness.

____ 6. The former Soviet Bloc Nations.

____ 7. Columbia.

____ 8. Increasing productivity and living standards.

____ 9. Criteria used to assess human suffering.

____ 10. Chinese capitalism.

FILL IN THE BLANK QUESTIONS

1.   A key insight gained from world systems theory is "our ____ is their ____.

2. Nations on the periphery have little control over their ___ and quickly become ___.

3. More than two-thirds of the world's population live in countries with extreme or high measures of ___ ___.

4. It seems that in coming decades, competition between the ___ and ___ will be overshadowed by that between the ___ and the ___.

5. The three forms of dependency are ___ dependency, ___ ___ dependency and the classic ___ ___.

6. The power and wealth of the U.S. make us a ___ ___.

7. The new process of reforming the Soviet economy is called ___.

8. The undesirable consequences of foreign capital penetration into Third World economies serves to exacerbate ___ , ___ and ___ ___.

9. On a global basis ___ operates with less restraint than it does within any single nation.

10. ___ ___ ___ theory is a conflict analysis of the economic relationships between developed and undeveloped countries.

11. With the decline of Soviet Communism, the ___ ___ may be the new source of peril.

12. The ___ ___ are aimed at ridding society of low productivity associated with the "iron rice bowl" system.

13. The major reason for foreign capital penetration is ___ ___.

14. Nicaragua aimed to develop ___ industries that will manufacture raw materials into ___ goods.

15. Except for arms sales, the ___ ___ has not been a serious competitor in the world Capitalist system.

CHAPTER 22

MULTIPLE CHOICE

1. Not included as a facet of development:

    a.   productivity.
    b.   life expectancy.
    c.   education.
    d.   military power.

2. The ____ consists of rich nations with high degrees of economic and political autonomy.

    a.   Third world.
    b.   Second world.
    c.   First world.
    d.   Developing world.

3. ____ societies dominate the world system.

    a.   Peripheral.
    b.   European.
    c.   Third world.
    d.   Core.

4. The classic form of dependency in the world system:

    a.   industrial dependency.
    b.   foreign capital dependency.
    c.   cultural dependency.
    d.   "banana republic."

5. This has replaced the "iron rice bowl" system in China:

    a.   wooden bowl system.
    b.   private ownership of land.
    c.   individual responsibility.
    d.   equality for all.

6. Which is NOT a tie that binds together the nations of the world in the international system?

   a. economic.
   b. Christianity.
   c. joint dependency on the oceans and air.
   d. fear of the bomb.

7. Included in the First World:

   a. U.S., Japan, Western Europe.
   b. U.S., Japan, China.
   c. Japan, China, Russia.
   d. U.S., China, Japan.

8. Countries that would like to duplicate China's "four modernizations" would emphasize:

   a. agriculture, science, industry, defense.
   b. religion, education, science, defense.
   c. large families, science, education, defense.
   d. social services, sciences, sports, education.

9. Which of these isn't a Third World country?

   a. West Germany.
   b. China.
   c. Zambia.
   d. Nicaragua.

10. If a political candidate in a developing country calls for a "Great Leap Forward" comparable to the one in China, he/she seeks:

    a. better athletic programs.
    b. decentralized planning.
    c. war with the weakest neighbor.
    d. more exports.

11. The Soviet Union development goal that calls for political openness:

    a.   glasnost.
    b.   great leap forward.
    c.   perestroikea.
    d.   four modernizations.

12. Countries in the First World have about ___% of the world's population and consume about ___% of the world's energy.

    a.   25%, 25%.
    b.   15%, 15%.
    c.   15%, 55%.
    d.   75%, 25%.

13. Modernization theory is linked to:

    a.   structural-functional theory.
    b.   symbolic interaction theory.
    c.   conflict theory.
    d.   world system theory.

14. The primary reason that less-developed countries have not followed our footsteps to modernization:

    a.   they face a different social and economic context.
    b.   they were initially too backward.
    c.   corrupt government.
    d.   ethnocentrism.

15. The prevailing ideology that supports the world systems division of labor:

    a.   socialism.
    b.   communism.
    c.   capitalism.
    d.   modernization.

16. Which is not an element of modernization theory?

    a. simple to complex societies.
    b. development as a natural unfolding of evolutionary process.
    c. exploitation by industrial core.
    d. structural-functional theory.

17. The chief actors in the world system's free market economy:

    a. educated elite.
    b. military leaders.
    c. small business managers.
    d. nation states.

18. Historically, the wealthy countries in the world system have switched from a ____ strategy to a strategy of ____ in their relationships with poor countries.

    a. industrial dependency, banana republic.
    b. foreign capital dependency, banana republic.
    c. foreign capital dependency, equal partner.
    d. banana republic , industrial dependency or foreign capital dependency.

19. The percent of world energy used and percent of gross world product produced by the Second World:

    a. 50 percent.
    b. 80 percent.
    c. 65 percent.
    d. 25 percent.

20. The estimated population of China the largest Third World country:

    a. one billion.
    b. fifty million.
    c. five hundred million.
    d. ten billion.

21.   Soldiers from this country occupied Nicaragua from 1919 to 1933:

    a.   Germany.
    b.   U.S.
    c.   France.
    d.   Spain.

22.   Nicaragua's development plan in the 1980s:

    a.   aid to contras.
    b.   increased exports of raw materials.
    c.   development of mixed economy.
    d.   an embargo on U.S. goods and services.

23.   The largest country in the First or Second Worlds:

    a.   Russia.
    b.   China.
    c.   Canada.
    d.   U.S.

24.   The richest country in the First World is:

    a.   Switzerland.
    b.   United States.
    c.   Germany.
    d.   Italy.

25.   Which characteristic is not descriptive of core societies?

    a.   highly specialized economies.
    b.   rich.
    c.   powerful.
    d.   autonomous.

26. Which kind of export would be least expected from a classic "banana republic?"

    a.   bananas.
    b.   cotton.
    c.   automobiles.
    d.   oil.

27. A negative effect of dependence on economies of Third World countries:

    a.   emphasis on manufactured goods.
    b.   income inequality.
    c.   expansion of the middle class.
    d.   emphasis on local investment of surplus capital.

28. This country has experimented with limited capitalism but now stands alone in its strict endorsement of Marxist-Leninism:

    a.   People's Republic of China.
    b.   East Germany.
    c.   Soviet Union.
    d.   Nicaragua.

29. The HSI is positively correlated with:

    a.   life expectancy.
    b.   GNP per capita.
    c.   percentage of labor force in agriculture.
    d.   cars per capita.

30. Given current trends, the HSI will continue to be highest in the:

    a.   northern hemisphere.
    b.   southern hemisphere.
    c.   eastern hemisphere.
    d.   western hemisphere.

CHAPTER 22

ESSAY QUESTIONS

1. What is the status and the future of the Soviet Union and Eastern Europe?

2. Explain the differences between the three "worlds."

3. Describe the relationship between foreign investment and dependency.

4. How might modernization theory be seen as ethnocentric?

5. Describe the basic assumptions of world systems theory.

CHAPTER 1

MATCHING

1.	B	p.11	5.	J	p.17	8.	L	p.12
2.	N	p. 21	6.	C	p. 8	9.	E	p.10
3.	I	p.15	7.	A	p. 7	10.	O	p. 9
4.	D	p. 8						

FILL IN THE BLANK

1. Positivism p.7
2. thesis, antithesis, synthesis p.8
3. Weber p.9
4. manifest p.13
5. disorganization, poverty p.6
6. poverty, inequality p.7
7. Weber, Marx's p.10
8. social problems, reform, scientific method p.11
9. practical, theoretical p.11
10. Stability, harmony p.13
11. functions, dysfunctions p.13
12. macro, micro p.20
13. symbolic interaction p.18
14. sociological imagination p.4
15. critical, systematic p.4

MULTIPLE CHOICE

1.	a,	4	11.	b,	5	21.	a,	11
2.	c,	4	12.	a,	10	22.	c,	20
3.	b,	6	13.	a,	17	23.	b,	10
4.	d,	7	14.	b,	15	24.	d,	23
5.	c,	8	15.	a,	8	25.	a,	4
6.	c,	10	16.	c,	9	26.	d,	21
7.	b,	4	17.	d,	17	27.	b,	4
8.	d,	4	18.	a,	13	28.	a,	6
9.	a,	8	19.	a,	6	29.	a,	10
10.	b,	8	20.	d,	11	30.	a,	9

ANSWER KEY

CHAPTER 2

MATCHING

1.	H	p. 29	5.	B	p. 34	8.	K	p. 53
2.	G	p. 32	6.	N	p. 36	9.	F	p. 31
3.	O	p. 29	7.	M	p. 35	10.	I	p. 37
4.	A	p. 37						

FILL IN THE BLANK

1.   common sense p. 28
2.   objective, critical, empirical p. 28
3.   description, explanation p. 29
4.   data, patterns, theories, hypotheses pp. 29-31
5.   biographical anonymity, personal harm p. 52
6.   incidence, trends, differentials p. 36
7.   Interviewing, participating, observing p.37
8.   participant observation p. 37
9.   representative subset p. 33
10. many flaws p. 47
11. lone, known p. 50
12. experiment p. 42
13. operational definition p. 32
14. more, less, more p. 44
15. lower, higher p. 43

MULTIPLE CHOICE

1.	a,	28	11.	c,	36	21.	c,	52
2.	a,	29	12.	c,	39	22.	d,	44
3.	c,	32	13.	a,	33	23.	c,	50
4.	b,	32	14.	c,	34	24.	b,	52
5.	d,	36	15.	c,	39	25.	c,	31
6.	b,	39	16.	d,	37	26.	a,	42
7.	a,	31	17.	d,	41	27.	c,	36
8.	c,	32	18.	d,	42	28.	c,	37
9.	c,	33	19.	c,	51	29.	a,	54
10.	a,	35	20.	d,	34	30.	a,	28

CHAPTER 3

MATCHING

1.	K	p. 63	5.	N	p. 71	8.	E	p. 69
2.	M	p. 68	6.	A	p. 65	9.	L	p. 66
3.	G	p. 65	7.	H	p. 76	10.	F	p. 76
4.	J	p. 60						

FILL IN THE BLANK

1. problem solving, relative, social product   p. 59
2. linguistic relativity hypothesis   p. 64
3. dominant cultural theme   p. 70
4. sanctions   p. 67
5. symbol   pp. 79-80
6. mores   p. 66
7. material culture   p. 58
8. language   p. 61
9. Conflict   p. 59
10. Sociobiology   p. 62
11. ethnocentric   p. 60
12. good family life   p. 73
13. self-fuifillment, work, consumerism   p. 74
14. accepted   p. 75
15. vocabularies, folkways   p. 75

MULTIPLE CHOICE

1.	a,	58	11.	a,	68	21.	a,	69
2.	c,	66	12.	b,	72	22.	b,	74
3.	b,	68	13.	a,	65	23.	d,	78
4.	c,	61	14.	a,	71	24.	b,	61
5.	d,	68	15.	a,	71	25.	b,	75
6.	d,	58	16.	b,	63	26.	c,	76
7.	c,	66	17.	c,	60	27.	b,	74
8.	b,	67	18.	a,	59	28.	a,	75
9.	d,	68	19.	a,	74	29.	b,	70
10.	a,	60	20.	d,	76	30.	c,	66

ANSWER KEY

PHOTO ESSAY: Environmental Damage: A Cultural Product

FILL IN THE BLANK

1.   3 5   p. 83
2.   culture, social structure   p. 83
3.   consumption, waste   p. 84
4.   utility   p. 85
5.   jobs, prosperity   p. 85
6.   biocentric   p.85
7.   political, economic   p. 86
8.   everybody   p. 86
9.   vested interest   p. 87
10. state   p. 87

MULTIPLE CHOICE

1.   b,   8 3
2.   d,   8 3
3.   b,   8 3
4.   d,   8 3
5.   c,   8 4
6.   b,   8 5
7.   b,   8 5
8.   a,   8 5
9.   c,   8 6
10. b,   8 7

CHAPTER 4

MATCHING

1.   F p. 99   5.   A p. 92   8.   H p. 103
2.   D p. 93   6.   L p. 93   9.   N p. 90
3.   G p. 90   7.   J p. 100   10. O p. 103
4.   K p. 96

CHAPTER 4, continued

FILL IN THE BLANK

1. consumers, producers   p. 107
2. black   p. 92
3. agriculture   p. 102
4. status   p. 90
5. social structures   p. 90
6. constraining, enabling   p. 90
7. role strain   p. 93
8. basic human needs   p. 96
9. status, role and institution   p. 90
10. interdependence   p. 97
11. social structure   p. 109
12. surplus   p. 102
13. sanctions   p. 94
14. resources, opportunities   p. 95
15. negotiated order   p. 95

MULTIPLE CHOICE

1.	a,	90	11.	c,	94	21.	c,	97
2.	c,	92	12.	c,	96	22.	b,	102
3.	c,	90	13.	c,	102	23.	a,	104
4.	c,	96	14.	a,	100	24.	d,	110
5.	b,	101	15.	b,	101	25.	b,	90
6.	a,	90	16.	d,	105	26.	d,	98
7.	c,	96	17.	c,	101	27.	c,	92
8.	a,	93	18.	b,	103	28.	d,	98
9.	b,	90	19.	a,	105	29.	b,	96
10.	c,	99	20.	d,	96	30.	a,	93

CHAPTER 5
MATCHING I

1.	E	p. 136	5.	I	p. 131	8.	C	p. 121
2.	K	P. 120	6.	D	p. 122	9.	B	p. 122
3.	G	p. 114	7.	N	p. 116	10.	M	p. 123
4.	H	p. 121						

ANSWER KEY

CHAPTER 5, continued

MATCHING II

1.	E	p. 133	5.	O	p. 124	8.	A	p. 134
2.	J	p. 130	6.	G	p. 116	9.	K	p. 124
3.	B	p. 131	7.	C	p. 131	10.	H	p. 132
4.	M	p. 134						

FILL IN THE BLANK

1.   competition, conflict pp. 115-116
2.   small groups p. 129
3.   norm of reciprocity p. 114
4.   cooperation p. 115
5.   secondary groups p. 124
6.   size p. 118
7.   efficiency p. 133
8.   voluntary associations p. 128
9.   cohesion, solidarity p. 129
10. social structure, dependency p. 116
11. exclusion p. 120
12. behavior, perceptions and values p. 117
13. expressive activity p. 122
14. social cohesion p. 119
15. all channel network p. 119

MULTIPLE CHOICE

1.	c,	115	11.	a,	131	21.	b,	125
2.	a,	121	12.	b,	127	22.	a,	128
3.	a,	122	13.	c,	128	23.	b,	130
4.	b,	124	14.	c,	130	24.	a,	132
5.	c,	133	15.	c,	132	25.	b,	116
6.	a,	116	16.	d,	124	26.	a,	123
7.	b,	116	17.	a,	119	27.	a,	129
8.	b,	121	18.	c,	124	28.	b,	136
9.	b,	121	19.	d,	119	29.	d,	132
10.	a,	128	20.	c,	121	30.	b,	126

CHAPTER 6

MATCHING I

1.	C	p. 159	5.	J	p. 144	8.	F	p. 146
2.	D	p. 160	6.	I	p. 146	9.	B	p. 146
3.	G	p. 145	7.	E	p. 144	10.	H	p. 157
4.	A	p. 150						

MATCHING II

1.	C	p. 158	5.	M	p. 147	8.	G	p. 142
2.	E	p. 146	6.	K	p. 152	9.	H	p. 145
3.	L	p. 147	7.	N	p. 149	10.	D	p. 159
4.	A	p. 157						

FILL IN THE BLANK

1. Identity salience hierarchy   p. 149
2. structural   p. 149
3. values, personalities   p. 150
4. adolescence, adulthood   p. 153
5. unstable, untrained, child to staff   p. 155
6. personality, role   p. 152
7. generalized other   p. 147
8. interaction   p. 145
9. role identities   p. 149
10. Anticipatory socialization   p. 155
11. motivations, normative   p. 142
12. socialization   p. 152
13. parents, friends   p. 156
14. self concept   p. 156
15. self esteem, self esteem   p. 156

CHAPTER 6, continued

MULTIPLE CHOICE

1.	a,	144	11.	a,	148	21.	b,	159
2.	c,	152	12.	c,	155	22.	d,	142
3.	d,	145	13.	a,	143	23.	a,	160
4.	a,	152	14.	d,	149	24.	c,	160
5.	a,	152	15.	c,	154	25.	c,	144
6.	b,	155	16.	a,	156	26.	c,	147
7.	a,	142	17.	b,	157	27.	a,	153
8.	a,	145	18.	b,	157	28.	d,	147
9.	a,	149	19.	b,	144	29.	b,	155
10.	d,	158	20.	a,	145	30.	a,	161

CHAPTER 7

MATCHING

1.	C	p. 177	5.	J	p. 183	8.	H	p. 178
2.	L	p. 170	6.	E	p. 167	9.	F	p. 170
3.	K	p. 174	7.	B	p. 172	10.	D	p. 179
4.	A	p. 182						

FILL IN THE BLANK

1. social status p. 167
2. dialectic p. 170
3. Thick description p. 170
4. interaction p. 168
5. frame p. 172
6. nonverbal cues p. 174
7. identity negotiation p. 173
8. identity work p. 179
9. story telling p. 183
10. withdrawing, pass p. 182

MULTIPLE CHOICE

1.	d,	167	11.	d,	183	21.	c,	181
2.	c,	170	12.	d,	183	22.	a,	182
3.	a,	172	13.	b,	168	23.	d,	184
4.	a,	178	14.	c,	168	24.	c,	184
5.	d,	179	15.	b,	174	25.	a,	167
6.	b,	182	16.	c,	177	26.	c,	179
7.	a,	169	17.	d,	178	27.	b,	183
8.	a,	174	18.	a,	181	28.	d,	171
9.	b,	175	19.	d,	166	29.	b,	187
10.	a,	179	20.	d,	174	30.	b,	184

ANSWER KEY

CHAPTER 8

MATCHING I

1.	G	p. 202	5.	D	p. 197	8.	C	p. 206
2.	L	p. 202	6.	H	p. 206	9.	O	p. 209
3.	B	p. 202	7.	F	p. 202	10.	J	p. 206
4.	K	p. 209						

MATCHING II

1.	G	p. 212	5.	J	p. 212	8.	L	p. 203
2.	N	p. 204	6.	F	p. 211	9.	E	p. 210
3.	A	p. 211	7.	M	p. 212	10.	C	p. 212
4.	H	p. 202						

FILL IN THE BLANK

1. formal, informal   p.   192
2. internalize   p.   192
3. nonconformity, deviance   p.   193
4. ritualism   p.   195
5. differential association, deviance, deviance, conformity   p.   196
6. inequality   p.   210
7. so label   p.   198
8. primary deviance   p.   198
9. self esteem   p.   197
10. male, young, minority group members   p.   204
11. Lower, middle   p. 206
12. abnormal   p. 201
13. anomie   p. 194
14. substantive law   p.   210
15. Less   p.   199

CHAPTER 8, continued

1.	a,	192	11.	c,	204	21.	a,	216
2.	c,	193	12.	b,	210	22.	a,	211
3.	a,	193	13.	a,	194	23.	d,	213
4.	c,	198	14.	b,	195	24.	a,	214
5.	b,	204	15.	b,	195	25.	a,	198
6.	b,	210	16.	b,	196	26.	d,	202
7.	b,	192	17.	a,	210	27.	d,	199
8.	a,	195	18.	c,	212	28.	c,	202
9.	b,	209	19.	a,	202	29.	b,	205
10.	a,	202	20.	d,	203	30.	b,	214

ANSWER KEY

CHAPTER 9

MATCHING

1.	N	p. 222	5.	O	p. 226	9.	G	p. 244
2.	A	p. 223	6.	J	p. 231	10.	L	p. 224
3.	F	p. 224	7.	D	p. 239	11.	I	p. 245
4.	B	p. 225	8.	M	p. 240	12.	C	p. 233

FILL IN THE BLANK

1. caste, class   p. 222
2. individuals   p. 234
3. False consciousness, class consciousness   p. 224
4. class, status, power   p. 224
5. rewards/incentives   p. 231
6. intergenerational mobility   p. 222
7. Conflict   p. 233
8. coordination, authority   p. 235
9. managers   p. 235
10. real income, public services   p. 230
11. occupational, individual   p. 236
12. indirect inheritance model   p. 237
13. achievement motivation, intelligence   p. 237
14. Ideology   p. 239
15. working   pp. 242-4

MULTIPLE CHOICE

1.	b,	222	11.	b,	247	21.	c,	227
2.	b,	223	12.	c,	248	22.	a,	229
3.	d,	226	13.	a,	224	23.	b,	241
4.	d,	237	14.	c,	231	24.	c,	240
5.	a,	247	15.	c,	234	25.	c,	237
6.	b,	247	16.	a,	234	26.	a,	224
7.	c,	227	17.	c,	249	27.	a,	237
8.	a,	229	18.	a,	222	28.	b,	243
9.	b,	239	19.	a,	227	29.	b,	242
10.	a,	245	20.	d,	226	30.	b,	240

CHAPTER 10

MATCHING I

1.	M	p. 262	5.	L	p. 258	8.	O	p. 258
2.	F	p. 254	6.	K	p. 254	9.	H	p. 258
3.	I	p. 257	7.	J	p. 263	10.	A	p. 261
4.	B	p. 259						

MATCHING II

1.	F	p. 263	5.	K	p. 264	8.	A	p. 268
2.	G	p. 263	6.	D	p. 273	9.	O	p. 270
3.	E	p. 268	7.	B	p. 271	10.	H	p. 268
4.	M	p. 260						

FILL IN THE BLANK

1. social p. 254
2. majority, minority p. 257
3. acculturation p. 257
4. social distance p. 258
5. Prejudice, discrimination pp. 258-261
6. authoritarianism, scapegoating p. 259
7. female headed families, low earnings p. 266
8. involuntary, earliest p. 264
9. Native Americans p. 273
10. Jews p. 270
11. residential segregation, intermarriage pp. 273-4
12. blacks p. 274
13. indirect inheritance model, majority rule p. 262
14. Asians p. 271
15. black p. 266

CHAPTER 10, continued

MULTIPLE CHOICE

1.	b,	254	11.	b,	262	21.	b,	261
2.	a,	258	12.	b,	264	22.	c,	264
3.	d,	257	13.	b,	258	23.	d,	274
4.	b,	259	14.	c,	259	24.	c,	268
5.	d,	262	15.	a,	258	25.	d,	255
6.	d,	263	16.	b,	263	26.	b,	263
7.	d,	258	17.	b,	258	27.	a,	266
8.	b,	272	18.	a,	257	28.	c,	268
9.	a,	257	19.	a,	260	29.	b,	270
10.	c,	257	20.	b,	261	30.	d,	269

CHAPTER 11

MATCHING

1.	E	p. 303	5.	B	p. 300	8.	A	p. 288
2.	I	p. 282	6.	K	p. 282	9.	F	p. 296
3.	L	p. 282	7.	C	p. 300	10.	D	p. 303
4.	H	p. 284						

FILL IN THE BLANK

1. gender roles   p. 282
2. children   p. 288
3. gendered jobs, different qualifications, discrimination   p. 289
4. Men, women   p. 294
5. small low-profit   p. 291
6. 65   p. 289
7. social institutions   p. 292
8. conservative, religiously fundamentalist   p. 297
9. support, prove   p. 305
10. segmented labor market   p. 298
11. Pornography   p. 306
12. nurturance, sharing, intuition   p. 303
13. Expectation states theory   p. 299
14. quid pro quo   p. 300
15. role strain   p. 304

MULTIPLE CHOICE

1.	b,	282	11.	a,	302	21.	d,	291
2.	d,	284	12.	c,	293	22.	d,	285
3.	b,	297	13.	a,	285	23.	c,	282
4.	a,	300	14.	c,	286	24.	c,	300
5.	b,	289	15.	b,	297	25.	a,	282
6.	b,	289	16.	b,	300	26.	b,	283
7.	c,	284	17.	d,	302	27.	a,	286
8.	a,	282	18.	b,	298	28.	d,	296
9.	c,	290	19.	d,	283	29.	c,	304
10.	d,	295	20.	a,	286	30.	c,	302

ANSWER KEY

CHAPTER 12

MATCHING

1.	F	p. 323	5.	B	p. 315	8.	H	p. 328
2.	J	p. 311	6.	A	p. 311	9.	I	p. 319
3.	M	p. 313	7.	L	p. 314	10.	O	p. 331
4.	C	p. 330						

FILL IN THE BLANK

1. social structure p. 310
2. cohort p. 311
3. four p. 312
4. job, marrying, raising a family p. 314
5. roles, absence p. 317
6. healthy p. 317
7. youth p. 318
8. image, demeanor, argot p. 319
9. 17 p. 320
10. elderly p. 322
11. female, minority p. 324
12. children, elderly p. 327
13. 9 p. 332
14. employment, quality of work p. 319
15. working p. 321

MULTIPLE CHOICE

1.	b,	311	11.	a,	331	21.	c,	333
2.	a,	311	12.	c,	327	22.	b,	313
3.	d,	313	13.	a,	323	23.	a,	318
4.	a,	317	14.	a,	325	24.	c,	331
5.	d,	319	15.	c,	329	25.	a,	311
6.	b,	314	16.	d,	330	26.	c,	314
7.	d,	310	17.	b,	328	27.	b,	313
8.	a,	310	18.	b,	328	28.	a,	317
9.	d,	311	19.	d,	310	29.	c,	317
10.	d,	325	20.	d,	313	30.	b,	332

CHAPTER 13

MATCHING

1.	I	p. 347	5.	E	p. 351	8.	K	p. 365
2.	F	p. 342	6.	A	p. 342	9.	H	p. 348
3.	G	p. 356	7.	N	p. 361	10.	C	p. 366
4.	L	p. 344						

FILL IN THE BLANK

1. family, kin group p. 341
2. Marriage p. 341
3. economic opportunity p. 358
4. personal freedom, economic security p. 353
5. unmarried p. 353
6. night care p. 354
7. very close p. 358
8. cohabitation p. 351
9. egalitarian p. 351
10. sex p. 352
11. multiple problems p. 359
12. parenthood p. 354
13. gender role agreement p. 353
14. divorce p. 365
15. parent p. 366

MULTIPLE CHOICE

1.	a,	341	11.	c,	351	21.	b,	347
2.	d,	341	12.	a,	344	22.	d,	355
3.	b,	342	13.	b,	349	23.	d,	351
4.	c,	342	14.	c,	353	24.	c,	344
5.	d,	344	15.	b,	352	25.	a,	343
6.	b,	344	16.	a,	356	26.	c,	344
7.	d,	341	17.	c,	349	27.	c,	344
8.	b,	342	18.	d,	361	28.	a,	360
9.	a,	349	19.	a,	340	29.	a,	351
10.	b,	348	20.	b,	341	30.	c,	354

ANSWER KEY

CHAPTER 14

MATCHING

1.	O	p. 390	5.	H	p. 381	8.	M	p. 373
2.	D	p. 389	6.	I	p. 381	9.	F	p. 392
3.	C	p. 374	7.	B	p. 388	10.	L	p. 391
4.	N	p. 379						

FILL IN THE BLANK

1. parental, labor, social control p. 370
2. parental involvement p. 380
3. conformity, independent thinking p. 374
4. inequality p. 391
5. hidden curriculum p. 391
6. increases, decreases p. 378
7. mental ability, cultural deprivation p. 377
8. cultural capital p. 374
9. female, male p. 385
10. middle-class p. 393
11. tolerant, prejudiced, more p. 387
12. vocational, academic p. 371
13. excellence, dropout p. 394
14. teacher expectations p. 395
15. credentialism p. 392

MULTIPLE CHOICE

1.	b,	370	11.	d,	387	21.	b,	381
2.	a,	371	12.	c,	390	22.	b,	385
3.	b,	373	13.	d,	375	23.	b,	374
4.	d,	375	14.	c,	375	24.	d,	392
5.	c,	376	15.	a,	378	25.	b,	390
6.	b,	389	16.	b,	382	26.	a,	375
7.	c,	370	17.	d,	383	27.	b,	378
8.	c,	392	18.	d,	391	28.	a,	375
9.	a,	375	19.	a,	372	29.	c,	394
10.	a,	380	20.	c,	373	30.	c,	393

CHAPTER 15

MATCHING

1.	E	p. 414	5.	M	p. 413	8.	O	p. 402
2.	F	p. 400	6.	K	p. 401	9.	B	p. 411
3.	I	p. 408	7.	A	p. 420	10.	N	p. 417
4.	C	p. 401						

FILL IN THE BLANK

1. Power, coercion p. 400
2. public, interest group p. 412
3. state autonomy model p. 415
4. jurisdiction, coercion p. 404
5. pyramid p. 411
6. democracies p. 405
7. authoritarianism. p. 406
8. winner take all rule p. 409
9. power elite p. 414
10. conflict/dialectic p. 414
11. race p. 420
12. age p. 419
13. income inequality p. 406
14. PACs p. 413
15. fundamental cleavages p. 407

MULTIPLE CHOICE

1.	c,	400	11.	b,	407	21.	b,	421
2.	c,	400	12.	d,	406	22.	d,	418
3.	b,	401	13.	a,	406	23.	a,	419
4.	b,	409	14.	c,	413	24.	d,	416
5.	b,	414	15.	c,	415	25.	b,	405
6.	c,	400	16.	a,	416	26.	a,	422
7.	b,	401	17.	c,	423	27.	a,	406
8.	a,	402	18.	a,	415	28.	a,	421
9.	d,	401	19.	b,	405	29.	d,	420
10.	a,	401	20.	d,	419	30.	d,	418

ANSWER KEY

CHAPTER 16

MATCHING

1.	J	p. 431	5.	B	p. 440		8.	D	p. 430
2.	A	p. 445	6.	H	p. 429		9.	F	p. 436
3.	I	p. 440	7.	C	p. 440		10.	L	p. 433
4.	O	p. 430							

FILL IN THE BLANK

1. preindustrial p. 428
2. primary, secondary p. 430
3. tertiary sector, primary, secondary p. 430
4. informal economy p. 437
5. socialism p. 432
6. Education p. 432
7. Communism p. 433
8. cooperative, competitive p. 436
9. industrial core, periphery p. 438
10. unemployment p. 439
11. pink collar p. 440
12. working class p. 442
13. false consciousness p. 444
14. intrinsic, extrinsic p. 442
15. deskilling, displacement, supervision p. 445-6

MULTIPLE CHOICE

1.	a,	428	11.	d,	447	21.	a,	433
2.	a,	431	12.	b,	444	22.	b,	433
3.	c,	433	13.	a,	430	23.	a,	434
4.	b,	440	14.	c,	430	24.	b,	448
5.	b,	443	15.	c,	432	25.	c,	430
6.	c,	444	16.	b,	433	26.	c,	430
7.	c,	428	17.	d,	439	27.	b,	430
8.	d,	430	18.	c,	446	28.	c,	441
9.	a,	437	19.	a,	422	29.	a,	436
10.	c,	432	20.	c,	446	30.	d,	442

PHOTO ESSAY: SPORTS: AN EMERGING INSTITUTION

FILL IN THE BLANK

1.   universal   p. 451
2.   macro, micro   p. 451
3.   racism, sexism   p. 452
4.   self-concept, self-esteem   p. 452
5.   competition, teamwork   p. 452.
6.   lower-class, minority   pp. 452-3
7.   3   p. 453
8.   secondary, institution   p. 455
9.   cathedrals, stadiums   p. 455
10. institutions   p. 455

MULTIPLE CHOICE

1.   d,   451
2.   c,   451
3.   b,   452
4.   d,   452
5.   c,   452
6.   b,   452
7.   d,   452
8.   a,   453
9.   b,   453
10. a,   455

ANSWER KEY

CHAPTER 17

MATCHING

1.	L	p. 460	5.	B	p. 464	8.	D	p. 461
2.	O	p. 463	6.	G	p. 460	9.	C	p. 467
3.	N	p. 466	7.	I	p. 464	10.	E	p. 468
4.	M	p. 472						

FILL IN THE BLANK

1. sacred, profane, beliefs, rituals p. 460
2. change p. 463
3. wealth p. 462
4. Marx, Durkheim p. 463
5. Eccleasia, sects pp. 464-467
6. churchlike p. 465
7. church, sect p. 464
8. Protestant ethic p. 462
9. churchlike, sects, cults p. 475
10. secularization p. 478
11. Civil religion p. 477
12. fundamentalism p. 479
13. decline p. 479
14. New Christian Right p. 480
15. negative opinions p. 482

MULTIPLE CHOICE

1.	b,	458	11.	d,	467	21.	d,	478
2.	c,	460	12.	a,	472	22.	c,	475
3.	b,	477	13.	c,	458	23.	c,	473
4.	a,	479	14.	a,	460	24.	b,	467
5.	c,	480	15.	b,	463	25.	b,	465
6.	b,	482	16.	c,	461	26.	d,	464
7.	a,	458	17.	a,	480	27.	a,	479
8.	c,	462	18.	c,	465	28.	b,	475
9.	b,	462	19.	b,	471	29.	c,	483
10.	a,	468	20.	d,	479	30.	a,	468

CHAPTER 18

MATCHING

1.	C	p. 507	5.	A	p. 488	8.	D	p. 500
2.	E	p. 488	6.	K	p. 498	9.	L	p. 499
3.	G	p. 490	7.	I	p. 501	10.	H	p. 503
4.	B	p. 495						

FILL IN THE BLANK

1. 14   p. 504
2. sick role p. 510
3. illness p. 490
4. medicalization p. 490
5. individual characteristics   pp. 489-90
6. de-medicalized p. 490
7. women, men p. 490
8. gender role socialization p. 492
9. social class differences p. 506
10. decrease p. 494
11. fundamental inequalities p. 505
12. social institutions p. 506
13. personal care p. 498
14. Medicare, Medicaid p. 503
15. heterosexual, children p. 509

MULTIPLE CHOICE

1.	b,	489	11.	c,	498	21.	b,	491
2.	b,	489	12.	c,	501	22.	c,	489
3.	a,	490	13.	d,	511	23.	a,	503
4.	b,	492	14.	a,	490	24.	b,	503
5.	c,	496	15.	c,	492	25.	c,	488
6.	d,	497	16.	b,	493	26.	d,	492
7.	b,	491	17.	b,	505	27.	a,	491
8.	a,	495	18.	d,	506	28.	a,	504
9.	c,	496	19.	d,	488	29.	d,	509
10.	d,	498	20.	a,	490	30.	d,	506

ANSWER KEY

CHAPTER 19

MATCHING

1.	F	p. 523	5.	K	p. 525	8.	E	p. 522
2.	C	p. 522	6.	J	p. 525	9.	H	p. 527
3.	M	p. 527	7.	D	p. 529	10.	O	p. 542
4.	N	pp. 531, 535						

FILL IN THE BLANK

1. less p. 522
2. values, aspirations p. 523
3. standard of living p. 523
4. younger p. 527
5. small p. 528
6. individual, societal p. 531
7. modest p. 534
8. gender roles family p. 533
9. costs, rewards p. 533
10. fatherless p. 540
11. 34 p. 540
12. poverty p. 536
13. demographic transition p. 525
14. chain migration p. 543
15. immigration p. 541

MULTIPLE CHOICE

1.	d,	520	11.	b,	522	21.	d,	521
2.	a,	521	12.	c,	543	22.	b,	524
3.	a,	538	13.	c,	523	23.	a,	538
4.	b,	526	14.	a,	525	24.	d,	534
5.	d,	542	15.	d,	527	25.	c,	521
6.	a,	539	16.	c,	537	26.	d,	542
7.	c,	522	17.	d,	530	27.	d,	526
8.	c,	522	18.	c,	528	28.	c,	531
9.	b,	523	19.	b,	520	29.	d,	538
10.	b,	527	20.	a,	521	30.	b,	535

CHAPTER 20

MATCHING

1.	P	p. 558	5.	C	p. 551	8.	J	p. 568
2.	E	p. 550	6.	A	p. 550	9.	B	p. 559
3.	I	p. 571	7.	H	p. 556	10.	M	p. 555
4.	D	p. 566						

FILL IN THE BLANK

1. last p. 548
2. birthrate, deathrate p. 548
3. manufacturing, immobile p. 550
4. south, west p. 554
5. cities p. 556
6. manageable, knowable p. 558
7. attracted to, created by pp. 558-9
8. lonely, alienated, estranged p. 560
9. unlikely p. 560
10. political boundaries p. 568
11. Anglo p. 568
12. central city p. 570
13. Mexico City p. 557
14. disinvestment p. 567
15. live, work p. 562

MULTIPLE CHOICE

1.	a,	549	11.	c,	563	21.	a,	560
2.	c,	549	12.	c,	562	22.	b,	568
3.	b,	552	13.	a,	550	23.	b,	553
4.	b,	556	14.	a,	558	24.	d,	560
5.	b,	560	15.	d,	556	25.	c,	548
6.	b,	561	16.	a,	559	26.	a,	560
7.	b,	550	17.	c,	558	27.	b,	555
8.	a,	557	18.	c,	559	28.	c,	558
9.	a,	558	19.	a,	555	29.	a,	564
10.	b,	561	20.	c,	549	30.	c,	565

ANSWER KEY

PHOTO ESSAY: INFORMATION TECHNOLOGY: HOW WILL IT CHANGE SOCIETY?

MATCHING

1. social integration, social control, work   p. 576
2. world   p. 576
3. cultural differences   p. 576
4. social institutions   p. 577
5. monitor, control   p. 577
6. income generating work   p. 578
7. stress p. 578
8. self motivation, will power   p. 578
9. office, home   p. 578
10. women   p. 578

MULTIPLE CHOICE

1.   b,   574
2.   d,   574
3.   b,   574
4.   c,   575
5.   b,   577
6.   b,   576
7.   a,   577
8.   b,   578
9.   a,   578
10. c,   578

CHAPTER 21

MATCHING

1.	A	p. 584	5.	F	p. 591	8.	C	p. 592
2.	I	p. 598	6.	O	p. 584	9.	K	p. 586
3.	M	p. 582	7.	J	p. 582	10.	L	p. 593
4.	N	p. 596						

FILL IN THE BLANK

1. contagion p. 584
2. convergence p. 585
3. emergent norm p. 586
4. contagion p. 588
5. size p. 606
6. frame alignment p. 595
7. publicizing events, demonstrating techniques, providing rationales p. 602
8. relative deprivation p. 591
9. resource mobilization p. 592
10. Counter movements p. 598
11. Mobilization p. 598
12. Media coverage p. 602
13. men, women pp. 600-601
14. free riders p. 596
15. dominant emotional, organizational form p. 583

MULTIPLE CHOICE

1.	b,	582	11.	a,	600	21.	c,	595
2.	b,	582	12.	a,	595	22.	a,	593
3.	a,	583	13.	a,	584	23.	d,	598
4.	c,	582	14.	a,	584	24.	c,	599
5.	c,	583	15.	a,	585	25.	c,	597
6.	b,	595	16.	d,	591	26.	a,	585
7.	c,	582	17.	a,	592	27.	d,	592
8.	a,	587	18.	a,	595	28.	b,	594
9.	a,	582	19.	b,	601	29.	a,	591
10.	c,	594	20.	d,	588	30.	b,	599

ANSWER KEY

CHAPTER 22

MATCHING

1.	L	p. 619	5.	D	p. 611	8.	I	p. 610
2.	N	p. 612	6.	C	p. 611	9.	H	p. 614
3.	M	p. 613	7.	A	p. 617	10.	E	p. 623
4.	B	p. 610						

FILL IN THE BLANK

1. prosperity, poverty   p. 616
2. economics, dependent   p. 616
3. human suffering   p. 614
4. East, West, North, South   p. 616
5. industrial, foreign capital, banana republic   p. 616
6. core society   p. 616
7. perestroika,   p. 629
8. poverty, inequality, political instability   p. 620
9. capitalism   p. 613
10. World system theory   p. 613
11. Third World   p. 633
12. four modernizations   p. 623
13. low wages   p. 619
14. secondary, export   p. 626
15. Soviet Union   p. 628

MULTIPLE CHOICE

1.	d,	610	11.	a,	629	21.	b,	625
2.	c,	610	12.	c,	611	22.	c,	626
3.	d,	613	13.	a,	612	23.	a,	627
4.	d,	616	14.	a,	612	24.	a,	629
5.	c,	623	15.	c,	612	25.	a,	613
6.	b,	610	16.	c,	612	26.	c,	617
7.	a,	610	17.	d,	613	27.	b,	619
8.	a,	623	18.	d,	619	28.	a,	624
9.	a,	611	19.	d,	611	29.	c,	620
10.	b,	622	20.	a,	621	30.	b,	616

ANSWER KEY

ANSWER KEY